FRAMED BY GENDER

CECILIA L. RIDGEWAY

FRAMED BY GENDER

How Gender Inequality Persists in the Modern World

OXFORD
UNIVERSITY PRESS

Oxford University Press, Inc., publishes works that further
Oxford University's objective of excellence
in research, scholarship, and education.

Oxford   New York
Auckland   Cape Town   Dar es Salaam   Hong Kong   Karachi
Kuala Lumpur   Madrid   Melbourne   Mexico City   Nairobi
New Delhi   Shanghai   Taipei   Toronto

With offices in
Argentina   Austria   Brazil   Chile   Czech Republic   France   Greece
Guatemala   Hungary   Italy   Japan   Poland   Portugal   Singapore
South Korea   Switzerland   Thailand   Turkey   Ukraine   Vietnam

Copyright © 2011 by Oxford University Press, Inc.

Published by Oxford University Press, Inc.
198 Madison Avenue, New York, New York 10016

www.oup.com

Oxford is a registered trademark of Oxford University Press

Library of Congress Cataloging-in-Publication Data
Ridgeway, Cecilia L.
Framed by gender : how gender inequality persists in the
modern world / Cecilia L. Ridgeway.
p.   cm.
Includes bibliographical references and index.
ISBN 978-0-19-975577-6; 978-0-19-975578-3 (pbk.)
1. Sex role—United States.   2. Social interaction—United States.
3. Women—Social conditions.   4. Women—Economic conditions.
5. Equality—United States.   I. Title.
HQ1075.5.U6R54 2011
305.42—dc22   2010017994

1 3 5 7 9 8 6 4 2
Printed in the United States of America
on acid-free paper

Contents

Acknowledgments

THIS BOOK HAS been on my mind for a long time, but it didn't become a reality through my own efforts alone. I am fond of telling my students that knowledge is a coral reef built out of the accumulated contributions of many. This book is no exception to that.

I started thinking about the arguments behind this book more than a dozen years ago in response to nagging questions students asked in my classes on gender. Exactly how does gender inequality keep reshaping itself for new eras? But it was the Center for the Advanced Study of the Behavioral Sciences, where I was a Fellow in 2005–2006, that actually pushed me to finally begin writing it. The Center is the kind of place that challenges yet also inspires you to take on the bigger questions and really try to work them through. And it offers a near-magical mix of stimulation, collegial support, and focused time to think and work. I am especially indebted to several of my fellow Fellows at the Center that year who generously gave me their thoughts and encouragement: Jennifer Eberhardt, Lauren Edelman, Paula England, Annette Lareau, Cathrine Mackinnon, Laura Beth Nielsen, Claude Steele, Pamela Walters, and Min Zhou. Stephen Morris and Arne Ohman also helped me with key literatures. And years later, when I finally finished the book manuscript, Annette Lareau helped me again with invaluable advice and connections for contacting publishers.

From the time I first began thinking about these questions many years ago to the final development of the arguments that I present in this book, I have been helped along by the insights, intellectual dialogue, and encouragement of my fellow gender scholars. I am particularly grateful to Barbara Risman, who has encouraged me in this line of thought for years; to my colleague Shelley Correll, who helped me develop many of my arguments; and to Lynn Smith-Lovin, who is as interested in gender and interaction as I am. I am also indebted to Cynthia Epstein, who read one of my first statements of these arguments in a 1997 article in the *American Sociological Review* and said to me, "You should do a book on this." Alice Eagly, as well, has over the years been a constant source of sharp thinking and systematic, scientific reasoning about gender that has kept me thinking and kept me honest to the empirical data. And as I completed a draft of the book, several graduate students gave me invaluable suggestions and assistance in locating references and assembling the bibliography: Sara Bloch, Susan Fisk, Justine Tinkler, Jamillah Bowman, and Tamar Kricheli-Katz.

There are longer and broader paths to projects like this as well. I would never have become a gender scholar if it hadn't been for the example of my mother, Jaqueline Ridgeway, who has always been a determined intellectual and a natural feminist. And I would never, never have managed to sustain a project like this without the daily support, faith, wit, and sharp thinking of my partner and fellow sociologist, Robert Nash Parker. I am extremely grateful to all these people.

Cecilia L. Ridgeway
Stanford University

FRAMED BY GENDER

ONE

The Puzzle Of Persistence

ENDER HAS MANY implications for people's lives, but one of the most consequential is that it acts as a basis for inequality between persons. How, in the modern world, does gender manage to persist as a basis or principle for inequality? We can think of gender inequality as an ordinal hierarchy between men and women in material resources, power, and status. A system of gender inequality like this has persisted in the United States despite major transformations in the way that gender, at any given time, has been entwined with the economic and social organization of American society. A gender hierarchy that advantages men over women survived the profound social and economic reorganization that accompanied the transition of the United States from an agrarian to an industrialized society. By the end of this major transition, the material base of gender inequality seemed to rest firmly on women's relative absence from the paid labor force, compared with men. Yet as women in the succeeding decades flooded into the labor market, the underlying system of gender inequality nevertheless managed to refashion itself in a way that allowed it to persist. More recently, women have moved not simply into the labor market, but into formerly male jobs and professions, like physician, manager, or lawyer, but again, a pattern of gender hierarchy has remained in which men continue to be advantaged not only in employment but also throughout much of society. What is the dynamic of persistence that allows gender inequality to survive like this?

These social and economic transformations have not left gender untouched. Each brought substantial changes in social expectations about how men and women should live their lives. The degree of inequality between men and women in material dependence, social power, and status has also gone up and down over these transitions (cf. Padavic and Reskin 2002, pp. 17–28). Yet the ordinal hierarchy that advantages men over women has never entirely faded or been reversed. This is a bit of a puzzle.

Gender, like race, is a *categorical* form of inequality in that it is based on a person's membership in a particular social group or category, in this case, the categories of females and males. As we will see, social scientists generally agree that categorical inequalities in a society are created and sustained by embedding membership in a particular category (e.g., being a man or woman) in systems of control over material resources and power (e.g., Jackman 1994; Jackson 1998; Tilly 1998). If, for instance, in an agrarian society, men have greater control over ownership of land or, in an industrial society, men own the factories and occupy better jobs, these sources of wealth and power create and maintain gender inequality. Theoretically, then, when the system of resource control on which gender inequality is based in a given period is upset by technological and socioeconomic transformation, the gender hierarchy itself should be at risk of collapse. Yet this collapse has not happened in American society. How—that is, through what means—has gender inequality managed to persist?

When I ask this question, I am not asking for a story of the specific, contingent historical events through which gender hierarchy has been reestablished in the transitions from one socioeconomic period to another. Instead, I am asking a more abstract and analytical question. Are there any general social processes through which gender inequality manages to reinscribe itself in new forms of social and economic organization as these forms emerge in society?

Notice, too, that I am not asking the ultimate, sweeping question of *why* gender inequality has persisted, but rather the more proximate, means-focused question of *how* it has persisted. The "how" question is essential to any effort to intervene in the perpetuation of gender inequality. Even the how question is a very large one, however. To bring it down to a manageable scale, I will focus on its more specific, modern version. In this book, I ask how gender inequality persists in the contemporary United States in the face of potentially leveling economic and political changes, such as men's and women's increasingly similar labor market experience, antidiscrimination legislation, and the growing convictions of many that boys and girls should be raised to have equal opportunities in life. This more specific question about contemporary persistence is especially relevant for understanding the current challenges faced by those seeking greater gender egalitarianism.

There can be little doubt that gender inequality still does persist in the United States. Evidence of gender inequality in employment is particularly revealing since in the contemporary United States, paid labor is the major means by which individuals gain access to material resources, authority, and social status. Women's labor force participation rates rose relative to men's throughout the 20th century, but they have leveled off since 1990, when 74% of women in the prime working ages of 25–54 were in the paid labor force. In 2000, that figure was still 74% for women, compared with men's 86% participation rate in the prime working years (Cotter, Hermsen, and Vanneman 2004). Since 2000, the gender gap in labor force participation has held steady rather than substantially narrowed (U.S. Bureau of Labor Statistics 2009). Although men and women have similar education levels, women's annual wages for full-time, year-round work were still only 77% of men's in 2008 (Institute for Women's Policy Research 2010). Furthermore, the jobs and occupations that people work in are still quite sex segregated in that most women work in jobs filled predominantly by other women, and most men work in jobs filled predominantly by other men. While the movement of women into men's occupations has significantly reduced sex segregation, the decline has slowed since the 1990s. At present, the elimination of the sex segregation of occupations would still require 40% or more of all women in the workforce to change occupations (Charles and Grusky 2004; Cotter et al. 2004; Tomaskovic-Devey et al. 2006). Women are also less likely to be in managerial or supervisory positions in the workplace, and when they are, their positions carry less authority and power than those occupied by men (Reskin and McBrier 2000; Smith 2002). Only 15% of top executive positions in Fortune 500 companies are filled by women (Catalyst 2008).

Some women, of course, do not choose to participate in the paid labor force, at least for a period of years, choosing instead to devote their time to raising a family. There is evidence, however, that persistent gender inequality continues to taint social judgments of this choice, too. A study of contemporary American stereotypes showed that such "housewives" were perceived to be in the lower half of all social groups in social status, below blue-collar workers and women in general and well below men in general. Housewives in this study were seen as similar in competence to the elderly and disabled (Fiske et al. 2002). A subsequent study further confirmed that contemporary Americans rate housewives as well below the average for social groups in social status (Cuddy et al. 2007; Cuddy, personal communication).

Gender inequality persists as well in who does the work at home. Whether or not women work in the paid labor force, they continue to do more work in the household than men (Bianchi et al. 2006). Furthermore, women's share of the housework compared with men's is not dramatically changed by increases in the hours they put in on the job (Bianchi et al. 2000; Coltrane 2000). As a result, the burden of juggling the management of household duties with employment continues to fall on women (Bianchi et al. 2006). The weight of this burden, particularly that of caring for dependent children, affects how women fare in the labor force as well. At present, studies show that mothers of dependent children suffer a "wage penalty" in the labor force of about 5% per child compared with similar women without children (Budig and England 2001).

Gender inequality in the contemporary United States, then, continues to be widespread. Evidence from the world of work suggests that progress toward greater equality has actually slowed or stalled since the 1990s (Cotter et al. 2004; Padavic and Reskin 2002). Such evidence suggests that present levels of gender inequality are not merely dead artifacts of the past that have not yet been fully worn away. Instead, it is more reasonable to view present levels of gender inequality as a product of competing forces, some acting to perpetuate inequality in the face of others that act to erode it.

This book is about a set of social processes that, I argue, play a critical part on the perpetuation side of the competing forces that shape gender inequality in contemporary America. The processes I will describe are hardly the only ones that act to maintain inequality, but they are among those that are most central. These processes, I argue, must be understood if we are to achieve greater gender equality in the future.

To address the question of the contemporary persistence of gender inequality, I will outline in this book an analytic perspective on the way that gender acts as an organizing force in everyday social relations. By social relations, I mean any situation in which individuals define themselves *in relation* to others in order to comprehend the situation and act. That is to say, social relations are situations in which people form a sense of who they are in the situation and, therefore, how they should behave, by considering themselves in relation to whom they assume others are in that situation. In social relational situations, they implicitly say to themselves, for instance, "That is a traffic policeman and I am a driver and therefore. . . ."

Everyday social interactions, either in person or through some other medium like a computer or a telephone, are of course social relations by this definition. However, situations in which individuals act alone—evaluating a resume, for instance, or taking a qualifying test—can also be social relational if the individuals imaginatively consider themselves in relation to others to decide how to act because they feel their behavior or its consequences will be socially evaluated. From the perspective of individuals, social life and society itself are made of up of social relations of this sort, happening over and over again across multiple contexts (Ridgeway 2006b). It is worth keeping in mind that societal patterns of gender inequality are actually enacted through social relations.

Gender inequality's staying power, I argue, derives from people's use of *sex* (that is, the physical status of being male or female) and *gender* (shared cultural expectations associated with being male or female) together as a primary frame for organizing that most fundamental of activities: relating to another person. I argue that people use sex/gender as an initial, starting framework for defining "who" self and other are in order to coordinate their behavior and relate, whether they do so face-to-face, on paper, over the Internet, or on a cell phone. The everyday use of sex/gender as a basic cultural tool for organizing social relations accounts, I'll argue, for why cultural meanings associated with gender do not stay within the bounds of contexts associated with sex and reproduction. Instead, the use of gender as a framing device spreads gendered meanings, including assumptions about inequality embedded in those meanings, to all spheres of social life that are carried out through social relationships. Through gender's role in organizing social relations, I'll argue, gender inequality is rewritten into new economic and social arrangements as they emerge, preserving that inequality in modified form over socioeconomic transformations. In a very brief form, that is the argument I am going to make, spelling out its implications as I go along.

As this abbreviated account suggests, some general aspects of my arguments about gender and social relations might be applied in some degree to societies other than the contemporary United States. Caution is required in this regard, however, since, as I have already implied, the social structure of gender is virtually always specific to a particular societal and historical context. Although I will pose some parts of my argument in general terms, the details address gender in the contemporary United States, and I limit my focus in this book to that context.

Before I turn to my specific analysis of gender as an organizing force in social relations, there are some questions that need to be addressed. It will be useful, first, to inquire more closely into gender as a form of inequality in contemporary society. A more detailed understanding of the nature of gender inequality will help us assess what a plausible explanation for the persistence of gender inequality might entail. This inquiry will also clarify why an approach that focuses on the way people use gender as a framework for organizing social relations might be appropriate to the problem of persistence.

Second, it will be helpful to position the social relational analysis of gender's persistence within a more encompassing picture of gender as a system of social practices in society to better understand what aspects of gender will be the focus of this book. Third, to clarify the premises from which this book proceeds, I need briefly to describe my opinion on the biology question that inevitably arises when people debate the persistence of gender inequality. Debating the complex and difficult questions that are involved in this issue would be the topic of a very different book. Instead, I will make a few simple, evidence-based assumptions about this issue in relation to which I develop my social organizational analysis of the persistence of gender inequality. As we shall see, I understand gender to be a substantial, socially elaborated edifice constructed on a modest biological foundation.

Fourth, although my focus is on the persistence of inequality, discussions of inequality are inevitably entwined in people's minds with assumptions about the nature of gender differences (or "sex differences," as they are often called). For this reason, it also will be useful to outline very briefly the evidence about contemporary sex differences in social behavior. This evidence will provide an empirical foundation with which my subsequent arguments must be consistent. These questions occupy the rest of this chapter. Once we have them in hand, I will turn in the following chapters to my analysis of gender as a primary frame for social relations.

GENDER AS A FORM OF INEQUALITY

Gender is frequently referred to as a social role that males and females play. If gender is a social role, however, it is unlike other roles as we commonly use the term. In contrast to other roles such as, say, teacher and student, boss and worker, or leader and follower, gender is not inherently attached to a defined set of positions in specific types of organizations or institutions. Instead, gender is about *types* or categories of people who are defined in relation to one another. We can think of gender as *a system of social practices within society that constitutes distinct, differentiated sex categories, sorts people into these categories, and organizes relations between people on the basis of the differences defined by their sex category* (Ridgeway and Smith-Lovin 1999). I use the intermediate term, *sex category*, in this definition to refer to the social labeling of people as male or female on the basis of social cues presumed to stand for physical sex (West and Zimmerman 1987). Physical sex itself is more complex than the dichotomous social labels of sex category. However, it is typically the social labeling of someone as male or female rather than direct physical sex that triggers gendered social practices.

Distinctive Aspects of Gender

Although gender is a categorical distinction among people, like race or ethnicity, even in this regard it has some distinctive characteristics that have implications for understanding gender as a form of inequality. Unlike those who differ in race or ethnicity, males and females are born into the same families. People who differ in sex, unlike most who differ in race or ethnicity, also go on to live together in the same households. These mixed-sex households are distributed throughout every economic spectrum so that there are always rich as well as poor women, just as there are rich as well as poor men. Finally, there are roughly equal numbers of men and women in the population so that neither sex constitutes a distinct statistical minority or majority in society.

These distinctive aspects of gender have two implications for inequality that are relevant here. First, in comparison with those who differ on other significant categorical distinctions like race, men and women interact together all the time and often on intimate terms. Consequently, while there is an interpersonal, relational aspect to any form of inequality, including those based on race and social class, the arena of interpersonal relations is likely to be especially important for gender inequality. This means that processes taking place in everyday social relations have the potential to play a powerful role in the persistence or change of gender inequality.

Second, because both men and women are distributed throughout all sectors of society, gender inequality can never be a matter of all men (or women) being more advantaged than all women (or men). Instead, gender inequality is a state of affairs in which the average member of one sex is advantaged compared with the average member of the other sex. Even when gender inequality favors men on average, there will always be some women who are more privileged than many men. But even rich, powerful, high-status women will not be as rich, powerful, and high in status as the most privileged men.

Positional and Status Inequalities

As I stated at the outset, gender inequality is an ordinal hierarchy between the average man and woman in valued resources, in power, and in status. As the early-20th-century sociologist Max Weber (1946) famously described, resources, power, and status constitute three interrelated but slightly different dimensions of inequality in societies. It is worth unpacking these related dimensions to better understand how gender inequality is constituted in the modern world. How gender inequality is constituted has implications for how it might or might not be undermined by changing social and economic arrangements in society. First, we need some conceptual tools for thinking about resources, power, and status. Next, we need to understand the nature of gender inequality in relation to these interrelated forms of inequality.

The relationship between the resources and power dimensions of inequality is especially close. While the possession of wealth, information, or other valued resources is not the same as power over people and events, it is easy to see how one might lead to the other. In fact, research based on the sociological theory of power dependence has shown that power arises between people from the dependence of one person on another for valued resources (Emerson 1962, 1972; Cook, Cheshire, and Gerbasi 2006). As power dependence theory has also shown, access to valuable resources and power over others develops from the relative positions actors hold in social networks and organizations.

In societies, social organizations of all sorts are the major producers and distributors of the resources most of us seek, from the basics of food and shelter to more abstract resources like money or information (Tilly 1998). Employment organizations are obvious examples, but so are households, government institutions, unions, educational institutions, and so on. Organizations are made up of a structure of related social positions, such as teachers and students in educational institutions and managers and workers in a business firm. Some of these positions have greater control over the resources that the organization generates and carry more power than other positions. These unequal resources and rights to power are vested in the positions themselves, independent of the individuals that occupy them. The CEO position in a business firm carries resources and power that are a function of the position rather than the person. Because resources and power in the contemporary United States are largely attached to such *positional inequalities* in organizations, inequalities in the organizational positions individuals occupy result in inequalities between them in resources and power (Jackson 1998; Tilly 1998).

The third dimension of inequality, social status, is a bit different from that created by positional inequalities. *Status inequalities* are distinctive in that they are rooted in *shared cultural beliefs* about the respect, social esteem, and honor associated with types or categories of people compared with other types or categories of people. In an achievement-oriented society like the United States, social esteem is represented and expressed by corresponding assumptions about differences in these people's competence at the things that "count most" in society (Berger et al. 1977; Ridgeway 2006d).

Status inequalities, then, are based on cultural presumptions about the traits of people in some social categories compared with others rather than directly on the nature of the positions they occupy in society. Since gender is a categorical distinction based on cultural assumptions about differences between people in one sex category compared with the other, it is at root a status inequality. When cultural beliefs (i.e., stereotypes) about men and women incorporate assumptions about status and competence differences between the sexes, they base gender inequality on categorical membership itself. One is unequal *because* one is a man or woman and not just because one occupies a particular set of organizational positions in society. In fact, contemporary gender stereotypes in the United States do incorporate beliefs that men are worthier of status and more generally competent than women (Fiske et al. 2002; Glick et al. 2004; Rudman et al. 2009). Because such gender status beliefs color our impressions of people, a woman in a certain social position—say, a CEO in a business firm—is not quite equal to an equivalent man in that position, despite the structural equivalence of their positions.

The pattern of gender inequality that we see in American society at any given time is a result of the relationship between these two types of inequality working together (Jackson 1998). It is a joint result of status inequalities between people *because* they are men rather than women and positional inequalities between people who *happen to be* men or women. Of these two types of inequality, however, it is the status dimension that causes patterns of inequality between people who happen to be male or female, but who also have many other social identities, to be understood as *gender* inequality rather than some other form of inequality. Consequently, the status dimension, rooted as it is in beliefs about the nature of men and women, is especially significant for the persistence of gender as a distinctive form of inequality with its own social dynamic.

The Dependence of Gender Status on Positional Inequalities

As almost all sociologists agree, however, status inequalities are effective only if they are embedded in positional inequalities in society (e.g., Jackman 1994; Jackson 1998; Tilly 1998). If people who are thought to differ in status and competence do not usually also differ in positions of power and resources, the significance of the status difference becomes difficult to sustain. As the saying goes, "If you're so smart, why aren't you rich?" The persistence of gender as a status inequality, then, is dependent on the persistence of positional inequalities between men and women in society.

To see this dependence more clearly, let us go back to the indicators I used earlier to describe current levels of gender inequality in the United States. Differences in labor force participation, wages, sex segregation of jobs, the likelihood of being in a managerial position, and even differences in the household division of labor all reflect positional inequalities between men and women in the organizations that make up American society. Taken-for-granted acceptance of beliefs that men are more socially esteemed and generally more competent than women depends on people's daily experience with positional inequalities like this that appear to provide evidence for these beliefs (Eagly, Wood, and Diekman 2000; Ridgeway and Smith-Lovin 1999).

It is gender status beliefs, then, that cause inequalities between people to be distinctly *gender* inequality—that is, organized on the basis of people's social classification as males or females rather than in terms of their other attributes or roles. Yet gender status beliefs depend on positional inequalities that create resource and power differences between men and women. As a result, when social, technological, and economic changes begin to undermine the positional inequalities between men and women on which gender inequality has rested in a particular historical period, pressure builds on gender status beliefs, and the gender hierarchy itself is at risk of eventual collapse.

Sociologist Robert Max Jackson (1998), in his book *Destined for Equality*, argues that this is precisely what has been happening over the last century in the United States and perhaps elsewhere as well. He attributes the erosion of positional inequalities between men and women over this period primarily to a cascading series of effects set in motion by the emergence of large-scale, modern economic and political organizations and their increasing dominance of economic and political life in America. The last hundred years has seen the growth of the large corporation and the development of equally large institutions of government. Large modern organizations, whether economic or political, are bureaucratically organized and seek to rationalize their procedures in the pursuit of greater profits, more votes, and more institutional power. Traditional distinctions between people based on gender have become increasingly at odds with organizational procedures and priorities based on rationalized, universalistic conceptions of workers and citizens. While these organizations are created and run by people who think of themselves as men and women, when they put on their hats as capitalists or politicians, they take actions that have the effect, whether intended or not, of undermining traditional positional inequalities between men and women.

Accompanying these organizational changes have been persistent pressures for women's rights coming from two related sources. The first has derived from women's own political efforts to improve their position in society. The second has come from a growing cultural logic of individual "civil" or "human" rights. These processes in turn have led to an array of laws prohibiting gender discrimination in education and employment. Such laws create further incentives for organizations to treat men and women similarly, intensifying the pressure on positional inequalities between them.

Jackson argues that these mutually amplifying processes have now progressed so far that they are effectively unstoppable. Whether men and women like it or not, their daily lives in the United States will become more and more similar, making gender status beliefs increasingly untenable. The ultimate collapse of gender hierarchy in the United States is now inevitable as a consequence, Jackson argues. He bases this conclusion not only on the power of the institutional processes he describes but also on that fact that he sees no compelling process that actively reconstructs gender inequality in the face of these leveling forces.

Several aspects of Jackson's analysis are useful for us here. He makes a persuasive case that the overall thrust of powerful social forces currently acting at the institutional level in the United States is to undermine gender inequality. Equally persuasive is his underlying premise that, although gender is at root a status inequality, its persistence ultimately depends on embedding gender in positional inequalities in organizations of all sorts. As a distinctive principle of inequality, gender will disappear only when gender status beliefs have faded, but the way to erode those beliefs is through the elimination of resource and power differences between men and women. On the other side, if gender inequality is to persist, some process must continually reembed gender in the positional inequalities of new organizational forms as they develop, despite countervailing processes that suppress such inequalities in established, bureaucratically well-organized contexts.

A Dynamic of Persistence?

History, of course, has shown that gender inequality has remarkable resilience. In the past, it has indeed managed to reconstitute itself in new social and economic forms as older ways of organizing things have collapsed. To do so, gender as an organizing principle of inequality must have had some independent dynamic that caused people to reestablish it in new contexts in a way that propelled gender inequality into the future. The questions for us here then become: of what might such a dynamic consist, and is it likely to be still operating now? If such a dynamic is still operating in a powerful way at present, then it would work as a counterforce to the leveling processes that Jackson describes, slowing progress toward gender equality. The effects of such a counteracting gender dynamic need not mean that gender equality cannot or will not be achieved in the future. However, the existence of such a dynamic would suggest that progress toward equality can be assured only by taking it into account.

What processes might maintain gender inequality, separate from positional access to resources and economic and political power? Some might point for an answer to gender's role in organizing heterosexuality, reproduction, and the family. In one version of such arguments, for instance, sociologist Mary Jackman (1994, p. 101) argues that the core of gender inequality lies in a very special form of resource dependence and power: control over sexual access and reproduction. The assumption is that men's greater average size and upper body strength gives them power over women in sexual matters.

The primary point Jackman (1994) wishes to make, however, is that the ongoing system of gender inequality that we see in society cannot be a simple reflection of such an underlying physical power dynamic. I agree. If it were, we would see gender as a combination of relationships in which large men control small women but large women control small men. Furthermore, as Jackman argues in detail, control based on coercive power like this is inherently unstable unless it is secured through a broader pattern of unequal resources, positions of power, and legitimating status beliefs. It is a matter of controversy whether control over sexual access is an underlying basis of gender inequality (see Wood and Eagly 2002). Even if it is, however, this analysis suggests that it, too, would be threatened and destabilized by the elimination of resource and power differences between men and women.

Of course, there are other ways that gender's relevance for sex, reproduction, and the family might play a role in maintaining gender inequality in the face of leveling economic and political factors. For my own part, I consider that analyses based on sex and reproduction provide only partial answers to the puzzle of gender inequality's independent staying power, primarily because such analyses do not fully address gender's effects as a status inequality. As we have seen, it is the development and persistence of gender status beliefs that constitute gender as a distinct principle of inequality based on membership in sex category alone. My own analysis of gender inequality's dynamic of persistence focuses instead on a set of intermediate processes that partially result from gender's role in reproduction and the family but that carry gender to relationships beyond the family and sustain it as a status distinction.

These intermediate processes derive, I will argue, from gender's deep-seated role as a cultural distinction that individuals use to organize their social relations with others. As we have seen, interpersonal relations play an especially large part in the enactment of gender as a system of difference and inequality because men and women, unlike people of different races or classes, interact so frequently and often on intimate terms. To understand how gender persists as a distinct principle of inequality, I argue that we need to look to this crucial social relational arena.

It is not a coincidence that the social relational arena is also central to the way status works as a process of inequality. Status inequalities are rooted in shared cultural beliefs that associate greater social esteem and competence with people in one social category or group than with people in another. Status inequalities have a dual aspect, however.

In addition to an evaluative ranking between groups in society, status can also be thought of as a hierarchy between individuals based on esteem, influence, and deference (Goffman 1959, 1967). Status between social groups and status between individuals are linked in the social relational arena. Decades of research have shown that status in social relations between individuals is largely determined by the way their distinguishing social attributes, such as gender, race, or occupation, evoke cultural beliefs about the esteem and competence of those in the social categories to which they belong (Berger et al. 1977; Strodtbeck, James, and Hawkins 1957; Wagner and Berger 2002). In turn, cultural status beliefs about social groups affect inequality largely by shaping interpersonal influence and status hierarchies in a manner that directs some individuals toward positions of greater resources and power than others. If gender is fundamentally a status inequality and status is carried out most directly through interpersonal relations, we should expect gender's effects on social relations to play an important role in the persistence of gender as a status distinction.

Social Relations and the Gender System

I have defined *gender* as "system of social practices" that constitutes males and females as different and organizes relations between them on the basis of the presumed differences. Gender inequality exists to the extent that this system of social practices organizes gender relations on unequal terms. The social practices that constitute males and females as different and unequal involve social processes at several levels of analysis (Lorber 1994; Ridgeway 1997; Risman 1998, 2004). They involve economic, political, and cultural processes at the organizational and institutional level (see, for instance, Acker 1990; Epstein 1988; Jackson 1998; Lorber 1994). They involve interpersonal expectations and behaviors at the social relational level. They also involve the socialization of self and identity at the individual level.

In developing an analytic perspective about gender as a primary frame for organizing social relations, I will focus on a defined range of the broader system of social practices that make up the full phenomenon of gender in the contemporary United States. There will be many vital aspects of gender that I will not address. I will say little, for instance, about the intricacies of gender and the self or the complexities of sexual identities. Instead, I will focus on key processes at the interpersonal level and, on a more macro level, on institutionalized cultural beliefs about gender that shape expectations for behavior at the interpersonal level.

As I develop my analytic perspective on gender and the organization of social relations, my goal throughout will be to prosecute a specific argument about processes that I claim are central to the persistence of gender inequality in the modern context. To build this argument, I will draw extensively on several theories of interpersonal processes and refer to a diverse body of evidence on contemporary gender processes. I will not, however, attempt to review more generally the full spectrum of contemporary gender scholarship or the broad array of theories of gender in sociology and psychology. Rather than an overview of the full workings of the contemporary gender system, then, this book is an effort to isolate and identify a specific set of social processes that, I argue, are especially important for the persistence of gender inequality in the modern world.

For some readers, however, it may be useful for me to briefly locate the approach I will take in relation to dominant perspectives on gender in sociology and psychology. In sociology, most scholars take either a primarily materialist approach to gender inequality that emphasizes structures of resources and power (e.g., Epstein 1988) or a more cultural, institutional approach (e.g., Acker 2006). As my previous discussion of the nature of gender inequality demonstrates, my own approach is positioned between the materialist and culturalist stances. I put great emphasis on cultural status beliefs about gender that, I argue, constitute gender as a distinctive form of inequality. But I also argue that these beliefs are created, maintained, and most important, changed through structures of material resources between men and women. From the standpoint of this intermediate perspective, I am distinctively concerned with the way these cultural gender beliefs and material contingencies are implicated in the organization of social relations at the interpersonal level and the enactment of gender through these relations. In this sense, my approach, despite other differences, is closer to the interactional "doing gender, doing difference" perspective in sociology (West and Fenstermaker 1993; West and Zimmerman 1987). In regard to psychological perspectives, my approach will draw most heavily from cognitive and social psychological approaches to gender, in contrast to more developmental or personality approaches (see Eagly, Beall, and Sternberg 2004).

In narrowing my focus to the interpersonal level of the gender system, I do not mean to imply that gender processes at other levels of analysis are necessarily less important for the structure of gender inequality as we see it today. On the contrary, the evidence suggests that the most obdurate features of gender inequality in contemporary America, such as the household division of labor and the sex segregation of jobs, are overdetermined in the gender system (Reskin, Branch McBrier, and Kmec 1999; Ridgeway and Correll 2004b; Ridgeway and Smith-Lovin 1999; Risman 1998). That is to say, these features are created and maintained by multiple complementary processes acting simultaneously at different level of analysis.

Although processes at multiple levels of analysis are involved in the patterns of gender inequality we see around us in contemporary America, I focus on processes at the interpersonal level because I believe these to be especially implicated in the *persistence* of gender inequality at this moment in time. As Jackson shows us, the thrust of economic and political processes at the institutional level at present is to undermine gender inequality. As Risman (2004) notes, the contemporary emphasis on raising girls to have as many chances in life as boys is similarly reducing the impact of socialization practices at the individual level that might perpetuate inequality. In this context, processes at the level of interpersonal expectations and behavior become especially important in sustaining gender inequality.

Of course, gender processes at any level of analysis implicate some processes at other levels of analysis, and this is true as well for gender processes at the interpersonal level. As we shall see, gender processes at the interpersonal level draw on widely shared gender status beliefs that are macro-level cultural phenomena but that in turn are learned by individuals at the micro level and used to frame their social expectations. But the interpersonal approach distinctively focuses on how these cultural beliefs and individual expectations play out in social relational contexts to affect gender inequality.

THE BIOLOGY QUESTION

As I mentioned at the outset, this is a book about *how* gender inequality persists in the modern world, not about *why* it persists. It is not an effort to adjudicate the ultimate causes of gender inequality. The actual origins of gender inequality in Western society are lost in the past, and of course, causes of the historical origin need not be causes of contemporary persistence. Nevertheless, questions about ultimate, biological causes are often in the back of people's minds when the persistence of gender inequality is discussed. Given this, it may be helpful to clarify from the beginning how the arguments presented in this book relate to assumptions about ultimate biological causes for the persistence of gender inequality.

The first point to make clear is that the social relational processes that I will describe as *mediating* the persistence of gender inequality would continue to have an effect *even if* it were the case that strong, genetically determined factors predisposed gender inequality among humans. If such determining genetic factors do exist (and this is not my personal assumption), these become the ultimate causes of the persistence of gender inequality. Even such factors, however, must work through more proximate social processes to actually create and continually re-create social structures of gender inequality. Since my argument describes these more proximate social processes that rewrite gender inequality into new social forms, the validity of my argument neither rests on nor is undercut by assumptions about biological factors that predispose gender inequality.

Although my argument does not logically depend on particular assumptions about the power or nature of biological causes of gender inequality, it nevertheless may be useful for me at this point to clarify my own background assumptions in this regard. While the logical validity of my arguments may not depend on these assumptions, they do frame the explanatory significance I attach to the arguments I put forward.

Before entering into a discussion of biological sources of sex differences in social behavior and dominance, it is worth remembering that such discussions are always difficult and controversial for at least two reasons. First, of course, when a sex difference in behavior or social outcome is attributed to biology, it is perceived in the common discourse as unchangeable, inevitable, and "natural" (Eagly 1995). Such biological claims become especially sensitive when they are taken to suggest that women's lesser power and status in contemporary society is inevitable. Despite the common discourse, it is useful to keep in mind that it is not necessarily the case that if some behavior has a genetic cause, it is unchangeable or inevitable. Genes interact with the environment in very complex ways in their effects on an organism's behavior. Even something as biologically basic as an animal's tendency to mate and reproduce may be biologically turned down or even turned off in an environment in which there is a severe lack of the resources necessary to sustain reproduction. That said, behaviors that are genetically determined, if not unchangeable, are nevertheless relatively persistent and more difficult to change.

Arguments about biological causes of sex differences in social behavior are controversial for a second reason as well. There are substantial empirical difficulties involved in ascertaining when a predisposing genetic cause is present. These problems remain despite tantalizing recent advances in knowledge about human genes and how they work, about the brain, and even about sex differences in the aspects of the brain that men and women appear to be using under various circumstances. There are many problems in sorting out biological causes, but some of the most intractable derive from the close physiological relationship between organisms and their environment. For people, this includes a close physical attunement to the *social* environment on which we all depend for so much of what we want and need. Thus, correlations, for instance, between physiological states, such as sex hormone levels or brain scans, and social behaviors or attributes do not in themselves answer questions about the direction of causality between biology and social environment (see Wood and Eagly 2010). Due to such difficulties, at present we simply do not yet have much strong, highly reliable evidence one way or the other about biological sources of behaviors or attributes relevant for gender inequality.

What, then, are my own underlying assumptions about the biology question? I do not think it reasonable to assume that biology plays no role in producing sex differences in behavior. Whatever biology contributes, however, it never acts alone, but in concert with a wide variety of social processes. I suspect that biology is only rarely determinative in itself. In particular, I am personally unconvinced that there are any unchanging biological factors that make male dominance inevitable among humans. Rather, I believe that the diverse patterns of gender difference and inequality that we see around us in American society are not only not primarily rooted in biology but also not necessarily a simple product of the internal dispositions of individuals. Instead, these patterns, I believe, result from complex interactions between individuals, social relations, and social structures. I assume, then, that the social system of gender is a "biosocial" system of amplifying cultural practices built on modest and flexible biological material. The arguments I put forth in this book focus entirely on the amplifying cultural practices of gender.

Since the biology question is so often on people's minds when they think about the persistence of gender inequality, I will briefly clarify the empirical bases of my assumptions to suggest why I believe they are not unreasonable. To do so, I will describe recent efforts to evaluate determinative biological models of gender inequality against cross-cultural evidence about gender differences in social behavior. This description will also serve the purpose of showing why I think the extant evidence in regard to this issue does not contradict the social relational analysis I present in this book.

The Cross-Cultural Evidence

The contemporary approach that attributes the persistence of inequality most directly to biologically driven sex differences derives from evolutionary psychology (Buss and Kenrick 1998; Crawford and Salmon 2004). While there are many evolutionary approaches, those with the most direct implications for the persistence of inequality posit evolved sex differences in dispositions that give men a greater proclivity for violence, competition, and risk taking and women a greater tendency to nurture and choose mates with greater resources (see Buss and Kenrick 1998; Eagly and Wood 1999). If biologically driven (rather than more socially shaped) dispositions of this sort exist, they would make persistent male dominance likely as men compete with each other for resources and women depend on their ties to men to gain access to these resources.

Direct scientific evidence to either support or reject a deterministic genetic basis for such dispositional differences is not yet available. As a result, researchers in sex differences have turned to cross-cultural evidence to adjudicate the question as well as possible at present. Wendy Wood and Alice H. Eagly (2002), in particular, have assembled a wide variety of cross-cultural evidence on gender behavior and inequality and systematically compared it with predictions from an evolved dispositions approach versus approaches that more heavily weight the impact of social processes. The evidence they drew on is anthropologists' ethnographies of a substantial number of nonindustrial societies that have been coded for the presence or absence of various characteristics to allow systematic comparisons among them. Some of the societies in this sample were relatively simple hunting and foraging societies whose circumstances of living approximated the conditions in which evolutionary psychology theories have posited that gender differences in dispositions were genetically selected for in the past.

On the basis of this cross-cultural data, Wood and Eagly (2002) conclude that the evidence for evolved sex differences in dispositions that predispose gender inequality is not strong. In fact, the simple societies that most closely correspond to those in which these dispositions are supposed to have evolved are in general the most gender egalitarian of the societies in the sample. Some of these small societies, especially the ones that rely primarily on foraging, appear to show little evidence of an overall gender hierarchy at all. That is, there were few overall differences between men and women in power or status, even though men and women differed in their spheres of influence and power. In general, male dominance and gender inequality was associated in this sample of societies with the development of more complex economies and social structures and with warfare.

The cross-cultural data, however, did reveal one apparent gender universal in these nonindustrial societies, and that was a "sex-typed division of labor or coordination between men and women in the performance of daily life tasks" (Wood and Eagly 2002, p. 707). Divisions of labor were sex typed in that a majority of tasks in each society were considered men's tasks or women's tasks and performed primarily by people of that sex. Which sex did which tasks varied substantially between societies. There were a few tasks, however, that were almost always performed by men (e.g., hunting large animals) or by women (e.g., cooking vegetal food).

Wood and Eagly (2002) conclude that, rather than a model of evolved dispositions, the cross-cultural evidence, including that on the gendered division of labor, supports a "biosocial model" of sex differences in which physical sex characteristics set certain constraints on gendered behavior but in which social processes are dominant. The cross-cultural evidence, they argue, suggests that the gendered division of labor is rooted in the cooperative, functional interdependence between men and women for reproduction and survival. Men and women must coordinate and cooperate to raise children, and in the interests of efficiency, they develop a division of labor. What men and women do in a given society—that is, the gendered division of labor—in turn, shapes cultural assumptions in that society about men's and women's dispositions (Diekman and Eagly 2000; Eagly and Diekman 2003; Eagly and Steffen 1986).

The gender division of labor people develop can vary greatly but may also be shaped in some degree by sex-typed biological characteristics, such as men's greater upper body strength or the physical constraints faced by lactating mothers. Wood and Eagly's (2002) cross-cultural evidence suggests that these biological attributes have greater or lesser impact on the division of labor in different resource and technological environments. Joan Huber (2007), another social scientist, makes the case, for instance, that the physical constraints on lactating mothers posed by the need for frequent suckling in premodern societies played a profound role in the development of widespread male dominance in human societies. Yet Huber also argues that there is no reason that the physical state of being a lactating mother must necessarily predispose male dominance in the richer and technologically more complex conditions of modern advanced industrial societies.

In sum, even though the social relational account I offer for how gender inequality persists at present holds even if ultimate biological causes are involved, current evidence is not in favor of such necessary, determining causes for male dominance. The cross-cultural evidence does, however, suggest a role for biology, in combination with social processes, in shaping the pattern of gender differences and inequality in a given society. This role is one that is congenial with the account of the persistence of inequality in the modern world that I develop in this book. Note that Wood and Eagly locate the primary nexus of gender as a social phenomenon in a *social relational* process, the organizational need for men and women to work together to some degree, which in turn has roots in men's and women's biological dependence on one another for reproduction. Although my account of the use of gender as a primary frame for organizing social relations focuses primarily on proximate processes by which gender inequality persists in the modern world, it is compatible with the conclusions Wood and Eagly draw. To the extent that the account I offer reaches back to basic causes, it does so in terms that are consistent with the Wood and Eagly account.

In the next section, I consider what can be said about the nature of empirically measured sex differences in social behaviors as we see them in the contemporary United States, whatever their causes. As should be clear from the biosocial model we have just discussed, this evidence can tell us little about the biology question. Instead, it provides a picture of the empirical variation in behavior with which any model of gender processes in the contemporary United States must be consistent. Since gender is a system of difference and inequality, it will be helpful to begin a discussion of the contemporary persistence of inequality with a foundation of descriptive knowledge about contemporary sex differences.

A PERSPECTIVE ON CONTEMPORARY SEX DIFFERENCES IN BEHAVIOR

Two psychologists, Janet Hyde (2005; Hyde and Plant 1995) and Alice Eagly (1987, 1995; Eagly, Wood, and Diekman 2000), have conducted influential projects to pull together the empirical evidence about sex differences in significant social behaviors. These efforts rely on a statistical technique called meta-analysis that systematically aggregates the results of whole bodies of research to more reliably estimate the underlying nature and size of sex differences in particular behaviors.

I rely heavily on the results of these meta-analytical efforts in what follows.

Several points are important to keep in mind from the onset as we consider this evidence. First, these meta-analytic studies seek to describe *presented* differences in behavior by (primarily) adult males and females in contemporary North America, whatever their cause. Thus these are *not* studies about the biological causes of behaviors but, rather, about the patterns of sex differences for which we could seek causes. Second, these studies focus on sex differences in *individual* attributes, dispositions, and behavioral tendencies and do not attempt to measure social patterns of behavior, like military experience, on which the sexes may differ due to the way the society is organized by gender. Third, not all studies of individual sex differences attend to the way these differences are affected by the context in which people are acting, but those that do show substantial contextual effects, as we shall see. These contextual effects are especially congenial with my account of gender as a primary frame for organizing social relations.

Hyde's (2005) comprehensive review of the evidence on virtually all traits that have been examined in meta-analyses shows that sex differences are often smaller than popularly assumed. In 78% of these meta-analyses, the mean sex difference was in the close to zero or small range, meaning that the sexes differed on average by less than a third of a standard deviation. Nevertheless, both Hyde's (2005) and Eagly's (1995) assessments of the evidence suggest that in contemporary North America, there are systematic, small to moderate mean differences between women and men in some gender-related social behaviors, such as helping behavior, aggressive behavior, and smiling. These patterns of differences consist of overlapping bell-shaped curves with a different mean point for men and women. The typical mean sex difference for social behaviors is estimated by Eagly (1995) to be about 0.35 of a standard deviation. Figure 1.1 displays a typical pattern of difference like this.

As both Hyde and Eagly point out, mean sex differences of this size are big enough to notice and matter in social life. This is just what we would expect if gender is a system of social practices for constituting males and females as different and organizing relations between them on the basis of that difference. On the other hand, there are men and women at both extremes of the distributions of these behavioral tendencies so that differences between people of the same sex are always much greater than the average difference between men and women.

The overlapping distributions of men's and women's tendencies to engage in various social behaviors have an important implication for us

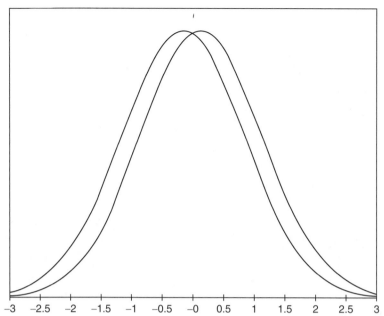

FIGURE 1.1 Typical mean sex differences (standardized units) on psychological attributes. (Either sex may have higher score.) (Source: Maccoby 1998, p. 80, based on Eagly 1995 findings.)

here. They suggest that sex differences in individual traits or dispositions are too small to fully account for some of the highly gendered social patterns we see in the contemporary United States. Recall that gender is a multilevel system of social practices. As a result, the enacted patterns of gender difference and inequality that make up American society are not just an expression of sex-differentiated attributes of individuals, however these are formed. Rather, such enacted patterns result from complex social processes at the interpersonal, organizational, and social structural levels that affect individuals' behaviors and outcomes over and above their personal traits.

To see this point more clearly, consider aggressive behavior, which is often suggested to be sex linked in some way, through biology, social expectations, or both. Could a sex difference in individual tendencies to aggression account for the highly gendered structure of violence in American society? Could it fully explain why in the contemporary United States more than 90% of those in prison for violent crime are men?

Meta-analyses suggest that, in American society, men as individuals, on average, do have a greater tendency to engage in aggressive behavior in a given situation than women (Hyde 2005). The difference is moderate in size, in the range of a third to six-tenths of a standard deviation, which, as we have seen, is bigger than most sex differences in individual attributes. Yet even with a moderate mean difference like this, the distributions of men and women in individual aggressiveness overlap by about two-thirds (Eagly 1995). In other words, there are out there a good number of both rather aggressive women and not so aggressive men. Such a pattern does not lead straightforwardly to the overwhelmingly gendered structure of violence we see in society. Clearly, a complex set of social processes intervenes beyond individual tendencies to aggression to produce the extreme gender differences in violent behavior and incarceration that we see in the United States.

If enacted patterns of gender differences in social behavior do not result simply from stable sex differences in individual dispositions, then the gendered nature of men's and women's social behaviors must be affected by the social contexts in which they are acting. The evidence confirms this. Since we were speaking of sex differences in aggressiveness, consider a study by psychologists Jennifer Lightdale and Deborah Prentice (1994). These researchers measured college men's and women's aggressiveness by their willingness to drop bombs in an interactive video game. When participants completed the video game measure in a social context in which they knew their behavior was monitored by others, the men were significantly more aggressive than the women. But when participants completed the same measure anonymously, there were no significant sex differences in aggression, and women were actually slightly more aggressive than men.

Not surprisingly, then, meta-analyses have clearly shown that the nature of the sex differences studies find is powerfully affected by the context in which behaviors are measured (Eagly 1995; Hyde 2005). In general, sex differences in social behaviors are larger in contexts that are *social relational* in that participants are aware that they are being observed and, thus, are subject to gendered social expectations. Sex differences in social behaviors are typically smaller and sometimes nonexistent in more anonymous situations (see Hyde 2005 for a review). In her comprehensive review of the meta-analytic evidence, Hyde (2005, p. 589) concludes that "the magnitude and even direction of gender differences depends on the context."

My argument in this book focuses on the persistence of gender inequality, not on the explanation of gender differences. Status inequalities like gender, however, as inequalities between "types" of people, rest on cultural assumptions about differences between the types.

Consequently, accounting for the persistence of gender inequality necessarily involves discussions of the social shaping of gender differences. My account of how people use gender as a primary frame for organizing social relations speaks in particular to the role of interpersonal processes in shaping or changing enacted gender differences in behavior. As we will see in future chapters, this account is entirely consistent with meta-analytic evidence that demonstrates how social relational contexts affect the nature of behavioral sex differences.

CONCLUSIONS AND A LOOK AHEAD

In the modern world, then, gender inequality is at root a status inequality. That is, it is based in widely shared cultural beliefs about gender (i.e., gender stereotypes) that have embedded in them assumptions that men are higher status and effectively more competent at most things than are women. It is these status beliefs that constitute gender as a distinct principle of inequality with its own dynamic potential to change or persist. As a result, the persistence of gender inequality in the modern context is at core a question about the persistence of gender status beliefs. As we have seen, however, what allows gender status beliefs to persist is that they are supported in people's everyday experience by positional inequalities between men and women that provide men with more resources and power, on average, than women have. This brings us to the point with which we started. Social, technological, and economic changes that undermine positional inequalities between men and women put pressure on gender status beliefs and, in the process, put the gender hierarchy at risk. How, then, has gender hierarchy managed to persist in contemporary America despite a number of potentially leveling legal, institutional, and political processes?

There is no question that gender inequality does continue to exist in the United States at present. Is it simply an artifact of the past that has not yet fully worn away, or are there processes that actually perpetuate it in the present? The evidence of recent years is that progress against gender inequality has slowed or even stalled in some respects. I argue that the best way to understand contemporary levels of gender inequality is to view them as a product of competing forces. Some of these forces act to level positional inequalities between men and women, while others act to maintain such inequalities in existing organizations and, critically, to reestablish new positional inequalities between men and women in emergent forms of social and economic organizations as these develop in society.

This book is about what I argue is a powerful process on the perpetuation side of these competing forces. Individuals use gender, I will argue, as a primary cultural tool for coordinating their behavior with others and organizing social relations with them. Since most of what people do, they do through relations with others, their use of gender as a primary frame for organizing these relations has widespread consequences. It causes people to carry cultural meanings about gender well beyond contexts of sex and reproduction to all activities that people carry out through social relations. As people use trailing cultural beliefs about gender to frame new social contexts that they confront, they reinscribe the status assumptions embedded in these cultural meanings into the new setting. In this way, I will argue, people rewrite gender inequality into new social and economic arrangements as these are created, preserving that inequality in modified form in the face of ongoing socioeconomic changes that work to undermine it. My argument, then, is that people's use of gender as a primary frame for organizing social relations is a central part of the processes by which gender inequality persists in the modern context.

As we have seen in this chapter, gender is a system of social practices that entails social processes at multiple levels from large-scale institutional arrangements and cultural beliefs to interpersonal relations to individual selves and identities. But gender has several distinctive aspects, including the high rate of interaction between men and women and their dependence on each other for reproduction, that increase the significance of events that take place at the interpersonal level. It is not a coincidence that interpersonal relations are also a central arena for status processes, including those associated with gender. For these reasons, among others, the interpersonal level of social relations is a plausible place to look for processes that play an important role in the persistence of gender inequality.

The account that I will develop about the use of gender as a primary cultural frame for organizing social relations focuses on proximate, mediating causes of the persistence of gender inequality. This account, I have argued, does not depend on assumptions about ultimate causes for gender inequality, including arguments from biology. I have argued that an account of gender as a primary frame for social relations is not inconsistent with cross-cultural evidence about how gender difference and inequality vary or with contemporary evidence about the nature and variation in sex differences in social behavior in North America.

The major point, however, is that contemporary patterns of gender inequality cannot be explained without reference to mediating social processes that create and sustain status beliefs about men and women. It is these mediating processes that I address in my arguments about the social processes through which gender inequality is reinscribed into new forms of social and economic organization as they emerge. To say that there are powerful social relational processes that act to perpetuate gender inequality is not to say that gender inequality cannot be overcome in the modern world. Rather, it is to say that we are unlikely to overcome gender inequality even in the modern context if we do not take these powerful processes into account.

In the next chapter, "A Primary Frame for Organizing Social Relations," I go to the heart of the social relational account of gender that I have only alluded to so far. I describe what it means to say that sex/gender is a "primary frame" for social relations and examine the evidence that it is so. In doing so, I consider the underlying problems of organizing social encounters and how these encourage the cultural development of "common knowledge" categories of social difference, some of which must be "primary" difference systems. I also consider evidence for how cultural difference frames such as gender can be transformed into frames for status inequality as well as difference.

Chapter 3, "Cultural Beliefs and the Gendering of Social Relations," describes how the use of gender as a primary frame shapes people's behavior and judgments in social relational settings in ways that vary systematically by context. In this chapter, I look closely at "common knowledge" cultural beliefs about gender, which are effectively gender stereotypes, and describe how these constitute the "rules" of gender in social relations. I develop a model of how cultural beliefs about gender shape behavior and judgments in ways that create systematic patterns of inequalities between otherwise similar men and women. I then compare this model with the empirical evidence. This chapter develops a set of predicted effects of the gender frame that I then apply in future chapters to consequential organizational settings where positional inequalities between men and women are at stake.

Chapter 4, "Gendering at Work," applies my model of the effects of the gender frame to one of the great battlegrounds over the future of gender inequality: the workplace. I describe how the framing effects of gender on workplace relations act to both reproduce existing gendered structures of jobs and procedures in the work world and create new ones. I consider how the background frame of gender shapes the job-matching process on both the demand side, as employers seek workers, and on the supply side, as individuals seek jobs. Then I consider examples of how gender frame effects occurring in key workplace social relations can lead to the development of new workplace procedures, such as pay systems, that preserve positional inequalities between men and women in work organizations.

The other great battleground over gender inequality in the modern context is the home. This is the focus of chapter 5. The family household, especially the heterosexual household, is a wellspring of cultural beliefs about gender. I develop an account of how the gender frame shapes the household division of labor in the face of the changing material terms on which men and women confront one another in the contemporary American family. I then compare the implications of this account to evidence about the gender organization of household labor at present. This comparison shows how cultural beliefs about gender powerfully shape household work in ways that not only reconfirm those beliefs but also structure men's and women's availability for paid work. The contribution of these effects to the overall maintenance of gender inequality in contemporary America is difficult to overstate.

Chapters 4 and 5 give us a beginning of an answer to the persistence question by showing how the framing effects of gender on social relations at work and at home often blunt the impact of social and economic change on gender inequality in these key organizational sites. The leading edge of change in society, however, consists of sites outside established institutions where new forms of work or new types of social unions are innovated. Chapter 6, "The Persistence of Inequality," examines the persistence question in these settings. First I describe evidence that changes in cultural beliefs about gender follow, but lag behind, changes in material arrangements between men and women. Then I consider how people implicitly draw on lagging gender beliefs to help organize behavior under the uncertain conditions at sites of innovation. Examination of examples of high-tech start-ups and emerging new types of heterosexual unions demonstrates how gender inequality is transmitted forward into new forms of social and economic organization that reinvent it for a new era.

Each of these central substantive chapters (chapters 2–6) contains its own "summary and conclusion" section. Close readers who are familiar with gender scholarship may wish to skim these sections and move on to the next chapter. For others who are new to this material, however, these sections may provide a useful capstone. For yet others, who may wish to read some sections of the book more closely than others, these summaries offer a guide to the progression of the argument.

My goal in this book is to reveal often unrecognized forces that contribute to the persistence of gender inequality even in the contemporary context. It is natural, however, to ask what the implications of my framing perspective are for the future of gender inequality. Since the previous chapters have their own summaries, the last chapter is not a final summary of the argument. Instead, this chapter, "Implications for Change," provides a brief consideration of the prospects for the ultimate achievement of equality, given the framing argument. I make the case that the change process will be an iterative and uneven one but that the framing effects of gender need not be incompatible with considerable progress toward gender equality.

A Primary Frame For Organizing Social Relations

IT IS STRIKING that people find it almost impossible to relate to a person that they cannot classify as male or female. This doesn't happen often, of course, because most of us try to present ourselves to others as clearly male or female. But when it does, it is profoundly unsettling and, more to the point here, *disorganizing* of the social situation. We don't even know how to address a person we can't place as male or female. If we can't begin to address the person, how can we coordinate our behavior with that person in a social encounter? All our taken-for-granted routines for dealing with others are brought up short. In fact, people seem to find it difficult to complete even a routine, trivial social exchange with someone they cannot label as male or female.

The television program *Saturday Night Live* ran a comedy sequence several years ago that memorably evoked the social quandary we face when dealing with a sex-unclassifiable person. In these skits, "Pat," a perfectly androgynous person, engages someone in a routine social exchange—Pat enters a hair salon and asks to have Pat's hair cut, Pat tries to buy shampoo, or Pat walks up to speak to a man or woman at a cocktail party. In each case, the other person is made nearly speechless with confusion and desperately seeks cues by which to categorize Pat as a man or woman in order to figure out how to treat him or her.

Simply by being innocently unclassifiable, Pat wreaks havoc with the routine organization of the social encounter.

These "Pat" skits were interesting not only for illustrating the social vertigo that a sex-unclassified person causes for others but also for the extreme audience reaction they provoked. Each time one of these skits was performed, the studio audience literally howled with nervous laughter that seemed to express as much anxiety as amusement. When I discussed the skits in my classes, one student commented that the skits made some of her friends so uncomfortable when they came on the dorm lounge TV that her friends literally left the room.

The social chaos and anxiety Pat creates shows us how deeply we rely on sex/gender as a basic category for making sense of others in order to know how to relate to them. This is what I mean when I say that sex/gender is a primary frame for organizing social relations. The anxiety we feel when confronted with Pat is not merely personal; it is social, a fundamental disruption in our basic cultural *rules* for making sense of another and organizing the social relation on the basis of that understanding.

Once I was having dinner in a restaurant with my sister; her 3-year-old son, who still had the soft, curly, collar-length hair of a child; and her more grown-up 6-year-old daughter. What happened next showed how our use of sex category as an organizing frame for everyday social relations is as much social-normative as personal. A middle-aged man came somewhat unsteadily from the bar past our table toward the men's room. As he did, he patted my nephew on the head and said, "Cute little girl." "I'm a boy," my nephew loudly replied. The man turned toward the rest of us in red-faced anger, as though we had tricked him, and shouted, "Get his hair cut!" My niece, somewhat endearingly, piped up, "You big bully." The man's righteous anger stemmed from his sense that his social stumble was our fault, not his, because we had violated the basic cultural rule that everyone's sex category should be clearly indicated so that interaction can be organized on the basis of that understanding. Perhaps this is why people put pink headbands on bald babies. They wish to clearly signal the baby's sex to frame the situation properly for everyone.

In this chapter, I explain in greater detail the concept of sex/gender as a primary framing device for social relations and begin to develop its implications for gender inequality. I begin with the underlying problems of organizing social encounters with other people and show how these encourage the development of shared social category systems for making sense of self and other in the situation in order to coordinate behavior. These shared category systems are a type of "common" or cultural knowledge. I then discuss how sex, as a dimension of physical variation among people, is especially susceptible to cultural amplification into a primary framing category for social relations of all sorts.

The utility of socially defined gender, as a cultural device for coordinating social relations, lies in the construction of shared beliefs about presumed differences that are associated with sex category. But as I discuss next in the chapter, beliefs about difference are easily transformed into beliefs about inequality and gender status. Once again, the problems of organizing social relations play a role in this transformation, I argue. Once shared beliefs about gender status develop, they transform the relational framing device of gender into a social frame for inequality as well as difference. In the final section, I discuss how the use of gender as a primary frame for social relations creates a distinctive set of gendered interests that affect the intensity with which people perform gender. These interests, I will argue, become a factor in the staying power of gender as a social form of difference and inequality.

SOCIAL RELATIONS AND THE PROBLEM OF COORDINATION

How is our use of gender as a fundamental way of making sense of people related to the problems of organizing social encounters with others? To answer this question, we need to begin with some basics about social relations themselves—why they are important and what they require. Humans are, after all, a social species. People depend on relations with others to get most of what they want and need in life, from the basics of food, shelter, and security to affection, social recognition, and achievement. We have families; we work together. In fact, nothing is more important to our very survival than our capacity to relate to others and engage with them in joint endeavors.

Relating to another, however, raises the fundamental problem of *coordination* (Brewer 1997). You must find some way to coordinate your behavior with another to engage him or her in the joint activity that even a superficial relationship entails. Engaging another in joint activity is something like a dance. If the other steps forward, you must step back, or you will stumble over each other. What you wish to do in the situation is inherently contingent on what the other will do.

As this suggests, then, coordinating your behavior with another in order to relate requires you to find ways to anticipate how the other will behave in a given instance so that you can decide how to act yourself. For this dance of coordination to work, the other similarly needs a means to accurately anticipate your behavior. Essentially, the two of you need to make your behavior mutually predictable.

Relating to another is an example of the more general coordination problems studied by game theorists (Chwe 2001). Coordination problems involve actors who want to engage in joint behavior, but exactly how they want to behave is contingent on how the other will behave. At first blush, one might think that the solution to coordination problems is simply communication between the actors. But if I tell you what I am about to do so we can coordinate, before I can act, I need to know that you correctly understood what I said, and I need to know as well that you know I know you understood, and so on, in a potentially infinite regress. For instance, let's say that I suggest that we meet at a given time and place. You reply by agreeing. But you still do not really know whether the meeting is on or not until you know that I have received your reply. And I am uncertain about the meeting until I know you know that I have received your reply. Until we both show up for the meeting, there is always some uncertainty and risk of a mix-up.

How do we get out of traps like this and effectively coordinate our behavior, as we do routinely in everyday social relations? Game theorists have used logical proofs to show that the only effective solution to coordination problems is shared or "common knowledge" (see Chwe 2001, pp. 13–18). Interestingly, sociologists known as symbolic interactionists have come to exactly the same conclusion from observations of how people organize everyday interaction (Goffman 1967; Mead 1934; Stryker and Vryan 2003). Common knowledge is not just knowledge that actors in a situation do share but knowledge that they each know or can reasonably presume that they share. Shared knowledge like this is in effect *cultural* knowledge. It is knowledge that is presumed to be consensually shared by a group of people—what "everybody knows"—and not just the private knowledge of individuals. The presumption that everybody in the group knows common knowledge gives it a kind of objective or public character (Berger and Luckmann 1967; Chwe 2001).

We do not solve the coordination traps of everyday social relations by relying on our own idiosyncratic judgments, then. We solve them by drawing on shared, common knowledge that has been constructed by our society and that we all know we know. Sociologist Erving Goffman's (1959, 1967) analyses of everyday social interaction show

how participants draw on common knowledge to develop an implicit "working consensus," through which they coordinate their behavior in a given situation. This consensus defines who each actor is relation to the others in the situation and what he or she can therefore be expected to do. Evidence in fact shows that actors' social interaction in a local situation depends on and is regulated by the shared definition of the local situation represented in this working consensus (Hardin and Conley 2001; Hardin and Higgins 1996). Goffman (1967) points out that actors need not fully buy into the working consensus to accept it as the implicit rules of the game on which the successful coordination of behavior in the local situation depends.

Cultural Category Systems Based on Difference

To get this process started and develop the shared definition of the situation that makes their interaction possible, Goffman's observations suggest that participants need to begin not just with any common knowledge but with a particular *type* of common knowledge (Bettenhausen and Murnighan 1985; Carley 1991; Ridgeway 2006c). Specifically, the participants need shared cultural knowledge that allows them to initiate the process of defining who the others in the situation are and, therefore, who in comparison they are in this situation and, thus, how each person can be expected to act. To define who someone is, we need to categorize that person in some way. And when we categorize another in some way, by implication we categorize ourselves as similar to or different from that other. This mutual categorization, in turn, carries suggestions for how we are likely to act in relation to that person. For this process of defining one another to effectively coordinate our *joint* behavior, it must be based on some common cultural knowledge that we share about ways of categorizing and making sense of people. This suggests that to begin to coordinate our behavior with another, we need to bring to the situation at least some commonly shared cultural systems for categorizing and defining one another.

Category systems by their nature are based on contrast. Something can only be perceived and understood as a particular thing in comparison with something else that it is not. A person is young and not old, black and not white, female and not male. Thus, category systems inherently focus on standards of difference by which things can be judged and classified. This basic observation has implications for our problem here. It suggests that the coordination problem of social relations directs people's attention to *differences* among them, differences on which they can form broadly shared cultural category systems for making sense of one another. As we shall see, sex provides just such a convenient difference upon which to create a shared cultural category system for defining and coordinating with another.

My argument, then, is that the inherent problem of organizing social relations in a population of people who must regularly deal with one another drives them to develop shared category systems based on culturally recognized standards of difference. Obvious examples in American society are shared category systems based on race, gender, age, occupation, and education. In other societies, the list might be slightly different and include categories such as religion, caste, tribe, or region. These cultural category systems are *social difference codes* that play an important role in organizing social relations in a society, not only at the interpersonal level but also in organizations and social institutions like employment firms and the government (Ridgeway 2000; 2006c). Social difference codes provide members of the population with common knowledge about the cues by which to classify self and others according to the code and the behaviors and traits that can be expected of someone of that classification. In this way, these difference codes provide publicly available cultural devices for managing the underlying coordination problems involved in relating to others in that society.

Societies have a variety of social difference codes. For people to interact with one another in real time, however, a few of these cultural category systems must be so simplified that they can be quickly applied as framing devices to virtually anyone in the population to start the process of defining self and other in the situation (Brewer 1988). Following psychologist Marilynn Brewer, I call these *primary* category systems. Primary categories need to be sufficiently broad and general in meaning to apply to virtually everyone.

We most often encounter others in a specific institutional context, say, a workplace or grocery store. Those institutional contexts typically contain defined social roles (e.g., coworker or boss, shopper or cashier) that give us clues to defining who self and other are in that context. But to use the roles an institutional context suggests, we need to already know the rules of that context. Also, each institutional context is different and has slightly different roles embedded in it, so there is a lot to know. Primary categories get us out of this trap by applying to everyone, rather than just to those in a particular institutional context or from a particular segment of society. Since they transcend the limits of institutional definitions of self and other, they allow us to act quickly in the time constraints of interaction wherever we are. Thus, primary categories jump-start the process of defining self and other in the situation by giving us an all-purpose starting place, an initial frame for figuring the other out, whether we encounter that other in a familiar institution or in an utterly unfamiliar context.

Just as primary category systems can be applied to everyone, they also must be so widely shared as cultural knowledge that people can presume that everyone in the population knows them. Furthermore, primary category systems need to be based on salient cues that can be quickly recognized so that the other can be immediately classified to initiate the coordination process. Psychologists' studies of how people perceive others suggest that primary categories are usually ones that can be based on visual cues, whether these are distinctive physical features of the person, like skin color, or visually distinctive social signs, like a caste mark (Fiske and Taylor 1991, p. 144).

As broad categories of difference, primary categories do not provide a very specific sense of who the other is, or who, by implication, self is in relation to the other. Furthermore, primary categories may not be the aspects of identity that personally are most important to either self or the other in the situation. But primary categories provide self and the other with a sufficient common knowledge base to begin the coordination process of relating to one another. They render the other sufficiently meaningful to self, and self to the other, to allow both individuals to take the additional steps necessary to further define each other in more specific and situationally relevant ways. Knowing that Pat is a woman (or a man), the hair stylist can now ask, "How would you like me to cut your hair?" and understand the answer. Thus the need for a few primary categories of identity, I argue, is social organizational as well as a result of people's needs for cognitive simplification, as psychologists have posited (Brewer 1988; Fiske 1998).

Sex/Gender as a Primary Category

As a form of human variation, sex/gender is especially susceptible to being culturally amplified into a primary framing category for social relations. It is associated with a bimodal distribution of physical traits that encourages a usefully simple, dichotomous category system. It can usually be identified quickly through visual cues. It can be applied to anyone. Furthermore, the resulting sex category system is of real interest to people both because it has relevance to sexuality and reproduction and because it delineates a line of difference among people who must regularly coordinate their behavior, not just as mates but in kin and other larger groups.

Given its relevance to sexual activity, reproduction, and the survival of the species, is the perceptual ability to sex-categorize others simply an innate reflex rather than socially driven? Clearly, the ability to sex-categorize others is something that we must be biologically prepared to learn. However, the biological imperative to be *able* to sex-categorize does not logically necessitate that we use sex category as a primary frame for organizing social relations of all sorts, rather than just those with reproductive implications. It may make biological sense to automatically sex-categorize anyone who is of an appropriate age to be a potential mate. Arguably, attention to the sex category of our children might also have implications for the survival of our biological line. But why do we automatically sex-categorize old people and other people's babies, and why can we not relate to them unless we do? Why, after all, did the man in the restaurant care whether he knew that my nephew, who was no one to him, was a boy or a girl? I am arguing, then, that the problems of organizing social relations encourage people to make much greater cultural use of sex categorization than biology alone could logically require. However, the fact that the ability to sex-categorize is something that we do learn early on makes it only more likely that sex/gender will be a dimension of individual difference that is culturally expanded into a primary device for framing social relations of all kinds (Zemore, Fiske, and Kim 2000).

The cultural transformation of sex/gender into a primary category for framing social relations expands sex categorization past its biological base in two ways. First, the transformation expands the social range across which we use sex as a focal category for defining people. Instead of a frame for relations of reproductive relevance, it becomes a primary frame for all concrete others to whom we relate, not only in person but also over the Internet or even imaginatively. Along with this expansion of range comes a transformation of the sex categorization process itself, from one based on a perceptual ability to recognize physical features to a culturally knowledgeable reading of social cues. As ethnomethodologists have demonstrated, in everyday social encounters, sex categorization is a socially constructed process that depends on social cues such as clothing, hairstyles, and conventional ways of speaking and moving that are culturally presumed to stand for underlying physical sex differences (Kessler and McKenna 1978; West and Zimmerman 1987). This, of course, is why the man in the restaurant mistook my nephew for a girl. It is precisely because routine sex categorization is so socially constructed that people as diverse as characters in Shakespearean plays and transgendered individuals are able to pass as a member of the other sex.

Second and importantly, the cultural transformation of sex categorization into a primary frame for social relations expands and diversifies the cultural meanings and expectations for behavior associated with men and women far beyond those necessitated by reproduction. As we shall see, it becomes possible to associate anything that males and females do in a given society with their sex category (Eagly and Steffen 1984; Wood and Eagly 2002). I argue, then, that the biological baseline of sex becomes culturally specific gender through two cultural amplification processes: expansion in range of application and expansion and diversification of associated behavioral expectations.

Evidence that Sex/Gender Is a Primary Category

The social confusion and anxiety evoked by Pat gives us a feel for how important sex/gender is for making sense of others. But what systematic evidence do we have that we actually use sex/gender as a primary category for making sense of anyone we try to deal with? In 1988, psychologist Marilynn Brewer proposed that limits on people's capacity to process information would require that they have a small number of no more than three or four superordinate or primary categories that they automatically use to make initial sense of others. Besides being easily perceptible and culturally meaningful, primary categories would be used so frequently as to be processed quickly and automatically without the need for conscious thought.

Following these criteria, Brewer reasoned that sex and age will virtually always be primary categories in any society, but other primary categories will vary across cultures. Subsequent research on how people cognitively make sense of others has confirmed that sex, age, and race are all primary categories of person perception in the United States (see Schneider 2004, p. 96, for a list of references). This research further shows that people use these categories to define who the other is, in terms of character and behavior, by drawing on shared cultural stereotypes associated with the categories.

In one of the earlier studies of this sort, Marilynn Brewer and Layton Lui (1989) asked study participants to sort 140 pictures of people into between 6 and 12 stacks, based on similarity in character or personality. The participants were then asked to describe what made the people pictured in each of their stacks similar in character. Half the pictures were men and half women, and half were young and half older, but otherwise the pictures were diverse in appearance. The researchers found that especially sex but also age powerfully predicted which pictures were stacked together. In fact, participants' groupings of people almost never crossed sex and age boundaries, suggesting that they relied very heavily on these categories to read character. Yet, when asked to describe why the pictures in their stack went together, the participants only rarely acknowledged either sex or age, further suggesting that they often used these categories unconsciously without realizing that they were doing so.

In another study like this, Charles Stangor and colleagues (1992) asked participants in a series of studies to examine 8 to 10 pictures of people identified by a name and a quoted statement. The pictures contained equal numbers of white and black males and females. A few minutes after studying the pictures, the participants were given a surprise quiz that asked them to match each statement with the person who made it. The researchers were interested in the errors participants made on the quiz because prior research had shown that people are more likely to mix up those that they have cognitively lumped together in the same category. The results showed that participants were overwhelmingly more likely to confuse people of the same sex and race, suggesting that both sex and race were functioning as primary categories. Furthermore, they were more likely to mix up people of the same sex but different races, but not the other way around, suggesting that people were using sex as their most fundamental category for making sense of the people in the pictures. The tendency for participants to confuse people on the basis of other aspects of appearance, such as black or white clothing, was sensitive to instructions that called participants' attention to that aspect, but not sex and race. These American participants categorized the people in the pictures by sex and race whether the instructions primed them to do so or not, as though they felt it was always necessary and useful in the United States to understand people in terms of their sex and race.

People not only sex-categorize others automatically but also do so literally in the blink of an eye, even when confronted with people who could potentially be classified in many ways according to other social characteristics, as studies of the speed of categorization show (Ito and Urland 2003; Zárate and Smith 1990). Furthermore, when people cannot instantly sex-categorize others, it interferes with their cognitive ability to process other things in the situation. Allison Wisecup, Miller McPherson, and Lynn Smith-Lovin (2005) had study participants sex-categorize faces just before working on a cognitively demanding task. When the faces were androgynous and difficult to categorize, participants' performance on the task was significantly reduced, compared with when the faces were easy to categorize.

Psychologists Sarah Zemore, Susan Fiske, and Hyun-Jeong Kim (2000) argue that sex categorization becomes so automatic, quick, and ubiquitous at least partly because, as a simple, dichotomous classification, it is one of the first social difference codes that small children's still developing minds are able to learn, at least in outline. As a first cultural tool, children apply it broadly to simplify their efforts to make sense of others in their environment.

Children learn to sex-categorize adult faces and voices in their first year and learn to reliably sex-categorize themselves at around 2½ years of age (see Maccoby 1998, pp. 157–163). Once children learn to reliably sex-categorize both self and other, they become cognitively able to use sex as a category for relational, self-other meaning. As developmental psychologist Eleanor Maccoby (1998) observes, it is only at this age that children for the first time begin to show preferences in the sex of their playmates. During the age 3 to 5 period, these preferential choices can be seen primarily in play settings outside the immediate family, such as in a preschool or neighborhood play area, where these youngsters encounter others of their age that they may not already know. In these settings, the youngsters act as though they are using the others' similar or different sex as an initial basis for figuring out how to relate to them. It appears that these youngsters are already beginning to use sex categorization to frame relations with unfamiliar others. Because it begins so early, Zemore and colleagues (2000) argue that the use of sex category as a primary way of making sense of others becomes automatic for children, even though their initial assumptions about the cultural meanings associated with sex category are oversimplified. Children only gradually learn the full content of cultural beliefs associated with sex categories.

Although we automatically sex-categorize people we try to make sense of or relate to, our use of sex categorization is not mere reflex but driven by the implicit goal relevance of another we must deal with (Fiske 1998; Schneider 2004, p. 96). Studies of the limits of sex categorization—that is, the few circumstances under which people can be exposed to a human face and not cognitively classify it as male or female—show these goal-driven aspects of sex categorization. Neil Macrae and colleagues (2005) asked study participants to classify names written in uppercase or lowercase (e.g., "peter" or "SUSAN") either in terms of sex (male or female) or case (upper or lower). In the background were either male or female faces, but participants were told to ignore this information as irrelevant to the task. When participants were classifying the names by sex, however, gender meanings were implicitly associated with their goals, and they were unable to avoid sex-categorizing the background faces despite their instructions. As a result, they slowed down when classifying names that were inconsistent with the sex of the faces in the background. When participants classified the names by case, however, gender meanings were completely irrelevant, and they showed no evidence of having meaningfully categorized the faces as male or female.

Although the use of sex/gender as a primary cultural device for making sense of another begins with a rapid, simple classification of the other as male or female, it does not end there. Research shows that labeling another by sex implicitly primes in the person's mind shared cultural stereotypes of males and females and makes those stereotypes unconsciously available to shape the person's judgments and behavior toward that other (Banaji and Hardin 1996; Blair and Banaji 1996). As we will see in the next chapter, the extent to which these stereotypes bias the person's judgment and behavior varies greatly and depends on the nature of the situation, but sex categorization makes these stereotypes cognitively available to do so (Kunda and Spencer 2003; Ridgeway 2001a; Wagner and Berger 1997). In addition, because sex category is typically the very first way that actors in a situation classify one another, their subsequent classifications of one another by institutional roles and so on are cognitively nested within their prior understanding of each other as a male or female and take on a slightly different meaning as a result (Brewer 1988). Consider, for instance, the slightly different meanings evoked by a male clerk and a female customer versus a female clerk and a male customer. If we can't comprehend someone sufficiently to relate to them without sex-categorizing them first (and making salient our own sex category by implication), then cultural meanings associated with gender are pulled in some degree into every sphere of social life that is enacted through social relations.

FROM FRAMING DIFFERENCE TO FRAMING INEQUALITY

Sex/gender works as a coordinating device for social relations through the construction of shared cultural beliefs about presumed differences in character and behavior that are associated with sex category. By this common knowledge, someone classified as female can be expected to behave in a specific way that is different from someone classified as male, and this provides an initial, orienting frame for coordinating behavior with them. Cultural beliefs about difference, however, are easily transformed into beliefs about inequality. Our next task is to examine how the organizational problems of social relations that encourage a focus on difference also play a role in this transformation of difference to inequality. If gender is a primary frame for social relations, then relational processes that transform beliefs about difference into inequality may be especially important for cultural beliefs about gender.

Beliefs about inequality, once they develop, shape, in turn, the nature of beliefs about difference in a recursive manner. Inequality, after all, presumes difference because men and women must be understood as different to be perceived as unequal. When widely shared cultural beliefs about gender become beliefs about inequality as well as difference, our use of sex/gender as a primary frame for social relations frames relations between men and women on unequal terms.

In what follows, we will first consider evidence that the problems of organizing social relations on the basis of a group difference tend to transform the difference into a status inequality when there is long-term mutual dependence among the groups. Next we will unpack one of the ways that this transformation can occur and consider its relevance to sex/gender. To do this, we will examine a theory and some evidence about how encounters between people from different social groups that are mutually dependent can cause the participants to form shared status beliefs about their difference that get spread among the population. In the final part of this section, we will apply this approach to different conditions of mutual dependence among the sexes and consider how it would sustain different sorts of gender status beliefs that imply greater or lesser gender inequality.

Mutual Dependence and Status Inequality

I have argued so far that the coordination problem of social relations encourages populations of people to attend to physical sex differences as a visible framework on which to construct a shared social difference code. A problem arises, however, from the fact that social difference codes are never purely neutral in their implications for the categories of people they define. Several decades of research by psychologists have demonstrated that the mere classification of another as different inherently evokes an evaluative response (for reviews, see Brewer and Brown 1998; Hogg 2001). This research has developed out of a theoretical approach called *social identity theory* that focuses on the way people's group memberships affect how they think about and act toward those within their group compared with those outside it (Hogg 2003; Tajfel and Turner 1986; Turner et al. 1987). When people classify themselves as a member of one social group compared with another, this research has shown, their first, typical response is to assume that their own group is "better." In some of these studies, for instance, researchers have divided participants into two groups on a purely arbitrary basis, such as the participants' relative preference for the paintings of Klee or Kandinsky (Tajfel and Turner 1986). Even such "mere differences" caused participants to evaluate members of their own group more positively than members of the other group. Furthermore, when given the chance, participants acted to favor their own group when dividing up resources. This research shows, then, that the use of a shared social difference code to make sense of and relate to another will also evoke an underlying tendency for in-group favoritism.

Notice, however, that in the context of sex/gender, this typical evaluative response to difference effectively creates competing views of the proper evaluative relation between males and females. That is, on the basis of mere difference alone, men should assume that men are better, and women should assume that women are better. If gender is a system of difference for coordinating joint behavior among individuals, then competing views of who is "better" are a problem. As an impediment to smooth mutual relations between men and women, competing views of which gender is better may be difficult to sustain over the long run.

Sociologist Mary Jackman (1994) has studied what happens when members of different social groups are bound together in society under conditions of long-term mutual dependence as, of course, men and women are. Using a variety of historical and contemporary data from the United States, she analyzes relations between groups based on race (blacks and whites), class (upper and lower classes), and sex (women and men). In each case, she argues, the mutual dependence between the groups has tended to transform their competing in-group preferences by one means or another into shared ideologies that constitute what we referred to in chapter 1 as *status beliefs*. When status beliefs develop, members of both groups come to agree (or concede) that, as a matter of social reality, one group is more respected, status worthy, and presumed to be more competent in some way than is the other.

For status beliefs to form, then, members of one group must overcome their tendency to in-group favoritism, at least in regard to status and competence, if not necessarily in liking (Rudman and Goodwin 2004). They must accept that the other group is more respected and thought to be more competent than they are.

Whether or not there was a preexisting inequality of resources or power between the groups, once status beliefs develop, inequality will be established because status brings influence, which is a type of social power, and it leads to resource advantages. Thus, to the extent that shared cultural beliefs about gender become status beliefs, gender is established as a dimension of inequality, as well as difference. Furthermore, since gender status beliefs associate group differences with presumed competence differences, they legitimize inequality between the sexes.

In comparison with groups created by most other social distinctions, including race and class, the mutual dependence between the sexes is exceptionally high. Heterosexuality, reproduction, the way that sex crosscuts kin relations, and the division of the population into two roughly equal-sized gender groups all increase contact and dependence between the sexes. These conditions put unusually strong structural pressures on gender as a system of shared beliefs about difference to also be a system of shared beliefs about the status ranking of men and women.

Social Relations and the Development of Status Beliefs

As Mary Jackman's analysis implies, there are likely to be many specific ways that status beliefs about a group difference might develop. A sociological theory called *status construction theory* claims, however, that processes that occur in the routine organization of interpersonal encounters are among the processes that can facilitate the emergence of status beliefs about group differences under particular conditions (Ridgeway 2006d). Given the high degree of contact between men and women under conditions of mutual dependence, these relational processes may be especially implicated in the construction or, if not in the initial creation, then in the everyday maintenance of status beliefs about gender. For this reason, we will examine this theory and the evidence behind it in more detail.

When people work together on a shared goal, whether it be planning a family vacation or devising a national health policy, a long tradition of research has shown that a hierarchy tends to develop among the participants in which some have more social esteem and influence than others (Bales 1950, 1970; Berger, Conner, and Fisek 1974; Ridgeway 2001b). A substantial body of research associated with a sociological theory called *expectation states theory* has delved into the way that such interpersonal status hierarchies work (Berger et al. 1974, 1977; Correll and Ridgeway 2003). This research has shown that such status hierarchies emerge from and are driven by the expectations participants form for their own ability to contribute to the group goal, compared with the ability of each other member. Thus, implicit assumptions about each member's relative competence at the group's goal activities underlie the members' influence and esteem in the group.

Since men and women must often cooperate with one another to achieve what they want and need, they frequently relate to one another in just the goal-oriented circumstances in which interpersonal status hierarchies tend to form. Since they will have also sex-categorized each other, this means that their cultural understandings of one another as men and women will be repeatedly juxtaposed to their understanding of one of them as more competent, esteemed, and influential in the situation than are others of them. Status construction theory argues that these are precisely the circumstances in which social encounters can induce their participants to form status beliefs about their social difference (Ridgeway 1991, 2006d).

Status construction theory is about the development and spread of status beliefs in a population of people. It is conceptually linked to the body of expectation states theory research on interpersonal status hierarchies that we just discussed (e.g., Berger et al. 1977; Correll and Ridgeway 2003). Although status construction theory is not a theory of gender, it can be usefully applied to understanding how cultural beliefs about gender difference often become beliefs about gender status inequality.

Status construction theory focuses on encounters in which people who differ on a salient group distinction, such as gender or race, come together to work on cooperative goals, and influence hierarchies develop. If, over multiple encounters like this, these influence hierarchies consistently associate those in one group with greater esteem and competence than those in another group, the theory argues that members of both groups will form status beliefs favoring the more influential group. Essentially, the repeated experience of seeing people different from them become more influential and apparently more competent in the situation than people like them talks the members of less influential group into accepting that "most people" would see their own group as less respected and competent than the other group. In this way, the members of the less influential group are implicitly pressured to overcome their in-group preference and concede, as a matter of social reality, that the other group has higher status than their own. Members of the more influential group agree that they are the higher status group so, in the end, the two groups share a status belief about their group distinction.

Do people actually form status beliefs in encounters in the way that status construction theory argues? I and my colleagues have conducted several studies that show that they do (Ridgeway and Correll 2006; Ridgeway and Erickson 2000; Ridgeway et al. 1998, 2009). In these studies, participants are told that they are going to work with a partner on a cooperative task. They are then given a "test" that classifies them as belonging to a different group than their partner in terms of "personal response style." Then they work with their partner, and an influence hierarchy develops between them. After this, they work on a second task with another partner who also comes from the other response style group, and the same type of influence hierarchy develops with this new partner. After just two experiences like this in which people in one response style group were consistently more influential than those in the other group, participants in study after study formed status beliefs about the response style groups. That is, they formed beliefs that "most people" would rate those from the more influential response style group as more respected, powerful, and competent but not as considerate as those in the other group. Participants formed these status beliefs even when the beliefs cast their own group as lower in status than the other group.

The fledgling status beliefs that individuals form from their encounters with socially different others have widespread significance only if they become part of the general cultural beliefs about that social difference that are commonly held in the population. The status beliefs, in other words, must spread widely in the population and become part of the accepted social difference code. Status construction theory argues that this will happen if some tipping factor develops that gives people from one group a systematic advantage in gaining influence over people from the other group in their goal-oriented encounters with one another (Ridgeway 1991, 2006d). Tipping factors could include a preexisting inequality between the groups in material resources, in technology, in information, in the means of physical coercion, or in any other factor that might shape the influence hierarchies that develop when people from the two groups meet. It is not necessary that the inequality in, say, resources or physical strength be such that all members of one group are richer or stronger than all members of another group. To act as a tipping factor, it is necessary only that there are more members of one group that are richer or stronger on average than there are members of the other group. Also, even a string of random events that results in a cluster of encounters in which people from one group gain influence over those from another group can snowball into a tipping factor (Mark 1999).

Once a tipping factor develops, it ensures that encounters in the population between people from the two groups will always produce more status beliefs overall that favor the advantaged group than the other group. This preponderance of beliefs favoring one group is amplified as people spread their beliefs to others. Studies show that people spread their beliefs by acting on them in future encounters (Ridgeway and Erickson 2000; Ridgeway et al. 2009). Eventually, the theory argues, status beliefs favoring the group advantaged by the tipping factor will overwhelm counterbeliefs and become widely held in the population. Computer simulations of these processes support these arguments of status construction theory. They confirm that if such a tipping factor develops, widely shared status beliefs would indeed be a logical result of the way people form and spread status beliefs in goal-oriented encounters (Ridgeway and Balkwell 1997).

These studies show how goal-oriented encounters facilitate the development of status beliefs about social differences. Such encounters do not inevitably transform a widely held social difference code into a status difference. This transformation requires the presence of a tipping factor that advantages people from one group in gaining influence over those from another in encounters. Also, other factors can disrupt the formation of status beliefs in encounters (Ridgeway and Correll 2006). However, if people in a society use gender as a primary cultural frame for organizing social relations, then goal-oriented encounters between men and women will continually expose their cultural beliefs about gender to the risk of being transformed into status beliefs. This is most likely to occur through the emergence of some tipping factor in a particular historical circumstance. The exposure of beliefs about gender difference to the risk of becoming beliefs about gender status is especially ongoing because men and women are not just mutually dependent in a material sense, as are people from different classes or races. Men and women also share intimate family ties that necessarily bring them together in cooperative goal-oriented encounters on a very frequent basis (Wood and Eagly 2002).

Specific and Diffuse Gender Status Beliefs

At least two different types of status beliefs might develop about gender through processes such as these: specific status beliefs and diffuse status beliefs (Berger et al. 1977; Wagner and Berger 2002). Specific status beliefs are beliefs that people from one group are more competent at a specific range of tasks and, therefore, more esteemed in that realm, but not in all realms. An example might be that people from one group are better at math, better at mechanical tasks, or better at child care than those from another group. Specific status beliefs advantage people in gaining influence and power in situations that are relevant to their presumed skills but do not advantage them in situations not connected to those skills. Being thought good at math is not a status advantage when the shared task is plumbing.

In contrast, diffuse status beliefs carry much broader implications for inequality. Diffuse status beliefs are beliefs that people from one group are not only more competent at some specific tasks but also more generally competent overall and, thus, more generally worthy of respect than are those from another group. As a result, diffuse status beliefs advantage (or disadvantage) people over an unlimited range of situations.

Different material circumstances in a society might cause goal-oriented encounters between men and women to give rise to specific rather than diffuse status beliefs about gender. Under material conditions in which cooperative dependence between men and women is especially intense in that they rely on one another for their very survival from day to day, beliefs about gender difference may be more at risk of being transformed into task-specific status beliefs. The material necessity for efficiency in task accomplishment is resolved through a gender division of labor that acts as a tipping factor that gives rise to specific status beliefs that favor men in some task areas and women in others (Wood and Eagly 2002). In such conditions of intense mutual dependence, however, neither men nor women can afford to minimize the contributions or skills of the other group. As a result, these specialized spheres of status and influence could result in a relatively egalitarian sharing of power between men and women rather than in a single, overall gender hierarchy. This argument is consistent with cross-cultural evidence that small, technologically simple societies, which are often foraging societies, tend to be relatively (although not necessarily entirely) gender egalitarian (Huber 2007; Wood and Eagly 2002). For interested readers, Maria Lepowsky (1993) describes just such an egalitarian gender arrangement in her ethnography of a small society in New Guinea.

Under conditions of greater social and material resources, however, the desperate interdependence between the sexes is lessened somewhat, and the egalitarian balance between gendered spheres of influence might be difficult to sustain. With more available resources, the risk is greater that one sex will gain greater access to these resources, creating a tipping factor that consolidates specific gender status beliefs into a diffuse status belief that broadly advantages that sex over the other. If this happened, the tasks at which the "losing" sex was thought to be more skilled would themselves become less valued than the tasks associated with the "winning" sex. In fact, the cross-cultural evidence shows that male dominance—that is, an overall gender hierarchy favoring men—is more closely associated with materially better-off societies than with the simplest societies (Wood and Eagly 2002).

The historical origins of male dominance in Western or other societies are unknown, and it is not my task here to uncover them. Many existing theories about these origins, however, posit some factor, such as superior strength or the physical constraints faced by lactating mothers, that could have given men a systematic influence advantage in their dealings with women at some particular time in the past through a resulting division of labor that allowed men a greater control of resources (cf. Huber 2007; Smuts 1995; Wood and Eagly 2002). The evidence we have about how status beliefs develop suggests that such a resource advantage would have led to widely held diffuse status beliefs that associate men not only with specific skills but also with greater competence and status worthiness overall than women.

Whatever their origin, however, once general status beliefs favoring men become established in a society's culture, they root male advantage in membership in sex category itself rather than in some physical or material advantage. As a result, diffuse gender status beliefs like this advantage men even over their female peers who are just as materially rich as them, just as strong as them, and not lactating mothers. Because such gender status beliefs root inequality in group membership, they constitute gender as a distinct organizing principle of inequality that is not fully reducible to other differences in power, material resources, or even sex-linked physical characteristics such as physical size or motherhood status. Gender status beliefs like this are characteristic of many societies, including the contemporary United States (Fiske et al. 2002; Glick et al. 2004; Williams and Best 1990). They transform the relational framing device of gender into a frame for gender inequality as well as difference.

GENDER INTERESTS

The cultural construction of sex/gender as a primary frame for social relations makes the performance of gender a cultural requirement for individuals. As we have seen, our use of gender as a category of meaning in social relations is automatic, unconscious, and nearly mandatory, socially. Research on person perception, however, has shown that individuals' automatic use of gender in relating to others is further intensified or undercut by their motivations in the situation (Fiske, Lin, and Neuberg 1999). These motivations reflect the personal interests they feel in playing the gender game in the situation.

As a primary cultural frame for organizing social relations on the basis of difference as well as inequality, sex/gender creates a distinct set of interests for individual actors. These interests become central to the staying power of gender as a socially significant form of inequality. They affect the energy with which individuals enact gender in different contexts and the likelihood that they will resist challenges to existing gender arrangements. Gender interests affect as well the likelihood that individuals themselves will act to undermine traditional gender enactments in social situations. Thus gender interests add a degree of individual agency to the otherwise automatic use of gender as a cultural frame for organizing social relations.

In any given situation, after all, people are never just men or women. They are also of a certain age, race, social class, region, occupation, and so on. As we will discuss in more detail in the next chapter, people's interests as men or women always coexist with multiple, other, often competing interests based on other identities. In any situation, then, people must allocate their energy over the enactment of these multiple potential identities. That they must make such implicit choices in allocating their energy gives a degree of interest-driven agency to the investment they make in the performance of gender in social relations.

What, then, are the interests that gender creates? Obviously, gender status beliefs that are incorporated within cultural conceptions of who men and women are give men an interest in maintaining the presumption that they are more status worthy and more competent than similar women. As we will see, these cultural beliefs advantage men in attaining positions of greater power and resources within a wide variety of social institutions (Reskin 1988; Ridgeway 1997). Some heterosexual women may also have an interest in maintaining these status beliefs if these women attain more resources through their alliances with status-advantaged men than they would in a world without male privilege.

The interests of most women in improving their lives, however, encourage them to push against male status dominance. Male privilege created by gender status beliefs, then, creates a somewhat divided set of interests in the populace.

Gender creates another, deeper set of interests for both men and women that are not divided, however. In my view, these additional interests are especially important to gender's contemporary staying power as a system of inequality. As a primary frame for social relations, gender is one of the most fundamental identities by which people render themselves comprehensible to others and to themselves in terms that are socially meaningful and valid (Ridgeway 2006b; West and Zimmerman 1987). This gives both men and women a deep sociocognitive interest in maintaining a reasonably clear framework of cultural beliefs that defines who men and women are by differentiating them. Thus, gender's embeddedness in the organization of social relations gives both men and women an interest in resisting a real erasure of gender difference. In the current cultural framework, however, maintenance of beliefs about gender difference sustains beliefs about status inequality. This is the difficult nexus that must be unwound to fully disrupt gender inequality.

For men, of course, the two sets of interests gender creates, the maintenance of status inequality and the maintenance of difference, work together. For most women, however, they compete. Not surprisingly, then, actions that intentionally or inadvertently work against current gender arrangements are more likely to come from women than from men. Feminist political movements are an obvious example, but so are everyday decisions by women to seek a promotion or apply for a better paying job. Men also occasionally take actions to undermine gender arrangements, however, since they, too, have other personal, political, or economic interests that may conflict with their gender interests. In subsequent chapters, as we examine how the framing effects of gender work to affect the persistence of gender inequality, we will repeatedly see the effects of the diverse interests that the gender frame creates for individual men and women.

SUMMARY AND CONCLUSION

Our goal in this chapter has been to unpack what it means to say that gender is a primary cultural frame that people use for organizing their social relations with other people. Since I have argued that gender's role as an all-purpose cultural tool for organizing social relations is at the heart of the processes by which gender inequality persists in the modern world, this is a concept that we need to understand. In this chapter, we examined the underlying processes that give rise to the gender frame and root it in cultural definitions of difference and inequality. Our purpose has been to set the stage for a more detailed analysis of the effects of the gender frame in subsequent chapters.

We started with the problems of organizing social relations and why they create the need for a few primary frames for categorizing and making sense of virtually any other and, by comparison, our self in relation to that other. To effectively coordinate our behavior with another, we must both act on the basis of common knowledge, that is, cultural information we can presume we share. In particular, we need shared cultural systems for categorizing and defining who the self and other are in the situation and, therefore, how each of us can be expected to act. Since categorization is based on contrast, these cultural systems will be based on social differences. A few (3–4) of these shared category systems must be so simplified that they can be quickly applied as framing devices to any person to initiate the process of defining self and other in the situation. Our organizational need for a few primary frames coexists with the fact that sex/gender is a dimension of human variation on which we learn to categorize one another early on, which has relevance for reproduction and sexuality, and that delineates a line of difference among people who must regularly coordinate their behavior. As a result, sex/gender is especially susceptible to cultural amplification into a primary framing category for social relations. Studies of social cognition confirm that sex, age, and race are primary categories in the United States. Studies show that we automatically and nearly instantly sex-categorize any concrete other that we consider in relation to ourselves. As we do so, we unconsciously prime our shared cultural stereotypes of gender. If we cannot relate to another without sex-categorizing him or her and implicitly evoking cultural beliefs about gender, then gender will be brought into all activities that we carry out through social relations.

Sex/gender coordinates social relations through shared cultural beliefs about presumed differences in the character and behavior of males and females. Cultural beliefs about difference, however, are easily transformed into beliefs about inequality, and when this happens, gender frames relations between men and women on unequal terms. We examined this transformation in greater detail.

When people cooperate to achieve a shared goal, as men and women frequently do, status hierarchies develop in which some individuals are perceived as more esteemed, influential, and competent than others. Since people in these situations will have sex-categorized one another, this means that their cultural understanding of one another as men or women will be repeatedly juxtaposed to their understandings of some of them as more esteemed and competent than others. This creates the possibility that, under some conditions, people might link these status perceptions with their gender beliefs and form either specific or diffuse gender status beliefs.

To consider this possibility more carefully, we turned to studies based on status construction theory, which is a theory about the development and spread of status beliefs in a population of people. This theory suggests that the problems of organizing social relations, alone, are not likely to create diffuse status beliefs that advantage males generally over females. However, in conjunction with particular historical circumstances, they may have this result. If a historical circumstance causes men to gain an advantage in control over material resources or some other factor that gives them a systematic influence advantage over women in their social relations, then the social processes of these encounters are likely to transform this resource advantage into widely shared status beliefs that favor men over women. Once such status beliefs develop, they advantage men even over women who are just as materially rich as they are or just as strong as they are. Gender status beliefs, however they develop, root inequality in the sex category itself and, thus, constitute gender as a distinct organizing principle of inequality that is not fully reducible to other differences in power, resources, or even sex-linked physical characteristics.

As a primary frame for social relations, the performance of gender is a cultural requirement for individuals. Nevertheless, the interests the gender frame gives individuals in maintaining or resisting gender arrangements can affect the energy with which they enact gender. While women and men usually differ in their interests in maintaining male status dominance, men and women often share an interest in maintaining a clear framework of cultural beliefs that defines who men and women are by differentiating them. Yet, in the current cultural framework, maintenance of beliefs about gender difference sustains beliefs about status inequality. We will trace the effect of these gender interests in future chapters.

THREE

Cultural Beliefs And The Gendering Of Social Relations

THE SOCIAL CATEGORY of sex works as a primary frame for social relations only because it carries with it "common knowledge" beliefs about men and women. These are cultural beliefs about the distinguishing characteristics and behaviors of typical males and females that we all assume we all know. Because we not only know these gender beliefs but also take for granted that others know them, we can rely on these beliefs to begin to coordinate the dance of social relations.

That is not all shared cultural beliefs about gender do, however. As we saw in the last chapter, these beliefs also disaggregate gender from other forms of inequality and constitute it as a distinctive system of difference and inequality with its own dynamic. I argued that gender in American society is a system of social practices for constituting males and females as different and unequal. Considered this way, our shared cultural beliefs about who men and women are clearly at the heart of our gender system. To understand how this gender system persists in the contemporary United States, along with the inequality it implies, we need to examine these cultural beliefs more closely and understand how they shape social relations. This is the project of this chapter.

The first task is to find out more about these beliefs themselves. How should we conceptualize these beliefs, and what does the evidence show about them? What, for instance, does research reveal about the content of contemporary gender beliefs? Are these beliefs consensually shared in society? What does the content of gender beliefs reflect? Are there dominant or alternative forms of these beliefs? What about sub-groups in society?

The second task is to examine the effects of these beliefs in social relational contexts. If these beliefs play a role in coordinating behavior, how do they do that, and how do their effects vary by context? In this chapter, we will examine the basic principles by which gender beliefs shape social relations and the evidence behind these principles. Then, in subsequent chapters, we will develop the implications of these processes for gender inequality in the workplace and in the home to further examine the question of persistence.

CONTEMPORARY CULTURAL BELIEFS ABOUT GENDER

The Rules of the Gender Game

We often think of widely shared cultural beliefs about men and women as simply stereotypes, reflected, for instance, in the popular phrase that "men are from Mars and women are from Venus." Commonly held cultural beliefs about gender are indeed stereotypes, but there is more to them than we often associate with that term. Shared gender stereotypes are cultural instructions or *rules* for enacting gender in American society.

The social theorists Anthony Giddens (1984) and William Sewell (1992) have argued that social structures of all sorts have an inherent "dual" nature. They consist on the one hand of the implicit rules or cultural schemas by which people enact the structure and, on the other hand, of the observable, material distributions of behaviors, resources, and power that result. The structure of the typical classroom, for instance, consists of the cultural conceptions or rules that students and teachers follow in shaping their behavior toward one another, as well as the observable distributions between students and teachers of behaviors, power, and resources that emerge from their actions.

Widely shared contemporary beliefs about gender are rules for structure in Giddens's and Sewell's sense. They are rules for enacting social relations in a manner that results in material arrangements between men and women that, in turn, uphold our current views of who men and women are and why they are unequal. We know how to act like a woman or a man precisely because we know our culture's taken-for-granted beliefs—its stereotypes—about who men and women are and how they behave. But by acting on these beliefs, we end up materially demonstrating the differences and inequality between men and women that these stereotypes suggest.

The Content of Contemporary Gender Beliefs

Gender stereotypes are variously measured by asking people to generate a list of traits that best describe men and women or to rate the extent to which a given trait is characteristic of men or women. Sometimes people make these ratings in terms of their own views of the typical man or woman, and other times they are asked to rate how men and women are viewed by society. A wide variety of research like this has demonstrated that people in the United States hold well-defined, largely consensual gender stereotypes (e.g., Broverman et al. 1972; Cuddy, Fiske, and Glick 2007; Diekman and Eagly 2000; Fiske et al. 2002; Glick et al. 2004; Koenig and Eagly 2006; Lueptow, Garovich-Szabo, and Lueptow 2001; Spence and Buckner 2000; Williams and Best 1990).

The traits people use to describe men, compared with women, can be summarized as those associated with *agency versus communion* or, as they are sometimes also termed, as instrumental versus expressive (Deaux and Kite 1993; Eagly 1987; Wagner and Berger 1997). Men are rated more highly than women on agentic qualities such as instrumental competence, assertiveness, confidence, independence, forcefulness, and dominance. Women are rated more highly than men on communal attributes such as emotional expressiveness, nurturance, interpersonal sensitivity, kindness, and responsiveness.

These stereotypes describe the traits or attributes that people associate with the typical man or woman. In that sense, they are *descriptive* in nature, providing a thumbnail sketch of what people take to be the way men and women behave on average. But as the rules of the gender game, gender stereotypes have a *prescriptive* quality as well. They include standards of behavior from which deviations will be punished (Diekman and Eagly 2008; Eagly and Karau 2002; Fiske and Stevens 1993; Rudman and Fairchild 2004).

The prescriptive edge of gender stereotypes derives from the way the maintenance of these stereotypes affects people's gender interests. Both men and women have an interest in maintaining clear gender beliefs as a basis for making sense of self and others and easing the coordination of behavior. Also, men and some women further benefit from the maintenance of a status quo from which men benefit (Glick and Fiske 1999a; Jackman 1994; Jost and Banaji 1994; Rudman et al. 2009). These gender interests drive the everyday enforcement of gender stereotypes as the rules of the gender game.

There are two sides to the prescriptive standards embedded in gender stereotypes. There are behaviors and traits that men and women *should* display (positive prescriptions) and those that they *should not* display (negative proscriptions) (Prentice and Carranza 2002). Interestingly, evidence suggests that men and women are especially likely to be punished for violating cultural assumptions about the behaviors people of their sex should *not* display (Rudman and Fairchild 2004; Rudman et al. 2009).

The prescriptive aspects of gender stereotypes are usually measured by further asking people to rate not only how typical a trait is of men or women but also how desirable or undesirable it is in one sex or the other. As we would expect, traits of communality (e.g., warm, emotional, sensitive to others) are seen as especially desirable in women, just as traits of agency (e.g., assertive, aggressive) are particularly desirable in men (Prentice and Carranza 2002; Rudman et al. 2009). Interestingly, however, the traits that are seen as especially *undesirable* in women are not those of insufficient warmth. Rather, the most undesirable traits in women are those like domineering and arrogant that violate the cultural presumption of women's subordinate status. Similarly, the traits viewed as most undesirable in men are those like weak and emotionally yielding that contradict the presumption of men's status superiority (Prentice and Carranza 2002; Rudman et al. 2009). The proscriptive aspects of widely shared gender stereotypes, then, embody and enforce gender status hierarchy.

As these studies show, contemporary gender stereotypes have dimensions of both inequality and difference. The stereotype of women is currently evaluated as more positive or "good" than that of men (Eagly and Mladinic 1989, 1994; Glick et al. 2004). Alice Eagly calls this the "women are wonderful" effect. The "goodness" of women is somewhat misleading, however. In fact, the stereotypic traits of men are evaluated as significantly higher status and more powerful than the stereotypic attributes of women, including their "goodness" (Glick et al. 2004; Rudman et al. 2009).

Psychologist Peter Glick and colleagues (2004, p. 724), for instance, asked a sample of American high school and college students to rate the typical traits of men and women in terms power and status on a scale of scale +3 (extremely high power/status) to -3(extremely low power/status). The typical traits of men were rated between 0.99 and 0.90 in power and status, on average. The equivalent ratings of women's typical traits were between 0.48 and 0.26, significantly lower in power and status. The traits of women, in other words, were perceived as only half as high in power and status as the traits of men. In another study, Laurie Rudman and her colleagues (2009) similarly found that contemporary American college students perceive the typical as well as desirable traits of men to be more closely associated with the traits of high-status people than are the typical or desirable traits of women. These studies provide further evidence that contemporary gender stereotypes imply male status superiority.

It is clear that contemporary gender stereotypes incorporate *status beliefs* as we have discussed them in previous chapters. Recall that status beliefs associate greater status and general competence with people in one social category than another, while granting those in each category some specialized skills (Berger et al. 1977; Berger, Rosenholz, and Zeldtich 1980). The competence embodied in status beliefs is really *performance capacity*, that is, the capacity to master events and successfully accomplish goals, either in general or in regard to specific tasks (Berger et al. 1977; Ridgeway and Correll 2004a). We have reviewed evidence that gender stereotypes link men with higher status than women; other studies document associated competence differences, by which we mean differences in general or specific performance capacity. In general, status and competence are highly correlated in contemporary American stereotypes of social groups. Gender is no exception (Cuddy et al. 2007; Fiske et al. 2002; Koenig and Eagly 2006).

Sociologists Lisa Rashotte and Murray Webster (2005) directly measured whether beliefs about gender differences in general and specific competence are still held by contemporary college students. They investigated this question because expectation states theory, currently the predominant theory of interpersonal status processes, argues that assumptions about differences in competence are at the core of status relations, including those based on gender (Berger et al. 1977; Wagner and Berger 2002). We will discuss this theory in detail later in the chapter.

Rashotte and Webster presented a sample of male and female college students with pictures of two males and two females of college age and average attractiveness. The students rated each person depicted on a series of questions about general competence, such as how intelligent he or she appeared to be and how competent he or she would be at most tasks. They rated each person on how well he or she would do at a specific task as well. The results showed that the students rated the pictured males as modestly but significantly higher in general competence than the depicted females. They also rated the males as likely to do substantially better at the specific task. This study suggests that modest but reliable differences in overall competence do still seem to be associated with typical men and women, and these beliefs about competence differences are stronger for the accomplishment of more specific tasks.

Understood as performance capacity, competence implies both underlying ability and the forceful agency and effort necessary to successfully accomplish goals. Other recent studies of gender stereotypes suggest that typical men and women are currently seen to differ hardly at all in underlying cognitive abilities like *intelligent* and *analytic*, even though such abilities continue to be viewed as more desirable in men (Cejka and Eagly 1999; Koenig and Eagly 2006; Prentice and Carranza 2002). However, men are still seen as substantially more forcefully agentic than women and thus more able to master events and successfully accomplish goals. It seems that status-based cultural beliefs about men's greater overall competence increasingly rely on assumptions about men's superior instrumental agency rather than on differences in cognitive abilities. Studies show that college students continue to see the typical college male as higher in agentic, instrumental competence than the typical college female, even though these students' ratings of their own personal instrumental competence differed little by gender (Spence and Buckner 2000).

As is typical of status beliefs, gender stereotypes also grant each sex some specialized skills and competences. The studies all show, for instance, that people continue to see the typical woman as clearly superior to the typical man in expressive competence (Lueptow et al. 2001; Rudman et al. 2009; Spence and Buckner 2000).

Contemporary gender stereotypes, then, have an "ambivalent" structure. Men are seen as higher status, more powerful, and more agentically competent than women, especially at the things that count most in society. Yet women are seen as "nicer" and more competent at the positively evaluated but lower status tasks of caring and communality (Conway, Pizzamiglio, and Mount1996; Glick and Fiske 1999b; Jackson, Esses, and Burris 2001). As sociologist Mary Jackman (1994) points out, beliefs like this stabilize status inequalities by attributing some compensatory positive, if lesser valued traits to the low-status group while maintaining the overall superiority of the high-status group.

People hold these gender stereotypes about how men and women are typically viewed in society even when the stereotypes differ from the way that they describe themselves. In some studies, for instance, college women rate the typical woman as lower than men in instrumental competence but do not rate themselves that way (e.g., Spence and Buckner 2000). People also hold these gender stereotypes as beliefs about social reality—both the way that men and women typically are and the way that men and women are socially expected to be—even though people vary in the extent to which they personally endorse these stereotypes as the way they think the sexes ought to be. Studies show, for instance, that holding gender stereotypes as descriptive beliefs about how men and women usually are is only modestly correlated with ideological beliefs about gender egalitarianism (Blair and Banaji 1996; Rudman and Kilianski 2000; Spence and Buckner 2000).

In fact, basic gender stereotypes appear to be consensual knowledge in the United States in that virtually everyone knows the content of these beliefs and most people presume that "most others" in society hold these stereotypes (Diekman and Eagly 2000; Eagly, Wood, and Diekman 2000; Jackman 1994; Wood and Eagly 2010). Studies show that when people are asked to describe how the sexes are viewed by most others in their society, they have no trouble responding, suggesting that they believe they know what others think (e.g., Cuddy et al. 2007; Fiske et al. 2002; Koenig and Eagly 2006; Williams and Best 1990). There is good evidence, then, that basic gender stereotypes are indeed cultural common knowledge in the contemporary United States. That is, gender stereotypes are cultural knowledge that we can presume everybody knows. This is as we would expect if gender is indeed a primary cultural device for coordinating social relations.

The Material Foundations of Gender Stereotypes

The use of gender as a cultural device for framing social relations suggests that the common knowledge represented in shared gender stereotypes will focus on differences between men and women. Use as a framing device, however, does not in itself dictate the nature of the sex differences that are incorporated in stereotypes. As we saw in the last chapter, however, gender as difference is easily transformed into status inequality. Status inequality does dictate something about the nature of the sex differences that will be represented in gender stereotypes, namely, that men will be perceived as higher status and more generally competent than women. But contemporary American gender stereotypes contain considerably more specific content than that. Men are portrayed as strong and women as communal and good, and each sex is thought to have a number of specific skills related to these general attributes, such as mechanical ability for men and cooking for women. Where do these stereotypic images of men and women come from? Evidence suggests three interrelated material foundations: the gendered division of labor, the behaviors through which status hierarchies are enacted, and the experiences of dominant groups in society.

The Gendered Division of Labor

Alice Eagly and her colleagues argue that the content of gender stereotypes in a given society and at a given period of time reflects the gendered division of labor in that society and time (Diekman and Eagly 2000; Eagly 1987; Eagly, Wood, and Diekman 2000). Essentially, the idea is that people form their stereotypes from observations of the typical behavior of women and men around them in society. That behavior, in turn, is structured by the societal division of labor by gender, such as that between providers and homemakers. In inferring personal traits, Eagly argues that people tend to follow a well-documented psychological process of *correspondent inference* that causes them to assume that people are what they do. That is, people attribute personal traits to others that correspond to the others' behavior.

The gender division of labor in the United States results in more women than men acting in domestic caretaking roles as primary child rearers, a task that requires them to display interpersonal sensitivity, expressiveness, and kindness. Men, in contrast, act more exclusively in paid employment roles than do women, and they are more likely to be in both manual jobs and jobs that carry higher status and power than are women (Charles and Grusky 2004). Acting in employment roles like these requires men to display relatively assertive, forceful behaviors. From observations of these behaviors, Eagly argues, people infer that women are more communal and men are more agentic.

Eagly has supported her argument about the content of gender stereotypes with several types of evidence. With Valerie Steffen, she conducted an experiment in which participants judged the agentic and communal qualities of men and women generally, men and women in domestic homemaker roles, and men and women in paid employment roles. This study found that occupational role was a strong determinant of perceived communal and agentic qualities. Homemakers of either sex were viewed as even higher in communion and lower in agency than were women generally. Full-time employees of either sex were seen like stereotypic men in that they were high in agency and low in communion. Both men and women with higher status job titles were also seen as more agentic than men and women with lower status jobs (Eagly 1987, p. 22; Eagly and Steffen 1984). A subsequent experiment showed that part-time employees of either sex were seen as intermediate between full-time employees and homemakers in agentic and communal attributes (Eagly and Steffen 1986). A number of other studies have replicated these results (see Eagly, Wood, and Diekman 2000, p. 140).

The logic of Eagly's argument about how people infer stereotypic traits from their observations of typical behavior implies that not only gender stereotypes but also the stereotypes of other social groups should reflect the traits linked to the roles people in those groups usually play in society. Recent studies have shown this to be the case. The stereotypes of a wide variety of social groups in the United States, in addition to gender, similarly reflect the power, status, and caregiving activities associated with the jobs or roles that people in these groups typically hold (Johannesen-Schmidt and Eagly 2002; Koenig and Eagly 2006).

If people infer the stereotypic traits of men and women from the productive roles they perform in society, then people should infer that the typical traits of men and women will change as these roles change. Another set of studies by Amanda Diekman and Alice Eagly (2000) showed this effect. Several samples of students and adults were asked to think about an average man or woman in a year in the past (1950, 1975), the present, or the future (2025, 2050) and rate that person's personal characteristics. Participants were also asked to estimate for that year what the distribution of men versus women would be in several currently gender-typed occupations, as well as what the household division labor would be. Both students and adults agreed that men's and women's occupational roles were more different in the past but would become increasingly similar in the future. Correspondingly, students and adults expected that the personal traits of the sexes would converge sharply. In particular, women were expected to increasingly hold men's jobs and therefore change to become much more masculine and somewhat less feminine in their personal traits. Men's jobs and personalities were seen as changing less but in the direction of convergence with women.

Given the differing interests the gender system creates for men and women, it is not surprising that participants expected gender differences and inequality to be reduced more through the actions of women than of men. Interestingly, although participants anticipated steadily increasing equality in occupational roles, they still did not expect that full equality would be achieved by 2050. Overall, however, participants agreed that men's and women's stereotypic agentic and communal characteristics would change in track with changes in their social roles. We will return to the issue of how recent changes in women's social roles have affected gender stereotypes in chapter 6. As we will see there, the content of stereotypes does gradually respond to social changes. Several processes, however, slow the impact of material changes on consensual gender stereotypes so that the content of stereotypes lags behind changes in men's and women's material lives. And while they persist, lagging stereotypes remain the rules of the gender game.

Status Hierarchies

Eagly's argument about the gender division of labor focuses on differences between men and women in the productive roles they play in society, but nested within this account is an argument that the roles played by men are not only different but also frequently higher in status and power (Eagly 1987, pp. 23–24; Koenig and Eagly 2006). Peter Glick and Susan Fiske (1999b) concur that status differences between men and women, in combination with the cooperative interdependence between the sexes, are powerful determinants of gender stereotypes. They argue that men's higher status and greater control over material resources in society give rise to the perception that they are more agentic and competent than women. But men's cooperative dependence on women for intimacy at the interpersonal level fosters attributions that women are warm and communal. In several studies, Fiske, Glick, and colleagues provide evidence that the content not only of gender stereotypes but also of stereotypes of a variety of groups (e.g., races, occupations) reflect the status and cooperative versus competitive relations between those groups in the United States (Cuddy et al. 2007; Fiske et al. 2002; Glick et al. 2004).

There is strong evidence that the content of American gender stereotypes is heavily shaped by the attributes that are associated in North American culture with the performance of high- versus low-status roles in interpersonal hierarchies (Conway et al. 1996; Geis et al. 1984; Gerber 1996; Wagner and Berger 1997). Because of the way that gender is embedded in positional inequalities in economic, political, and even familial institutions, network studies show that men and women in the United States most frequently interact with one another in status-unequal role relationships, such as mentor and protégée, boss and secretary, and older husband and younger wife (see Ridgeway and Smith-Lovin 1999 for a review). Research based on expectation states theory, the major sociological theory of interpersonal status processes, has shown that status-unequal interaction has a characteristic structure (Wagner and Berger 1997). The high-status person sets the agenda, often talks more, sticks with his or her opinions, and is more influential. The low-status person reacts to the high-status person, pays close attention to his or her concerns, offers supportive comments, and defers when disagreements develop.

These distinctive patterns of proactive versus reactive behavior through which interpersonal status hierarchies are enacted in American society affect the impressions participants form of one another. High-status actors appear to be assertive, independent, and agentic. Low-status actors appear to be responsive, expressive, supportive, and other focused—in other words, communal. Gwendolyn Gerber (1996) demonstrated this effect in her study of mixed- and same-sex police partners. She found that independent of gender, the high-ranking members of these partner teams were perceived by themselves and their partners as more instrumental and agentic. Low-ranking members were seen as more supportive and expressive.

Conway and colleagues (1996) found similar effects in a set of controlled studies. They found that high- and low-status actors in status relations as diverse as gender, occupation (file clerk versus stockbroker), and hypothetical tribal status were each similarly perceived as agentic and instrumentally competent versus communal and expressive. Finally, as we saw in the last chapter, studies show that people readily form beliefs that people in one social category are higher status and more competent, but not as nice, as people in another social category from the influence hierarchies people experience in their social encounters with these categories of people (Ridgeway and Erickson 2000).

In contrast to people who differ by race or other forms of categorical inequality, men and women are especially likely to form their impressions of one another from direct interaction because they interact together so frequently. A great many of these interactions are structured as status inequalities, due to both the inequalities in the institutional roles they occupy and the status attached to gender itself. As a result, men and women most often observe one another in the kind of interaction that causes men to appear not only higher status and competent but also more assertive, independent, and agentic, while women appear not only lower status but also more communal and interpersonally sensitive.

To a substantial extent, then, what we commonly think of as the typical differences between men and women are in fact the result of the enactment of status inequality between them. The content of gender stereotypes corresponds closely to what other evidence suggests is the North American stereotype of high- and low-status actors generally (Berger, Ridgeway, and Zelditch 2002; Fiske et al. 2002; Jost, Burgess, and Mosso 2001; Rudman et al. 2009). In addition, however, women are considered to be not only more reactive and expressive, as all low-status groups are, but also uniquely warm and good. Eagly's evidence suggests that this is a distinctive effect of women's close association with child rearing in the division of labor.

Hegemonic and Nonhegemonic Gender Beliefs

The consensually shared gender stereotypes we have described represent themselves as universal depictions of males and females defined in terms of a simple, stylized set of features. The simplified, abstract nature of gender stereotypes is in striking contrast to the complexity of real, diverse, and multiattributed men and women in the United States. The cultural use of sex category as a quick, first frame for social relations, I would argue, encourages shared gender stereotypes to take on this schematic nature. But whose experiences of gender difference and inequality end up represented in these stripped-down distillations of male and female natures?

Whites, middle-class people, and heterosexuals are dominant groups in American society in that they have higher status and typically occupy positions associated with greater power and resources than people of color, working-class people, and homosexuals. People in dominant groups have more cultural resources and power available to them to shape the cultural images of men and women that become consensual in society (Ridgeway and Correll 2004b). As a result, the descriptions of men and women that become inscribed in the simple, abstract stereotypes that become consensual tend to be those that most closely resemble white, middle-class, heterosexuals, if anyone.

Because people in dominant groups hold relatively advantaged positions in organizations and institutions such as government, the media, and educational establishments, the stereotypic representations that correspond to their own group experiences of gender tend to become *culturally hegemonic* in society. That is, the descriptions of women and men that these stereotypes contain become the ones that are institutionalized in media representations, government policies, and normative images of the family. It is these hegemonic stereotypic images of men and women that implicitly inform legislation, television shows, magazines, educational policies, and the design of public spaces. Thus, while the gendered division of labor and status hierarchies create the behaviors that gender stereotypes interpret, it is the experiences of these things by dominant groups in society that become most directly enshrined in the institutionalized form of these stereotypes that "everyone knows." These institutionalized stereotypes become the default rules of the gender game in public settings.

Alternate forms of gender beliefs do exist in American society alongside hegemonic stereotypes, however. Different ethnic, class, or regional communities sometimes share beliefs about men's and women's traits that are slightly different from the dominant stereotype. There is some evidence, for instance, that African Americans have less polarized views of the sexes and, in particular, see fewer differences in general competence or agency between men and women (Collins 1991; Dugger 1988). Ideological groups such as feminists or other groups such as gays and lesbians may hold alternative gender beliefs as well. When people who hold alternative gender beliefs are around like-minded others, such as at a gathering of African Americans or feminists, it is their alternative gender beliefs that may be evoked and serve as the rules of gender in that setting, as some research suggests (Filardo 1996; Milkie 1999).

Yet people who hold alternative gender beliefs are also likely to be knowledgeable about the hegemonic stereotypes that are institutionalized and widely available in the society around them. As these people leave their like-minded gatherings and enter into more public settings or settings in which they do not know the others present, they are likely to expect to be treated by these dominant stereotypes. For these people as well, then, hegemonic gender stereotypes are a stubborn aspect of reality that must dealt with and often accommodated in many social contexts.

HOW DO CULTURAL BELIEFS AFFECT SOCIAL RELATIONS?

If hegemonic cultural beliefs about gender provide a blueprint for enacting gender in most relational settings in society, how exactly do they do that? What are the effects of these gender beliefs on people's behavior and on their judgments of themselves and others? This is the next question that we need to examine. The first task is to describe the overall nature of gender's effects on behavior and judgments in social relations. Then we will turn to an analysis of the specific impact of beliefs about gender status and about women's greater communality.

Gender as a Background Identity

As we saw in the last chapter, the routine process of sex-categorizing someone implicitly evokes gender stereotypes in our minds and primes them to shape our behaviors and our judgments of that person. As a result, the stereotypic rules of the gender game are virtually always implicitly available to shape behavior in social relations. As ethnomethodologists Candace West and Don Zimmerman (1987) have observed, gender is a social standard to which you can always be held accountable in social relations.

Yet, the very factors that support sex/gender's utility as an initial cultural frame for making sense of another—its abstract, dichotomous nature—also limit its ability to take you very far in figuring out who the other is and how best to relate to him or her. Psychological research on how people perceive others shows that after sex-categorizing another, people nearly always go on to categorize that person in multiple additional ways as well (Fiske, Lin, and Neuberg 1999). Race and age are also primary categories by which others are quickly defined in the United States (Fiske 1998). In some settings, these other primary identities provide more powerful definitions of self and other in that they have more detailed implications for behavior in the situation than does sex category. In addition, social relations are typically embedded in organizational or institutional contexts that involve specific roles for self and other, such as clerk and customer, manager and subordinate, or brother and sister. In contrast to sex/gender, these specific roles carry highly detailed expectations for behavior that are centrally relevant to the focal activities of the situation.

Not surprisingly, then, these specific roles are typically in the foreground of people's definitions of who self and other are in a given context and how, therefore, they should behave toward one another in that situation. In contrast, gender almost always acts a diffuse *background identity* in social relations that is not, in itself, the ostensible focus of the actors' attention (Ridgeway and Correll 2004b; Ridgeway and Smith-Lovin 1999). Gender's characteristic position as a background identity is important to the nature of its effects on social relations.

To gain a feel for this, think of how gender is a background identity in student-teacher relations in the classroom. The institutionally defined and situationally focal identities of student and teacher define the actors' central behaviors toward one another. But gender, as an implicit background identity, imports an added set of meanings that may implicitly modify how actors perform the activities defined by their focal student-teacher identities. The female teacher, for instance, moderates her authoritative performance as the knowledge expert with a gendered display of warmth and communal concern for the student. The male student tempers his deferential performance as the learner with a small gendered expression of independence.

Thus, actors moderate or exaggerate in gender-stereotypic ways the behaviors they perform for their focal identities as a way of enacting their background identities as males and females. This is one way of understanding the idea that gender is a "performance" (e.g., West and Zimmerman 1987). In most situations, rather than a coherent set of independent behaviors, gender becomes a bias in the way that other, nominally ungendered activities are performed, like teaching, playing a piano, or acting as a manager.

Gender Acts in Combination with Other Identities and Varies in Impact

It is clear, then, that sex/gender always acts *in combination* with other identities in shaping people's behaviors and judgments in social relations. Identities that are more specifically informative for behavior in the situation, often institutional roles, are weighted more heavily than less relevant identities in this combining process. Madeline Heilman and colleagues (1989) have shown, for instance, that in perceiving managers, people combine their expectations for the manager identity with their background expectations for males and females. The result is that female managers are perceived to be more like managers than like women in general, but less competent than similar male managers. Alice Eagly and Stephen Karau (2002) document a similar combining of expectations for leaders with background gender expectations. As we will see shortly, expectation states theory, which is the theory of interpersonal status processes that I will draw upon throughout this book, gives a detailed account of this combining process for the status and competence implications of gender stereotypes (Berger et al. 1977; Wagner and Berger 1997).

Because gender combines with other identities, the extent to which gender stereotypes modify or bias behavior and judgments in social relations *varies* from one situation to another (Deaux and Major 1987; Wagner and Berger 1997). Thus, while automatic sex categorization makes gender stereotypes implicitly available to actors in all social relations, the actual impact of these stereotypes on behavior can vary from imperceptible to substantial, depending on the context. The extent to which it varies, however, can be specified. These points are central to understanding the nature of gender's effects on social relations.

The extent to which gender stereotypes actually do modify people's behavior and judgments in a given situation depends on gender's *salience* or relevance for them, given the nature of the situation. The more salient gender is, the greater its effects on their behavior. Salience, in turn, depends on the extent to which gender in a given setting appears to actors to give them useful clues about how others in the situation are likely to behave, so that they can figure out how to behave themselves. The salience of gender for actors probably varies on a continuum from almost negligible in a situation that is rigidly scripted by a constraining institutional role to a central focus of attention in a highly gendered situation such as a date.

At a minimum, however, evidence suggests that gender is typically *effectively salient* for actors—that is, sufficiently salient to measurably affect behavior—in two broad classes of settings (Ridgeway 1997). Gender is effectively salient in mixed-sex settings because identities that are different or distinctive attract attention and appear informative, as studies show (Cota and Dion 1986; Wagner and Berger 1997). Gender is also effectively salient in settings that are culturally linked to gender or to the stereotypic skills of one sex or the other, as a variety of studies also have shown (see Deaux and LaFrance 1998; Wagner and Berger 1997). This means that gender may be effectively salient in same-sex settings, too, if the context is gender linked in the culture. For instance, if math is stereotypically considered a masculine task, then gender will be effectively salient even in an all-female math class.

Intersecting Meanings and Interests

One final point is worth noting about the consequences of the way that gender acts as a background identity in social relations. Since automatic sex categorization causes gender to be continually present for actors as a kind of ghost in the background, social relational contexts expose the cultural meanings of gender to those of other identities being enacted in the situation. As the research we discussed by Eagly and her colleagues shows, this is part of the way that gender stereotypes change as men's and women's institutional roles change (Diekman and Eagly 2000).

Social relational contexts, however, particularly expose the cultural meanings of gender to those of race and age because these other primary identities are also almost always implicitly present in the situation. The mutual exposure of these primary identities to one another in social relational contexts may encourage actors to creatively borrow distinctive cultural meanings from one primary identity and apply them to define distinctions between people based on another primary identity. Power differences based on race, for instance, may be referred to in gendered terms when white authorities are called "The Man." Or gender differences may be discussed like age differences when, for instance, women are described as childlike and dependent and men as mature and responsible.

The mutual enactment of gender, race, and age as primary identities in social relations has another important consequence as well. Like gender, each of these other primary identities is also associated with widely shared cultural beliefs about difference and inequality based on that identity. And like gender, each of these cultural systems of difference and inequality creates its own interests for actors. Since actors are inherently multiattributed, these sometimes overlapping, sometimes conflicting interests are simultaneously present for them in social relations. As a consequence, as individual actors try to negotiate their lives through social relations, these multiple identity-based interests *intersect* for them and affect one another in complex ways (Collins 1991; Glenn 1999).

Individuals sometimes intentionally or unintentionally advance their gender interests as women or men, for instance, by taking advantage of political openings created by racial politics. Or they may pursue their racial interests by engaging in gender politics. Sociologists Nicola Beisel and Tamara Kay (2004), for example, show how in the 19th-century United States, dominant white groups, threatened by growing immigration, pursued their racial interests in maintaining whites as a dominant proportion of the population through the promotion of laws to regulate women by banning abortion. The use of gender and race as primary cultural frames for social relations in the United States has bound gender and racial politics together in intricate ways, as many gender scholars have demonstrated (Collins 1991; Glenn 1999; Romero 1992). And since the cultural schemas of gender and race that are institutionalized and hegemonic reflect the perspectives of dominant groups in society, these racial and gender belief systems are also entwined with interests and inequalities based on social class.

Conclusion

In sum, gender always acts in combination with other identities and in a contextually variable manner in its effects on behavior and judgments in social relations. The extent of its impact depends on gender's salience in the situation. Even when gender is effectively salient, as it is in mixed-sex and gender-relevant contexts, however, its diffuse implications for behavior typically make it a background rather than focal identity. As a consequence, the effects of other differences in actors' identities, skills, and abilities will nearly always be greater than the effects of gender on actors' judgments and behaviors in most social relational contexts. Across multiple social relational contexts, the background effects of gender yield a larger pattern in which the range of behavior among people of the same sex is typically greater than the average differences between women and men. Yet cultural beliefs about gender, acting in the background, bias expectations for self and other sufficiently to produce detectable average differences in the behavior and evaluations of men and women who are in equivalent social positions (Ridgeway and Correll 2004b). As we saw in chapter 1, this is precisely the pattern that sex differences in social behavior take in the contemporary United States, as the evidence from meta-analyses has shown (Eagly 1995; Hyde 2005).

The Impact of Gender Status Beliefs

When gender is effectively salient in a social relational context, participants' expectations for their own as well as others' behaviors and evaluations will be measurably shaped by gender stereotypes. All aspects of gender stereotypes have an effect, but the status and competence beliefs they contain are particularly consequential for the enactment of inequality between men and women. Recall that gender status beliefs include assumptions not only about men's greater status and general competence (understood as performance capacity) but also about each sex's specialized skills. Since these include assumptions about women's greater communal skills, gender status beliefs evoke elements from both the agentic and communal aspects of gender stereotypes.

The best account of how gender status beliefs shape events in social relations comes from expectation states theory (Ridgeway and Bourg 2004; Wagner and Berger 1997, 2002). I have already made several passing references to this theory in discussing status and gender. It is now time to examine it in detail. It will be useful not only in this chapter for understanding how gender shapes interpersonal behavior but also in later chapters for analyzing the persistence of gender inequality in the workplace and in the home.

Expectation states theory is a sociological theory of status and influence in interpersonal relations that was originally developed by Joseph Berger and his colleagues in the 1960s and 1970s (Berger et al. 1974, 1977). In the decades since then, its arguments have been extensively tested through experiments and other studies (see Correll and Ridgeway 2003; Wagner and Berger 2002 for reviews). Once tested, these arguments have then been used in applied settings to analyze and sometimes address social problems involving status processes, such as social equity in classrooms (Cohen and Lotan 1997) and gender inequality in work (e.g., Correll, Benard, and Paik 2007; Gorman 2006). Through this program of research, expectation states theory has become the predominant account of how interpersonal status processes work.

The theory is particularly known for its description of how widely shared status beliefs about socially significant differences, including gender, race, age, education, and occupation, shape people's interpersonal judgments, behaviors, and influence (Berger et al. 1980; Webster and Foschi 1988). For this reason, even though expectation states theory is not itself a theory of gender, it has been extensively applied to the study of how gender status beliefs shape social relations (e.g., Carli 1991; Correll et al. 2007; Dovidio et al. 1988; Ridgeway 1993, 2001a; Ridgeway and Bourg 2004; Wagner and Berger 1997). This is the use we will put the theory to here.

The Theoretical Argument

Expectation states theory focuses on social relational situations in which participants are oriented toward the accomplishment of a shared, valued goal or task. These goal-oriented contexts include a wide variety of situations from family decision making to most workplace or educational settings. To decide how to act in these situations, whether to speak up or hesitate, and how to react when others disagree, the theory says people look for clues by which to anticipate the value of what others have to offer to the task, compared with them. In the process, they form implicit, often unconscious *self-other performance expectations* for themselves compared with each other in the situation. These self-other performance expectations are simply implicit senses about whether the other will have better (or worse) contributions to offer to the group task than self and, if so, how much better (or worse). Notice that these performance expectations develop as a by-product of the more general process of defining self and other in order to coordinate behavior, but under the specific conditions of coordination in regard to a shared task or goal.

In social relational contexts, automatic sex categorization makes gender status beliefs implicitly available to actors as they form these self-other performance expectations. Expectation states theory argues, however, that gender status beliefs measurably bias the performance expectations the actors form only when gender is effectively salient in the situation, that is, in mixed-sex and gender-relevant contexts. This means that in same-sex, gender-neutral contexts, gender status beliefs should have little effect on actors' performance expectations.

The theory further argues that the actors combine the positive and negative status and competence implications of *all* identities that are salient in the setting, including gender, each *weighted* by its relevance to the situational goal or task, to form *aggregated* self-other performance expectations for each actor in the situation, compared with the others (Berger et al. 1977; Wagner and Berger 2002). Thus, if gender, race, and occupational role (boss or employee) are all effectively salient in a work setting, the performance expectations actors form for one another will reflect the *combined* impact of all three status identities. Those status identities that are more directly relevant to the work task (e.g., occupational role) have a stronger effect on the performance expectations than those that are less relevant. Importantly, however, even the status identities that are not logically linked to the work task, such as race or gender, still have a measurable effect on actors' implicit expectations for each other's performance.

The theory argues, then, that even if gender is a background identity in a setting, as long as it is effectively salient due to, say, the mixed-sex context, gender status beliefs are still likely to modestly bias performance expectations for men compared with women who are otherwise similar to them. In settings or tasks that are culturally linked to gender, gender status beliefs bias performance expectations more strongly. Experimental tests support the validity of this weighted combining approach to the way people form self-other expectations from status information that is salient in their situation (Berger et al. 1992).

The implicit self-other performance expectations that actors form are powerful because they have self-fulfilling effects on actors' task-directed behavior and evaluations in the situation, as research shows expectations tend to do (Miller and Turnbull 1986). The theory's major argument is that, specifically, differences between actors' task-focused behaviors and evaluations in a given situation will be a direct function of the degree to which performance expectations held for them by self and others advantage or disadvantage them compared with another (Berger et al. 1977). Consider how this works. The lower my performance expectation for myself compared with you, the more likely I am to initially hesitate (because I doubt myself compared with you) rather than speak up and assert my own views and also the more likely I am to ask you for your ideas instead. And when you then give your ideas, the more likely they are to sound good to me. And the better I assume your ideas are, the more likely I am to change to agree with you when disagreements develop, so that, in the end, you gain influence and status in the setting, compared with me. In this way, self-other performance expectations shape the extent to which actors assert themselves, whether their views are heard, how they and their ideas are evaluated, and whether they become influential and respected in the context.

A Distinctive Pattern of Gender Status Effects

In sum, expectation states theory argues that differences in men's and women's task-directed behaviors and evaluations in a given situation are a function of the extent to which their self-other performance expectations are biased by the stereotypic assumptions contained in gender status beliefs. The extent of this bias, in turn, is a result of whether gender is salient in the context and, if it is, how strongly relevant it is to the shared goal or task. Putting these arguments together, the theory predicts a distinctive pattern of gender status effects on behaviors and evaluations in goal-oriented contexts (Ridgeway and Bourg 2004; Wagner and Berger 1997).

In mixed-sex settings with a gender-neutral task, the theory predicts that men will be modestly advantaged over otherwise similar women in performance expectations and, therefore, in task-directed behaviors and evaluations. In mixed-sex settings with a stereotypically masculine task (car repair), men's advantage over women in these behaviors will be even greater. When the task is stereotypically feminine (cooking) in a mixed-sex situation, however, women will be slightly advantaged over otherwise similar men. This is because cultural expectations about women's specific, task-relevant skills combine with assumptions about men's greater overall competence to give women a slight advantage over men in expected performance on feminine-typed tasks.

In same-sex settings, gender will not be effectively salient for actors unless the task or setting is gender typed. Therefore, the theory predicts that in these situations there will be no differences between otherwise similar men and women in their task-directed behaviors and evaluations. When the task is gender typed, however, there will be differences between men and women in same-sex groups that are similar to those seen in mixed-sex groups with the same sort of gender-typed task.

This predicted pattern of gender effects should hold for a broad range of task-directed behaviors and evaluations, but not necessarily for all gendered behaviors in social relational contexts. Task-directed behaviors include a wide variety of agentic behaviors, both verbal and nonverbal, by which interpersonal status hierarchies are enacted (Ridgeway and Bourg 2004). They include participation rates, task suggestions, visual dominance, assertive gestures, assertive rather than tentative speech, and most important, influence. Task-focused evaluations include agreeing with or positively evaluating someone's ideas, evaluating task performances, and inferring ability from performance. As this suggests, in addition to agentic behaviors, task evaluations involve some more communal behaviors, such as agreeing with or responding positively to another. However, they do not involve purely social and expressive behaviors such as smiling, laughing, or joking. We will return to these expressive behaviors later.

Task Behaviors and Evaluations—The Evidence

What is the evidence that sex differences in task behaviors and evaluations do vary by context according to the distinctive pattern that expectation states theory predicts? The evidence comes from individual experiments and from meta-analyses that statistically combine the results of multiple studies. All these studies compare the task-directed behaviors and evaluations of otherwise similar men and women under one set of contextual circumstances compared with another.

Studies of the behaviors by which people enact interpersonal status hierarchies look very much like the predicted pattern. Other things equal, men in mixed-sex groups talk more (Dovidio et al. 1988; James and Drakich 1993), make more task suggestions (Wood and Karten 1986), use less tentative speech (Carli 1990), display more assertive gestures (Dovidio et al. 1988) and more visual dominance (Ellyson, Dovidio, and Brown 1992), and are more influential than women (Carli 2001; Pugh and Wahrman 1983; Wagner, Ford, and Ford 1986). In one of these studies, John Dovidio and his colleagues (1988) further showed that when the discussion in mixed-sex dyads shifted from a gender-neutral topic to a stereotypically masculine topic, men's advantage over women on a wide range of these agentic behaviors increased. But when the topic changed to a stereotypically feminine task, the interpersonal hierarchy reversed, and women displayed modestly higher rates of these agentic behaviors than did men, just as expectation states theory predicts. In same-sex groups with a gender-neutral task, in contrast, studies show no differences between men and women in participation and task suggestions (Carli 1991; Johnson, Clay-Warner, and Funk 1996; Shelly and Munroe 1999) or in willingness to accept influence from others, as the theory also predicts (Pugh and Wahrman 1983).

Additional evidence supports the argument that these effects are indeed the result of status-based assumptions about gender and competence that in turn shape task-directed behaviors. Wendy Wood and Stephen Karten (1986) demonstrated that when performance expectations for men and women in mixed-sex groups are equalized, sex differences in task-directed behaviors disappear. Also, other status-linked social differences, such as race and education, have been shown to produce comparable differences in task-focused behaviors, and these differences, too, have been shown to be mediated by the effects of status on performance expectations (Driskell and Mullen 1990; Webster and Foschi 1988). The fact that these results occur not only for women but also for other lower status groups suggests that they are indeed a result of the gender status beliefs rather than something unique to sex/gender, such as evolved differences in men's and women's dispositions.

Evaluations of men's and women's task performances similarly show the predicted pattern of biases. In a meta-analysis of evaluation studies, Swim and colleagues (1989) found a modest overall tendency for the same task performance to be evaluated more positively when produced by a man rather than by a woman. This tendency was significantly stronger when the task was male typed, but it disappeared altogether when the task was one associated with women. There is also some evidence that women rate the quality of their ideas lower than men rate their own ideas in mixed-sex contexts but equally positively as men in same-sex contexts (Carli 1991). Finally, a meta-analysis of studies of the evaluation of resumes in simulated employment contexts found a moderate tendency for the same resume to be evaluated more positively if it came from a man rather than from a woman when the job applied for was male typed. However, when the job was female typed, the same resume was evaluated less positively if it was a man's rather than a woman's (Davidson and Burke 2000). Eagly and Carli (2007, p. 77) further analyzed Davidson and Burke's data and found that when the job was gender neutral, a resume from a man was still preferred over one from a woman, but the bias was less than that for a male-typed job.

Expectation states theory argues that gender status beliefs not only bias the evaluation of performance but also bias the inference of ability from a performance of a given quality. Essentially, people from lower status groups, because they are presumed to be less competent, must perform better than those from higher status groups to convince others that they have high ability. Studies confirm this effect. Women are held to higher standards to prove high ability than similar men are, and comparable results occur for African Americans compared with whites as well (Biernat and Kobrynowicz 1997; Foschi, Lai, and Sigerson 1994).

Willingness to attribute ability to a man or a woman based on performance also varies with the gender typing of the task, as expectation states theory predicts. Swim and Sanna (1996) conducted a meta-analysis of the relevant evidence. They found that biases in the attribution of success to ability rather than effort clearly favor men for male-typed tasks but disappear altogether for tasks culturally linked to women.

Gender status beliefs also bias the inferences men and women make about their own abilities based on their performances, as Shelley Correll (2004) has shown. In an experiment, she demonstrated that when a task was labeled as masculine, women rated their ability lower than men did on the basis of identical performances. When the same task was disassociated from gender, however, there were no differences in the way men and women rated their ability from the same performance.

Finally, there is evidence that self-other performance expectations, biased by gender status beliefs, can affect not only the evaluation of a person's performance but also the actual quality of that performance, independent of his or her real abilities. Knowing that others expect you to be less competent at a task can create anxiety that interferes with the ability to perform well (Steele and Aronson 1995). Studies show, for instance, that when women are exposed to stereotypic beliefs that they are less able in math, they perform less well on math tests than they do when gender is not salient in the situation (Spencer, Steele, and Quinn 1999). Men, too, have been shown to perform less well on female-typed tasks involving social and emotional skills when gender stereotypes are salient (Koenig and Eagly 2005). On the other hand, stereotypic beliefs that you are more able than others can boost confidence and improve performance, as studies have also demonstrated (Shih, Pittinsky, and Ambady 1999). These effects, too, have been found for racial groups as well as gender, supporting the argument that they are a result of status and competence beliefs embedded in gender stereotypes, as well as in racial stereotypes.

It is clear, then, that gender status beliefs create a predictable pattern of biases in men's and women's task-directed behaviors and evaluations in goal-oriented contexts. Task-directed behaviors and evaluations in social relations are especially consequential for inequality. In an achievement-oriented society like the contemporary United States, these behaviors and evaluations, as they play out in the classroom, in job interviews, and in the workplace, have the effect of directing people toward or away from organizational positions of power and resources. In the home, they similarly affect the extent to which family activities take place on a man's or woman's own terms or on the terms of others. As gender status beliefs bias these behaviors and evaluations over multiple, repeating social contexts, then, they create potentially significant forms of inequality between otherwise similar men and women.

Legitimacy, Leadership, and Authority

In addition to biasing task behaviors and evaluations, gender status beliefs have a second type of effect that also fosters gender inequality. When salient in the situation, gender status beliefs affect the extent to which women are seen as *legitimate* candidates for positions of leadership and authority, according to expectations states theory (Berger et al. 1998; Ridgeway and Berger 1986; Ridgeway and Bourg 2004). Leaders are high-ranking members of interpersonal status hierarchies who take on additional duties and rights not only to influence but also to *direct* the group's activities. Leaders are also people who occupy positions in organizations that require them to direct the activities of subordinates. The essential hierarchical element of gender status beliefs attaches greater status worthiness to men, as well as greater general competence. The theory argues that this hierarchical aspect, in particular, causes men to seem like more socially expected, appropriate, and legitimate candidates for authority and leadership, as well as more instrumentally competent candidates. As the more expected candidates, men are more readily accepted by others in leadership roles.

In comparison, gender status beliefs make authority seems less legitimate and proper for women. Recall that the traits seen as most undesirable in women, as stereotype research has shown, are those associated with forceful dominance (Prentice and Carranza 2002; Rudman et al. 2009). This implied cultural criticism undercuts women's efforts to act authoritatively to achieve and effectively exercise leadership. These legitimacy problems are greatest for women, according to the theory, in contexts in which gender status beliefs advantage men, which is to say, mixed-sex situations with a gender-neutral or masculine task. Women, however, may even face modest legitimacy problems in feminine task contexts where they are viewed as somewhat more competent than men but still not fully appropriate for strong, directive authority. It is especially problematic for women who seek leadership roles that the management role in organizations is seen in the United States as a masculine task (Heilman et al. 1989; Powell, Butterfield, and Parent 2002). We will discuss this issue in the next chapter when we look more closely at gender in the workplace.

The legitimacy problems evoked by gender status beliefs create a second level of obstacles for women who pursue influence and positions of power and resources. As we have seen, the first-level effects of gender status beliefs bias performance expectations and set in motion a web of self-fulfilling, subtle effects that undercut women's own and others' assumptions about women's competence, at least in contexts other than those defined in stereotypically feminine terms. Increasingly, however, more and more women are determined to resist the pressure of negative expectations for their competence. They are developing strong skills that they can be confident of and are acting assertively to push past such doubts and better their lives (Hoyt and Blascovich 2007). When they do, however, they sometimes encounter the second problem created by gender status beliefs. Their assertiveness contradicts the hierarchical aspect of gender status beliefs and, thus, violates others' implicit expectations about gender and authority. The gender status incongruity of their assertive behavior makes it seem illegitimate and rudely dominant. As a result, the women encounter a resistive, backlash reaction to their assertive claims for advancement.

A number of studies have shown this effect in mixed-sex contexts in which a woman attempts to gain influence by assertively putting her ideas forward (Carli 1990; Ridgeway 1982; Shackleford, Wood, and Worchel 1996). Linda Carli (1990), for instance, found that for women in same-sex groups and men in both same- and mixed-sex groups, assertive speech was more effective in gaining influence than tentative speech. But when women used assertive speech in mixed-sex groups, they were actually less influential than when they used tentative speech, and they were seen as less likable and trustworthy as well.

Laurie Rudman and Peter Glick (2001) found similarly negative reactions to women, but not men, who engaged in assertive, self-promoting behavior in a mock job interview. The assertive self-promotions enhanced the perceived competence of both women and men in the mock interviews. Unlike the men, however, the assertive women were also disliked and not recommended for the job. In a later study, Rudman and colleagues (2009) demonstrated that the hostile reaction to women's assertive, status-enhancing behaviors in this setting was triggered by people's perceptions that such behavior is exaggeratedly dominant (i.e., is domineering) when performed by a woman rather than by a man. It is perceived as violating the status-based proscriptions of gender stereotypes and, therefore, is subject to sanction.

If women encounter resistance when they assertively put themselves forward to advance, then this will be an impediment to their emergence or appointment as leaders (Eagly and Carli 2003). Studies show that women can sometimes assuage the illegitimacy of their claims for authority by combining their assertiveness not only with clear competence but also with social and expressive behaviors that present them as friendly and cooperative rather than self-interested (Carli 2001; Ridgeway 1982). Such techniques can help women achieve greater influence and rank, but they can be tricky to bring off. They are also costly in that they reinforce gender stereotypes that women must be "nice," as well as competent, to succeed.

The difficulties of managing such resistance reactions suggest that women will be less likely to emerge as leaders in mixed settings, and this is what the research shows. In a meta-analysis, Eagly and Karau (1991) found that women were moderately less likely than men to be chosen as leaders in mixed-sex contexts. Women's disadvantage in this regard was greater for masculine tasks but present even for feminine tasks. When leadership was defined in more masculine terms as strictly task oriented, women's disadvantage was also greater. Following the expected pattern, only when leadership was defined in social terms as group facilitation rather than as task direction were women slightly advantaged over men in being selected as leader.

A study by Barbara Ritter and Janice Yoder (2004) shows how these legitimacy reactions can constrain the achievement of leadership even by women who are assertive and dominant by disposition. They measured the personal dominance levels of men and women and created task-oriented dyads with one high- and one low-dominance member. When these dyads were either same-sex or mixed-sex with a dominant male, the member with the more dominant personality was much more likely to be selected as leader. The interesting results, however, were from the mixed-sex groups with a high-dominance woman and a low-dominance man. When the task was either gender neutral or masculine, the man in these dyads, despite his low dominance, was still more likely than the woman to be selected as leader. Thus gender status trumped personality in these situations, sometimes because the dominant woman would appoint the low-dominance man leader. Only when the task was feminine (planning for a wedding) was the high-dominance woman more likely than the man to become leader in these dyads. These findings replicate a well-known earlier study (Megargee 1969).

In addition to making it more difficult for women to emerge as leaders, the legitimacy problems gender status beliefs create increase the likelihood that women leaders will be judged more harshly than similar men. According to expectation states theory, such judgments will be harsher the more strongly status expectations in the situation favor men. Thus, they will be especially harsh in male-typed settings. Two meta-analyses confirm this pattern of effects. In a meta-analysis of leadership effectiveness, Alice Eagly and colleagues found no differences in how men and women leaders were rated when the results were averaged over all types of contexts (Eagly, Karau, and Makhijani 1995). But in male-dominated and military contexts, men were much more likely than women to be seen as effective. In contexts more closely associated with women, such as education, government, and social service work, women, in contrast, were modestly more likely than men to be rated as effective leaders.

Ratings of leadership effectiveness, however, confound potential differences in the leaders' actual behavior (were male and female leaders behaving the same?) with biases in the evaluation of that behavior (were similar behaviors judged differently?). In another meta-analysis that held constant leadership behaviors, Alice Eagly and colleagues again found a small overall tendency to evaluate women leaders more negatively (Eagly, Makhijani, and Klonsky 1992). Predictably, however, this tendency was considerably stronger in male-dominated contexts. Even more predictably, according to the legitimacy argument, when women leaders exercised their authority in a directive, autocratic style, they were particularly devalued in comparison with similar men.

Additional research supports the argument that resistive reactions to women's assertions of authority are legitimacy effects brought about by gender status beliefs rather than a product of cultural expectations distinctive to women, such as that they be especially warm or caring. Rudman and colleagues (2009) showed that such resistive reactions were explained by exaggerated perceptions of women's dominance rather than their insufficient warmth. A different study found that when high-ranking members of task groups were younger or had lesser educational backgrounds, they, too, were resisted and disliked when they attempted to go beyond influence to wield directive authority (Ridgeway, Johnson, and Diekema 1994). The evidence of this study suggests that status distinctions other than gender also produce similar resistive reactions.

Conclusions

Overall, then, the evidence about sex differences in task behaviors and evaluations and about reactions to men's and women's assertions of authority and leadership fits reasonably well with expectation states theory's predictions about the impact of gender status beliefs on social relations in goal-oriented contexts. As the theory predicts, when gender status beliefs are effectively salient in a situation, they do seem to bias the implicit expectations men and women hold for their own comparative competence in the situation, as well as the expectations others hold for them. These biased performance expectations held by self and others converge to cause otherwise similar men and women to engage in different levels of task behaviors and make and receive different performance evaluations. Due to the effects of status beliefs, the theory predicts that performance expectations in mixed-sex settings will modestly advantage men over similarly able women in gender-neutral contexts, more strongly advantage men in male-typed contexts, and weakly advantage women in female-typed contexts, but produce no sex differences in same-sex, gender-neutral settings. The evidence on sex differences in participation and task suggestions, assertive speech and gestures, influence, evaluations of performances, and attributions of ability by self and others all correspond to these predicted patterns in the main.

When gender status beliefs are effectively salient, as they are in mixed-sex and gender-typed settings, expectation states theory argues that they shape perceptions of the participants' comparative appropriateness for authority and leadership according to a similar pattern, except that men are advantaged over women for authority even in female-typed contexts. Again, although the total record of evidence is sparser, it largely corresponds to the predicted pattern. In contrast to men, women in mixed-sex contexts more often receive negative reactions to their assertive claims for advancement. Not surprisingly, then, men are more likely to emerge as leaders in mixed-sex settings, independent of their personal dispositions, and their advantage in this regard is stronger when the task is male typed. In comparison with female leaders, male leaders are also more positively evaluated for the same behavior, especially for more directive behavior, and are rated as more effective. These effects are strongest for male-typed contexts or tasks. Although performance expectations advantage women over men in female-typed contexts, status beliefs still do not fully advantage them for directive authority even in those settings. As a result, women are not systematically more likely to become leaders even in mixed-sex settings with a feminine task. However, when they do succeed in gaining leadership positions in female-dominated work contexts, they are perceived as modestly more effective in those positions than are men.

These multiple, mutually reinforcing effects on task behaviors, evaluations, and leadership are all produced through the implicit, self-fulfilling effects of gender acting as a background identity in social relational contexts. These effects come about because virtually everyone is aware of hegemonic gender stereotypes and recognizes them as a force to be contended with. Some people who do not fully endorse these hegemonic beliefs may occasionally consciously react to the pressure of these beliefs and seek to challenge them in a given situation. In most situations, however, it is difficult for people to resist the constraints on them created by gender beliefs both because of the implicit, background nature of their effects and because the institutionalized nature of these beliefs often means there are real costs to challenging them. As a result, while many occasionally resist in small ways, most people most of the time generally and often unwittingly comply with gender status expectations in most of their behavior. As a result, the enactment of gender in social relations continues to be also the enactment of inequality.

Expectations for Communality

Automatic sex categorization makes all aspects of widely shared gender stereotypes implicitly available to shape actors' behaviors and judgments in social relational contexts. As we have seen, the gender status beliefs that are incorporated within hegemonic gender stereotypes are especially consequential for shaping behavioral hierarchies of influence, esteem, and authority and for creating inequalities in outcomes for men and women in relational contexts. The behavioral differences between men and women created by gender status beliefs, however, mark status or standing in the situation rather than sex category per se and, thus, vary by context. Marking sex/gender as essential difference is also important for the social relational enactment of gender inequality, since, as we have argued, inequality rests on cultural presumptions of difference. Interestingly, stereotypic expectations for women's greater communality are the aspects of hegemonic stereotypes that seem most clearly to create behavioral effects in social relational contexts that mark sex category, rather than situational status. Through the impact of cultural beliefs about women's distinctive communality, the use of gender as a primary frame for organizing social relations creates behavioral displays of categorical difference, as well as status inequality.

A variety of evidence indicates that women in contemporary America engage in modestly more *positive socioemotional* behavior in social relations than do men (Guerrero, Jones, and Boburka 2006; Ridgeway and Smith-Lovin 1999). This is behavior that is supportive, friendly, and emotionally expressive. As traditionally coded, it also includes agreeing with others, a behavior that is actually task directed but has supportive, communal implications as well (Bales 1970; Ridgeway 2006a; Ridgeway and Smith-Lovin 1999).

Research on socioemotional behaviors is not as extensive and systematic as research on task behaviors and judgments. Nevertheless, the extant evidence shows that women have higher total rates of socioemotional behaviors than men in task-oriented groups (Anderson and Blanchard 1982; Carli 1989) and provide more social support in close relationships (see Eagly and Koenig 2006). Women also use verbal forms that support the speech of others more than men do (Aries 1996; Johnson et al. 1996), use more expressive intensifiers (Carli 1990), smile and laugh more (Hall 2006; LaFrance, Hecht, and Paluck 2003), and are nonverbally warmer (Hall 1984; Wood and Rhodes 1992). The size of these differences is variously estimated as modest (about 2–8%: Aries 1996; MacGeorge et al. 2004) to more substantial (10% or more: Burleson and Kunkel 2006, p. 150), which means that the differences are clearly noticeable although not overwhelming.

Some part of women's higher rates of socioemotional behavior, particularly their higher rates of agreements, is because they are more likely than men to be in lower status positions in interpersonal status hierarchies. As we noted earlier, lower status actors are cast into a reactive, supportive role that causes them to act in a more communal manner (Conway et al. 1996; Wagner and Berger 1997). There is indeed evidence that lower status actors in interpersonal hierarchies engage in more positive socioemotional behavior than do high-status actors (Ridgeway 2006a).

Status dynamics, however, cannot fully explain women's higher rates of positive socioemotional behaviors (Balkwell and Berger 1996; Ridgeway and Smith-Lovin 1999). In close relationships, women typically provide more sensitive emotional support both in same-sex relationships, where gender status beliefs are not necessarily salient, and in mixed-sex relationships, including marital ones, where gender status is salient (Burleson and Kunkel 2006). Furthermore, differences between men and women in positive socioemotional behaviors are frequently larger in same-sex than in mixed-sex groups (Anderson and Blanchard 1982; Carli 1989, 1990; LaFrance et al. 2003). Finally, in mixed-sex groups, sex differences in some of these behaviors (smiling and laughing) have been shown to be unaffected by the sex typing of the task, as status-related behaviors typically are (Dovidio et al. 1988; Balkwell and Berger 1996). Sex differences in positive socioemotional behaviors do not follow the patterns we would expect if they were purely status driven.

Alice Eagly, in her social role analysis of sex differences in social behavior, has assembled a large body of evidence that points to stereotypic cultural expectations for women's greater communality as the major cause of women's higher rates of positive socioemotional behavior in social relations (Eagly 1987; Eagly and Koenig 2006; Eagly et al. 2000). The particular pattern that sex differences in positive socioemotional behavior take in social relations suggests some further details about how people respond to these cultural expectations for communality. It appears that people use their gendered displays of socioemotional behaviors to, among other things, signal or mark sex identity as an essential difference that is stably present across varying contexts (Hall 2006). Adding additional positive socioemotional behaviors distinctly signals female rather than male in social relations in the United States. Consistent with this interpretation, Carli (1990) argues that people develop cultural schemas or norms for same-sex social relations, according to which all female interaction is expected to be distinctively high in positive socioemotional behavior.

It is interesting that this behavioral signaling of sex category in social relations is similar to the way that difference is distinguished in language and person perception (Fiske 1998; Tannen 1993). It is the exception to the dominant form that is marked by something extra (e.g., "judge" for a man, "woman judge" for a woman). As we will see, the social marking of difference as well as inequality plays an essential role in the enactment of gender inequality in the workplace and home and the persistence of this inequality in the face of social change.

SUMMARY AND CONCLUSIONS

The argument that gender is a primary cultural frame for coordinating social relations carries with it two central presumptions that focus on cultural beliefs about gender. The framing argument presumes that the social categories of male and female are linked with cultural beliefs about the distinguishing characteristics and typical behavior of the sexes that we all assume we all know. It also presumes that we draw on these gender beliefs as common knowledge to coordinate behavior, and, in so doing, those beliefs shape or gender our behavior.

Our project in this chapter has been to investigate these central presumptions both conceptually and empirically. The first task was to develop a more detailed conceptual analysis of the nature of cultural beliefs about gender, their relationship to material arrangements, how they become salient in social situations, and how they shape behavior. The second task has been to examine the empirical evidence that supports this conceptual analysis and tells us what contemporary cultural beliefs about gender are like.

We began with the observation that while shared cultural beliefs about gender are indeed gender stereotypes, there is more to them than we typically associate with that term. Shared gender stereotypes are the implicit cultural *rules* for enacting a material structure of gender relations in American society. That is, acting on these taken-for-granted stereotypes results in material arrangements between men and women that, in turn, uphold our current views of who men and women are and why they are unequal.

There is ample empirical evidence that contemporary Americans hold well-defined gender stereotypes that are consensual common knowledge known to virtually everyone. Contemporary stereotypes describe men as more agentic and women as more communal and have both descriptive and prescriptive aspects. Embedded in gender stereotypes are *status beliefs* that associate men and their traits with higher status than women and their traits, even though women are seen as nicer. The status implications of gender stereotypes associate men with greater overall competence, understood as the ability to master events and accomplish goals, while also granting each sex some specialized skills. Thus, the content of gender stereotypes implies not only difference between the sexes but also inequality.

Efforts to account for the content of gender stereotypes compare the way the content of gender stereotypes shifts with changes in material relations between men and women in society. They also examine whether the content of stereotypes of other groups in society shows comparable associations with material arrangements. As we would expect, this evidence suggests that the content of widely held gender stereotypes is rooted in three material aspects of everyday social relations between men and women: the gender division of labor, the behaviors through which status hierarchies are enacted, and the particular experiences of these things by dominant groups in society. Studies of how the productive roles that men and women play in society shape the traits people attribute to them suggest that men's greater involvement in higher status work roles and women's in caregiving roles contribute powerfully to stereotypic assumptions about agency and communality. The evidence also indicates that the content of gender stereotypes is heavily shaped by the attributes (proactive and competent versus reactive and expressive) that American culture associates with the performance of high-status and low-status roles in interpersonal hierarchies of all kinds. Finally, people in dominant groups have more cultural resources and power to shape the cultural images of men and women that become institutionalized in the media, government policies, and elsewhere. As a result, the content of gender stereotypes that becomes consensual and culturally hegemonic tends to more closely resemble white middle-class heterosexuals than other groups. Alternative gender beliefs are shared by racial, political, or other subgroups, but these appear to affect behavior most directly in gatherings of like-minded others. Hegemonic gender beliefs remain the default rules of the gender game in public settings.

The other side of the reciprocal relation between shared gender stereotypes and material arrangements addresses the question of how these stereotypes shape behavior in ways that accumulate to create material consequences in the lives of men and women. In this chapter, we gained an understanding of the basic processes by which gender stereotypes shape judgments and behaviors in relationships between individuals. Future chapters will examine how these processes play out in the worlds of work and home.

The routine process of sex-categorizing someone unconsciously primes gender stereotypes in our minds and makes them implicitly available to shape our judgments and behavior. Yet the very factors that support sex/gender's utility as an initial cultural frame for making sense of another—its abstract, simplified nature—also limit its ability to offer very specific information about the other person or how to relate to him or her. As a result, gender almost always acts as a diffuse *background identity* in social relations. Specific institutional roles (teacher, student) with clearer instructions for behavior are typically in the foreground of people's definitions of self and other in a situation. Background gender identities, however, import an added set of meanings that modifies how actors perform their focal institutional identities. Thus, rather than a coherent set of independent behaviors, gender becomes a bias in the way that other activities are performed.

Since gender is a background identity, it always acts in *combination* with other identities in shaping people's behaviors and judgments. As men and women's institutional roles change, this is part of the way that gender stereotypes also change. Acting in combination with other identities also causes actors' gender interests in social relations to intersect in complex ways with the interests created by other significant identities, such as race or class.

Because gender combines with other identities, the extent to which gender stereotypes bias behavior and judgments in social relations can vary from imperceptible to substantial, depending on the nature of the situation. The more *salient* gender is to actors in a setting, the greater the impact of gender stereotypes on their judgments and behavior. Evidence indicates that gender is *effectively salient* in that it measurably affects behavior in mixed-sex settings and in settings that are culturally linked to gender (a wedding) or to the stereotyped skills of one sex or another (nursing or the military).

To better understand how gender modifies behavior and judgments when it is effectively salient in a setting, we examined in more detail the impact of the status and competence assumptions (i.e., gender status beliefs) contained in gender stereotypes, as well as the impact of assumptions about women's greater communality. We relied on expectation states theory for an account of the impact of gender status beliefs. This theory argues that differences in men's and women's task-directed behaviors and evaluations in a given situation will be a function of the extent to which their *self-other performance expectations* are biased by gender status and competence assumptions. The more salient gender is in the setting and the more relevant it is to the shared goal or task, the stronger the biases.

Specifically, the theory predicts that performance expectations in mixed-sex settings will modestly advantage men over similarly able women in gender-neutral contexts, more strongly advantage men in male-typed contexts and weakly advantage women in female-typed contexts, but produce no sex differences in same-sex, gender-neutral settings. We reviewed a wide range of evidence and found that sex differences in participation and task suggestions, assertive speech and gestures, influence, evaluations of performances, and attributions of ability by self and others all corresponded to these predicted patterns.

When gender status beliefs are salient in a situation, they also disadvantage women by making them seem like less appropriate candidates for authority and directive leadership. Because of such *legitimacy* problems, women can face resistive backlash reactions when they make assertive claims for advancement or attempt to exercise directive authority. As the evidence we reviewed shows, legitimacy biases follow a similar pattern as biases in performance expectations, except that women are not fully advantaged over men, even in female-typed contexts.

The behavioral differences between men and women created by gender status beliefs are consequential for inequality but vary by context. In contrast, the behavioral differences created by stereotypic expectations for women's greater communality most clearly mark sex as a stable category of difference rather than a situationally variable status. The extant evidence suggests that women in the contemporary United States engage in modestly more *positive socioemotional* behavior than do men in both mixed- and same-sex social relations. Thus, through the impact of cultural beliefs about women's distinctive communality, the use of gender as a primary frame for organizing social relations creates behavioral displays of categorical difference, as well as status inequality.

At this, point, then, we have a more specific understanding of how cultural beliefs about gender, cognitively primed by sex categorization, act to gender behavior in social relations. The extent and direction of the gendering effects of stereotypes on behavior vary by situation but in ways that we can systematically specify. The next task is to see how these general principles by which cultural beliefs about gender shape behavior play out in the socially significant contexts of the workplace and home. Examining these questions will show us how cultural beliefs, acting through everyday social relations at work and home, continually reproduce material patterns of gender inequality and difference. Understanding this reproduction process will, in turn, start us on the path of answering the question of how gender inequality persists in the contemporary world.

FOUR

Gendering At Work

I N THE CONTEMPORARY United States, the world of paid work not only occupies much of our lives it also is the central arena through which we gain access to material rewards of all sorts and achieve positions that allow us to wield power in society. What happens in the workplace, then, is of enormous consequence for the structure of inequality among us as individuals and also among us as men and women in society. When people make claims about gender inequality in the contemporary United States, the first indicators they point to are typically from the world of paid work: the gender gap in wages, the underrepresentation of women in management and positions of authority, and so on.

People are right to point to labor market outcomes when they discuss gender inequality. Along with the home, the world of paid work is currently one of the primary battlegrounds of the forces that work to undermine gender inequality and those that act to reproduce it, with the future of gender inequality in the balance. As we saw at the outset, the distinct system of difference and inequality that we call gender is at root a status inequality—an inequality between culturally defined types of people—rather than just an inequality in the material resources and power men and women have as a result of the positions they hold in the labor force and elsewhere. But as we also saw, the cultural beliefs that make gender a status inequality do so by defining gender differences in terms of men's status superiority. Such beliefs can be sustained in the long run only if men and women generally do occupy positions that carry unequal rewards and power in organizations of all sorts. If the roles men and women play (or are blocked from playing) in the socially central arena of work do not structure people's experiences in ways that generally uphold cultural beliefs about gender difference and inequality, then those defining beliefs of the gender system will be under pressure to change.

If gender is a primary cultural frame for coordinating social relations among individuals, then it is easy to see that it would be pulled into the organization of social relations in the workplace as well. The world of paid work is actually carried out through myriad social relations among individuals. Potential workers train and apply for jobs, and employers and hiring agents seek, interview, and evaluate applicants for hire. Both these *supply*-side processes, in which applicants pursue jobs, and the *demand*-side processes, by which employers hire them, are inherently social relational in that actors on both sides must define themselves in relation to others to figure out how to act effectively. Together, these everyday work relations create the job-matching processes that allocate men and women to positions in employment organizations and shape the rewards and power they have access to. Once on the job, the work process itself is carried out through more social relations that further affect the activities they engage in, the social networks they join, how they perform on the job, how they are evaluated, and the promotions they receive.

In each of these work relations, actors automatically sex-categorize as part of the process of making sense of one another. As they do so, they implicitly nest their identities as job applicants and employers and workers within their prior background identities as men and women. At the same time, the inherently goal-oriented nature of work brings to the fore issues of coordinating judgments and actions with others to jointly organize and accomplish workplace tasks. It is no surprise, then, that actors draw in varying degrees on the culturally convenient coordinating device of gender beliefs as they carry out their work-related activities. The gender status beliefs and the beliefs about each sex's specialized traits that are repeatedly activated in the background throughout workplace relations offer actors an ever-available framework for filling in the details of an uncertain work task, setting, or person and for providing an overarching, simplifying interpretation of complex circumstances. Since these gendered workplace assumptions and interpretations are based on taken-for-granted cultural beliefs, they are easily shared among workers and employers alike, so that they implicitly aid the coordination of work activities. In this way, the organization of work becomes gendered in varying degrees. The task before us here is to understand more clearly how this process plays out in the workplace and what its implications are for gender inequality in outcomes.

The first step is to take into account an obvious but critical point for understanding how gender shapes the work world: Although the world of paid work is carried out through relations among individuals, almost all these relations take place within organizational and institutional structures that constrain what occurs. As we saw in the last chapter, the extent to which individuals draw on cultural beliefs about gender in fashioning their behavior and judgments in a relational context depends on the extent to which the situation makes those beliefs salient and relevant and allows the individual discretion to act on them. The nature of the institutional structure within which individuals are acting plays a key role at each of these steps that shape the extent to which the individuals implicitly rely on the gender frame.

To begin with, the surrounding institutional structure affects gender's salience and relevance in a relational context. Simply the mixed-gender composition of job applicants, workers, or employers in a work context is sufficient to make the gender frame at least diffusely salient for those involved. If the work carries a gendered cultural connotation like, say, manual labor or nursing, then that, too, will make the gender frame not only salient but also implicitly relevant to the goals and focus of workplace activities. The institutional organization of work itself, then, routinely triggers the gender frame for workplace actors in many work contexts and affects whether gender is just diffusely present for them or a more powerful backdrop to their activities.

The institutional structure of work also affects the freedom workplace actors have to act on the cultural biases the gender frame implicitly introduces into their perceptions and judgments. Institutional structures and procedures, such as job definitions, formal hierarchies, and work rules, define much of what goes on in the workplace. When these structures and procedures rigidly script workplace actors' behavior, as in routine, highly bureaucratic jobs, actors' behavior and decisions largely reflect the rule, with less scope for the expression of their own personal implicit biases. Other workplace structures and procedures constrain behavior in general ways but allow individuals considerable discretion in interpreting and carrying out their work activities, such as among teachers in the classroom or lawyers in evaluating cases. Workplace actors' behavior and judgments, then, are likely to most directly reflect their personal use of gender as a framing device for self and others in workplace contexts that make gender effectively salient, typically through the gender composition of the workplace or the gendered cultural connotations of the work, and that allow actors some degree of discretion in their actions.

Constraining or enabling individual gender biases is hardly the only effect of workplace structures and procedures on gendered outcomes in the labor force, however. These structures and procedures themselves also can represent logics that either embody cultural beliefs about gender in the way that they organize workplace actors and activities or resist framing workers in gendered terms. In the contemporary workplace, the demands of rational efficiency in businesses and other employment organizations encourage procedures that treat workplace actors as disembodied skill sets (e.g., "systems analyst") and role incumbents ("assistant manager") rather than in terms of traditional distinctions such as gender (Jackson 1998). Also, federal equal opportunity laws create incentives for most employers to use procedures that at least appear to be nondiscriminatory and universalistic (Petersen and Saporta 2004).

Yet, even a cursory examination of the taken-for-granted structures and procedures of the workplace shows that many of them embody stereotypic assumptions about the gendered nature of the actors who will carry them out (Acker 1990, 2006). To take one broad but telling example, the very structure of the traditional 40-hour, Monday-to-Friday workweek reveals embedded assumptions about the gendered nature of ideal workers. The rigid structure of work time that the traditional workweek involves implicitly assumes that ideal workers will not have direct personal responsibility for the daily care of dependent children. It implicitly suggests, then, that ideal workers will look more like stereotypic men than like stereotypic women who are expected to be the ones with primary responsibility for children (Acker 1990; 2006). Research shows that existing work organizations frequently have structures of power and control, divisions of labor, rules for behavior, procedures for evaluating workers, and so on that carry within them implicit cultural assumptions about the gender, as well as the race and social class, of the actors that will enact them (see Acker 2006 for a review).

This point should not surprise us. Recall from chapter 1 that power and resources in modern societies derive from the positions people hold in the organizations that make up the society. Dominant groups in a society by definition occupy more powerful positions and have more control over workplace organizations than do subdominant groups. A consequence of this greater control is that the structural forms that develop and become commonplace practices in the workplace often reflect the perspectives and interests of dominant actors in the assumptions these practices make about work and workers. Since class-advantaged white males have been the dominant actors over the historical period in which many standard contemporary institutional structures and practices have developed, these structures and practices often carry an implicit stamp of hegemonic cultural beliefs about gender.

When structures and procedures embody stereotypic gender assumptions, they themselves become independent agents of gender bias in the workplace. They empower the gender frame to become part of the cultural rules by which workers are expected to interpret and carry out their workplace activities (e.g., P. Martin 1996). In so doing, they constrain workplace actors to behave in ways that result in unequal outcomes for men and women, independent of the actors' personal biases.

The tension between the forces of bureaucratic rationalization, efficiency, and legal liability that push against gender distinctions in the workplace and those that maintain and create structures and procedures that embody gender stereotypes causes the world of paid work to be a dynamic battleground over the future of gender inequality. In this battle, what is the force that continually reproduces workplace structures, procedures, and activities that embody cultural beliefs about gender? I argue that it is the use of gender as a primary frame for relating to another person that is the basic, underlying force behind these gendered structures and procedures.

Although I will not argue a historical case here, my argument implies that the effect of the gender frame acting on workplace relations over the years has been the primary mechanism by which gendered assumptions have become embedded in the institutional structures of work that are commonplace today. The question of persistence, however, turns on processes that maintain gendered structures and procedures in the contemporary work world and create new ones. The project of this chapter, therefore, is to describe how the framing effects of gender on workplace relations act in the present both to reproduce existing gendered structures of work and to establish new ones.

I begin by briefly reviewing the ways in which the structure of the labor market and the structures and procedures of employment organizations embody gender assumptions. As we shall see, these structures and procedures are responsible for much of the inequality in labor market outcomes between men and women. Then, I turn to how the framing effects of gender on workplace relations that take place in the context of existing structures and procedures perpetuate those structures and generate unequal outcomes. Finally, I take up the key questions of how such workplace relations can create new gendered structures and procedures in workplaces.

THE GENDERED STRUCTURE OF PAID WORK

The most striking way in which the labor market is structured by gender is in the sex segregation of occupations and jobs. An occupation or job is sex segregated when most of the people in it are of one sex and not the other. Elementary school teachers, for example, are overwhelmingly female; plumbers are overwhelmingly male. The contemporary occupational structure in the United States is so sex segregated that most people work in occupations or jobs that are largely filled by members of their own sex (Charles and Grusky 2004; Cotter et al. 2004; Tomaskovic-Devey et al. 2006). At present, more than 40% of all women in the workforce would have to change occupations to eliminate the existing sex segregation. Sometimes an occupation as a whole, like physician, includes a mix of men and women, but these men and women are nevertheless located in sex-segregated specialties, such as pediatrics versus surgery (Reskin and Roos 1990). Furthermore, when we look beyond broad occupations to the specific jobs people hold within employment organizations, the degree of sex segregation we see is even greater (Petersen and Morgan 1995; Tomaskovic-Devey 1993).

The sex segregation of jobs does not necessarily mean that men and women do not encounter one another in the workplace. After all, nurses work with surgeons, and secretaries work with bosses. It does mean, however, that men and women in the workplace are less likely to encounter one another as peers in the same position than as actors in differently titled and often unequal positions. Furthermore, as the preceding examples suggest, the types of jobs in which men and women are concentrated often appear to reflect cultural beliefs about gender, including status differences between the sexes and stereotypic assumptions about each sex's specialized skills. In a study of occupational sex composition in the United States and other affluent nations, sociologists

Maria Charles and David Grusky (2004) found that men were more likely to be concentrated in occupations associated with stereotypic masculine skills, which include manual jobs, and in top jobs in any occupation, and that women were more often in occupations associated with stereotypic feminine skills, which include many service jobs, and in jobs of lesser authority more generally. This pattern is as we would expect if workplace actors were repeatedly drawing on the cultural frame of gender to help organize workplace relations.

These patterns of sex segregation in occupations reveal a deep gender structure to the organization of paid work. Furthermore, the deep structure of overall sex segregation in jobs and occupations has been slow to change in the face of recent gains in women's education and labor force participation (Charles and Grusky 2004, p. 5). This is remarkable, given that the economy is always changing, creating new jobs and occupations while eroding others. As the economy and the labor force change, the sex compositions of particular jobs do change, typically as women enter formerly male jobs and men begin to leave them (Reskin and Roos 1990). Residential real estate agents used to be mostly men, for instance, but now they are mostly women. The fact that the overall sex segregation of the occupational structure persists in the face of dynamic changes in individual occupations indicates that it is not merely a relic of a more traditionally gendered past. Instead, it is continually being reproduced in some degree as jobs change from being segregated men's jobs to being segregated women's jobs, and new jobs, too, become gender typed as men's or women's jobs (Reskin and Roos 1990).

The sex segregation of occupations and jobs provides the organizational framework within which much of the gender inequality in wages and authority occurs. Only a small proportion of the gender gap in wages is due to pay differences between men and women with exactly the same job title and rank (Petersen and Morgan 1995). Most of the wage gap results from the fact that jobs primarily filled by women pay less than jobs mostly filled by men. In fact, the more women predominate in a job, the less it pays (Barnett, Baron, and Stuart 2000). As studies by sociologist Paula England and others have shown, women's jobs pay less, even when they require just as much education and skill as men's jobs (England 1992, chapter 2; Kilbourne et al. 1994). Furthermore, the more closely a job is associated with stereotypic female skills such as nurturing, the less it pays compared with similarly demanding jobs (England, Reid, and Kilbourne 1996). Even men's wages are less when they take on jobs such as nurse or librarian that are filled primarily by women.

The sex segregation of jobs is also an important factor in the authority gap between men and women in the workplace (Smith 2002). Often the job ladders associated with women's jobs yield less advancement than those associated with men's jobs (Barnett et al. 2000). Jobs dominated by women are especially less likely to be on the ladder to upper level management positions. It is much easier to become CEO, for instance, if you work in sales or finance, typically more male-dominated divisions of companies, than if you work in human resources—traditionally the female ghetto of the corporate world.

The sex segregation of occupations and jobs is the deepest and most pervasive gender structure in the organization of paid work, but many other gendered structures and procedures are common as well (see Acker 2006, chapter 5). In professions such as law or the academy, for instance, the normative timing of promotion rituals (e.g., gaining tenure or making partner) takes place during the prime child-bearing years. This timing structure implicitly presents more challenges to successful promotion for women than for most men.

SOCIAL RELATIONS AND THE ENACTMENT OF GENDERED STRUCTURES AT WORK

The sex segregation of jobs is not created by formal rules that require hiring a particular sex for a particular job. Indeed, explicitly gendered rules are usually illegal. Rather, the sex segregation of jobs is an emergent structure that comes about through the job-matching processes by which applicants seek and employers place men and women into different positions in an employment organization. Hiring and promotion decisions are critical junctures in this matching of people to jobs, but these junctures are supplemented by the social dynamics of the workplace in which they occur. The social dynamics of the workplace can influence who is referred to apply for a job, whether men and women persist in a job once hired, the tasks they are assigned, how they perform and are evaluated, and, consequently, the promotions and job changes they pursue as well as receive.

To see how the gender frame shapes the social relations that make up the job-matching process and create the sex segregation of jobs, I first discuss the demand side of the process by which employers and their agents hire and promote employees. Next I consider the supply side by which job seekers apply for jobs. I then turn to the workplace floor and discuss how gender can frame work relations in ways that are consequential for the perpetuation of gendered structures and inequality. After this general discussion, I look more closely at two sites in the work world where the gender frame creates especially difficult obstacles for women compared with men. These sites are particularly consequential for contemporary inequality in workplace outcomes. The first is the glass ceiling that challenges women who seek positions of substantial authority in not merely middle management but top management. The second is the maternal wall that makes it harder for women who are the mothers of dependent children to rise in the work world (Williams 2000).

Throughout this discussion, we need to keep in mind how we would expect the gender frame to influence workplace social relations, given what we learned in the last chapter. Gender is usually a background identity in the workplace, whose effects depend on its salience and relevance in the work situation. The structure of the work setting itself is a major factor in determining gender's salience and relevance, typically through the gender composition of those involved and through the extent to which work itself carries gendered cultural connotations. When gender is effectively salient in a situation, it subtly and implicitly biases performance expectations for men and women. These biases favor men most strongly in male-typed contexts, only modestly favor them in gender-neutral contexts, and do not favor men and may even favor women for competence in female-typed contexts. Men, however, are favored for authority in all contexts, just as women can always be held to proscriptions against forceful dominance and prescriptions for communality. These direct effects of the gender frame on individuals occur most clearly in situations in which work procedures are ambiguous or allow discretion in judgments and actions. Now we need to see when and how these implicit biases play out through the gendered background of the myriad social relations that make up the workplace.

Employers' Preferences in Hiring and Promotion

Employers and their agents start the job-matching process by seeking to hire or promote people into jobs they need to fill. Following the cultural logic of rational efficiency that dominates the modern work world, employers typically want to hire the best workers they can for a job, given the pool of applicants available and the compensation they are willing to offer. Out of these considerations, employers and their agents implicitly develop a shared image of the competencies and traits of the *preferred or ideal worker* that they would like to hire (Acker 1990; Gorman 2005; Williams 2000). This image or schema may be stated explicitly but often is not. Nevertheless, it guides how the job is advertised to applicants and sets a standard against which applicants are evaluated.

Gendering the Preferred Worker

As we will see, a number of factors can cause gender to become effectively salient for employers as they engage in this relational process of imagining whom they would like to hire, given who might be available. To the extent that it does, the image of the preferred worker will be implicitly infused with cultural beliefs about gender, so that an ideal hire is described in terms that more closely overlap either the male or female stereotype. The subtle bias this introduces makes it more difficult for applicants of the other sex to appear equally competent and "ideal" for the job.

Within the existing sex-segregated structure of the labor market, the job to be filled is often one whose current incumbents either in the workplace or in the broader labor market are known to be mostly of one sex. This structure in itself is likely to make cultural beliefs about gender effectively salient for both employers and applicants in the hiring and promotion process. Research shows that the gender stereotype of the sex that predominates in a job tends to bias the image of the competencies and traits of the ideal worker for that job. Psychologists Mary Ann Cejka and Alice Eagly (1999), for instance, found that the extent to which college students rated gender-stereotypic male or female qualities as essential to success in 80 different occupations directly corresponded to the sex ratios students estimated for those occupations, as well as to the actual sex ratios of those occupations. When the job at stake is one that is predominantly filled by one sex or the other, as many jobs are, then the stereotype of that sex tends to frame the image of the ideal hire for the job.

Not only the existing sex composition of the job but also the stereotypically gendered nature of the work (e.g., nursing or manual labor) or the status of the establishment that the job incumbent is expected to connote can implicitly activate gender beliefs and color the image of the preferred worker. The job of server, for instance, is commonly filled by both men and women and, thus, need not be sex segregated in a given workplace. When an owner opening a new restaurant wishes to project an image of a high-status, expensive establishment, however, the greater status culturally associated with men can become implicitly salient and bias the employer's sense of the preferred worker. This will tilt the sex ratio of those hired and create anew sex segregation in the job. In fact, more expensive restaurants, some evidence shows, are more likely to employ male servers (Rab 2001, cited in Reskin and Bielby 2005). Since tips are greater in more expensive restaurants, the result is income inequality between male and female servers.

The status associated with the type of job itself, not just the establishment, can also make gender a relevant dimension of the preferred occupant. The job of manager is by definition associated with authority and status in our society, as well as occupied disproportionately by (largely white) men (Collinson and Hearn 1996). Organizational behavior scholar Madeline Heilman and colleagues asked a sample of managers to describe the required characteristics for the job of manager, as well as the typical characteristics of men and women. Both male and female managers' descriptions of the good manager substantially overlapped their descriptions of typical men but were less similar to their descriptions of typical women (Heilman et al. 1989). Other studies have found similar results, suggesting that there is a shared cultural image of managers in our society that is clearly male typed (Powell, Butterfield, and Parent 2002). Given the hierarchical element of gender beliefs that cast men as more appropriate for authority than women, these findings are not surprising.

The gender biases that infiltrate employers' images of the ideal worker set the stage for biases in hiring and promotions by making cultural beliefs about gender status and gender skills implicitly salient and relevant to the evaluation of workers' qualifications. The process does not end there, however. Even if an employer's preestablished image of the job is gender neutral, gender can shape an employer's sense of who is best for the job in other ways. Gender can become effectively salient at multiple points in the hiring process, as resumes are compared and applicants are interviewed. Given this implicit salience, the more subjectivity that is involved in the assessment of applicants' competencies and suitability for the job, the more likely it is that decision makers will draw on the available background of gender status beliefs to decide which applicants are better.

Sociologist Elizabeth Gorman (2006) studied large U.S. law firms in the 1990s and the decisions they made to promote their male and female lawyers to partner, which is the rank of decision makers in the firm. In some cases, the legal work the firm's partners were expected to do was varied and complex rather than relatively routinized. When work is more complex, assessments of legal competence involve more subjective judgments that allow greater scope for stereotype bias. Recall that stereotypic gender status beliefs include the presumption that men are diffusely more competent than women. It is not surprising, then, that Gorman found that the more a firm's work involved complex uncertainty, the more that male rather than otherwise similar female candidates were perceived to be best and promoted to partner.

Gender Matching Applicants to Jobs

For employers, then, the social process of matching jobs to applicants involves an implicit comparison of competencies and traits presumed to be required for the job (the preferred worker image) with the perceived competencies and traits of actual applicants to assess the fit between the two. The multiple processes of relating to others that employers and hiring agents go through to carry out the matching of jobs to applicants provide many opportunities in which gender biases can be infused into either or both sides of the comparison between preferred worker images and applicants. Any of these biases affect the perceived fit between the job and a particular applicant. To the extent that social relations infuse cultural beliefs about gender into the hiring and promotion process, then, job matching becomes a gender stereotype fit or stereotype matching process between applicant and job (Heilman 1983; Heilman and Stamm 2007).

A second study by Elizabeth Gorman (2005) shows how this stereotype matching process affected the hiring of lawyers by large U.S. law firms in the 1990s. Gorman coded the hiring criteria that each law firm listed for its jobs (e.g., high academic achievement, willingness to assume responsibility) for the extent to which they included stereotypically gendered traits. Stereotypically masculine traits (e.g., ambitious, assertive) were more common, but feminine traits (cooperative, friendly) were sometimes listed as well. Controlling for other factors that affected the percentage of men and women applying for these jobs, Gorman found that the more masculine characteristics listed in the hiring criteria, the less likely it was that a woman was hired for the job. The more feminine characteristics in the hiring criteria, however, the more likely it was that a woman was hired.

Another study demonstrates that the perceived fit between the gendered image of a job and an applicant biases evaluations of competence and promotability in just the way we would expect from the effects of the gender frame that we learned about in the last chapter. We learned there that the more male typed the job, the more directly relevant gender status beliefs will become for judging competence and, therefore, the stronger the biases favoring men for expected performance. Karen Lyness and Madeline Heilman (2006) used archival data from a large financial services corporation to study the performance evaluations and subsequent promotions that upper middle- and senior-level managers received over a two-year period. While all corporate manager jobs carry a male-typed image, the authors argued that this male typing is especially strong for managers in line positions that direct essential organizational activities, such as production and sales, compared with staff positions that provide support and expertise to line officers.

Consistent with this and our analysis of the biases introduced by the gender frame, Lyness and Heilman found that while women managers received lower performance evaluations than men in both line and staff jobs, their evaluations were especially low in the more male-typed line jobs. Furthermore, to actually have been successfully promoted, women managers had had to receive higher performance evaluations prior to their promotions than had men who had been promoted. In general, performance standards were more closely related to receiving a promotion for women than men, suggesting that women were held to stricter standards to prove their ability than were men. As we saw in the last chapter, such double standards for proving ability are a documented effect of gender status beliefs on evaluations. The effects Lyness and Heilman found directly mirror those we would expect if cultural beliefs about gender status and agentic competence, acting through workplace relations, were implicitly biasing decisions about male and female managers.

A final study shows with particular clarity how the social processes by which people relate to one another in the job-matching process provide the medium through which gender shapes the perceived fit between job and applicant. Roberto Fernandez and Lourdes Sosa (2005) studied how the telephone customer service center of a large bank hired for an entry-level service representative job. This job was 66% female before the study began but became even more female dominated (78%) by the end, even though the hiring agents stated that they had no intentional preference for women over men.

One way gender entered the job-matching process was through the social networks by which applicants were referred for the job. The bank drew on its employees' personal networks for referrals. Later, we will see that gendered social networks are important for workplace dynamics, as well as hiring. Because of the way gender shapes personal ties, most people's networks overrepresent members of their own sex

(McPherson, Smith-Lovin, and Cook 2001). As a result, the customer service center's more numerous women employees were especially likely to refer other women applicants. Interestingly, however, even male employees referred more women than men for the job, suggesting that they held an implicitly gendered image of the job as more stereotypically feminine in nature.

The referral of applicants, however, was not the most important point in the process at which gender bias seemed to enter. It was the interview process that made the biggest difference. Fernandez and Sosa argue that while the hiring agents did not have an explicit preference for women, they implicitly perceived that the best customer service agents had communal skills of empathy and warmth that made them adept at service calls. In the social relational contexts of interviews, in which the judgment of qualifications is somewhat ambiguous, this implicitly gendered image of the preferred worker apparently colored their assessment of the competence and suitability of otherwise similarly qualified men and women applicants. As a result, after the interview process, women, compared with men with similar qualifications, were clearly and significantly more likely to be offered the job.

Employer Preferences and Discrimination

As these studies suggest, the biases that the gender frame introduces into employers' evaluations and decisions are typically implicit and unintentional. Nevertheless, they have the effect of being a type of discrimination. To the extent that these biases cause employers to misjudge the actual average differences between men and women applicants' ability to perform the job, these biases create "error" discrimination (England 1992, chapter 2). More insidiously, however, the biases introduced by the gender frame can endogenously create the basis for "statistical discrimination." Statistical discrimination occurs when the employer observes that there really are differences, *on average*, in how men and women perform at a particular job. The employer then uses each applicant's sex as an estimate of his or her likely productivity. This is discriminatory if the individual applicant is not just average for his or her sex and actually would perform as well or better at the job than someone of the other sex.

Statistical discrimination is hard to eliminate because it appears to be based on actual differences in productivity and, as a result, is resistant to the leveling effect of market forces. The problem, however, is that the gendered performance expectations that implicitly bias employers' estimates about men's and women's typical productivity in a job may also, through their effects on social relations in the workplace, have self-fulfilling effects on men and women employees' actual average performance at the job. In this way, the biases that shape employer assumptions can also actually *create* productivity differences between male and female employees that match those assumptions, independent of the underlying abilities of those employees.

The effects of employer biases that sex categorization sets in motion in the hiring and promotion process can vary from imperceptible to substantial but are typically rather modest. Gender is, after all, a background identity in the workplace. However, the small effects of these biases repeat over multiple evaluations and decisions to create a noticeably gendered structure of opportunity for men and women that subtly steers them toward different and unequal positions in the world of work (Agars 2004).

The Supply Side: Applicant Preferences

The sex-segregated structure of jobs and occupations is not created by employer biases alone, however. Applicant preferences are also shaped by the gender frame, and this, too, contributes to the differences we see in the jobs men and women hold. Above all, the cultural frame of beliefs about gender biases the assessments people make about what they are good at and therefore the choices they make about training and jobs. The choices people make about the jobs they pursue also take place in a structure of material interests, and gender plays a complex role in shaping both the nature of these material interests and people's reactions to them (see, for instance, Charles and Bradley 2009).

Gendered Biased Self-Assessments of Ability

From childhood on, in the home and at school, gender frames the social relations through which people try out different tasks, compare their performances with others, and form impressions of where their talents lie. Among the things people learn early on are the kinds of tasks that are culturally linked to one sex or the other, and this provides a gendered context in which they judge their own abilities at these tasks (Eckles, Barber, and Jozefowica 1999). A good example is the so-called path to math, the process through which children develop interests and skills in mathematics. Steps taken early on in the path to math have serious occupational consequences because many well-paying, prestigious jobs, notably those in science and engineering, require a good background in math. Women are substantially underrepresented in science and engineering jobs, and the way gender frames the path to math is part of the problem.

Math is widely believed in our society to be a task at which men are better than women, despite the fact that the evidence for such beliefs is weak (Correll 2001; Hyde 2005; Nosek, Banaji, and Greenwald 2002). The masculine cultural connotation of math makes gender salient in the classroom and elsewhere as children learn mathematical tasks, take standardized tests, and so on. As a result, as girls approach mathematics, they are at risk of a stereotype threat process that boys don't face in the same degree. Knowledge that they are expected to perform less well may undermine their confidence and cause them to actually perform less well (Eckles et al. 1999; Spencer, Steele, and Quinn 1999). Even if their performance is not affected, gender beliefs may cause girls to be less willing than similar boys to attribute their performance to an underlying talent in mathematics rather than just hard work. Self-assessments of underlying ability in turn shape children's willingness to persist in the face of difficulties and continue on the path to math.

Shelley Correll (2001) documented this process with data from a representative national sample that followed students from high school to the first years of college. She found that girls who had the same underlying math ability as boys, as indicated by grades and standardized tests, assessed their own ability at math as less than the boys did. Furthermore, for both boys and girls, self-assessments of math ability, independent of actual ability, predicted the likelihood that they would take more advanced math courses, like calculus, and choose a quantitative college major. Thus, the effects of gender-biased self-assessments of math ability accumulated as students went through school to point equally able girls and boys toward different, stereotypically gendered occupational choices.

For young people in school, not only biased assessments of their own abilities but also a tendency to fall back on the ever-available gender frame when making life choices that define who they are may encourage students to pursue gender-typical fields of study (Charles and Bradley 2009). Given the way gender implicitly frames educational choices, perhaps it is not surprising that the sex segregation of college majors has persisted despite large increases in the number of women who earn college degrees (England and Li 2006). Recent patterns of change and persistence in the sex segregation of college majors mirror the patterns we see in the sex segregation of occupations to which they contribute. In the 1970s and 1980s, women surged into higher education and also into traditionally male business fields, and the sex segregation of majors declined. But men did not move into traditionally female majors. And then, beginning in the 1990s, the movement of women into male fields flattened out, stalling the desegregation process and leaving us with a persistent pattern of sex segregation in college majors (England and Li 2006).

Gendered Choices in the Job Market

In adulthood, self-assessments of ability and the training and experience they lead to frame the jobs people look for. The gender framing of job interests, however, occurs within a powerful context of material incentives and costs. In a work world in which men's jobs pay better and carry more authority, women have a substantial interest in pushing against the implicit biases that undercut their attraction to and performance at men's jobs. Women's material interests in resisting gender biases introduce a potential dynamic of change into the sex segregation of jobs. This change dynamic is slowed, however, by the fact that men do not have a similar incentive to resist gender biases in order to enter women's lower paying jobs.

Other aspects of the rewards and costs of jobs, as currently structured by gender, work against change by encouraging job seekers of both sexes to act in ways that maintain the sex segregation of jobs. Because most women earn less than most men in the current structure, a particular not-very-well-paying women's job may look like a reasonable alternative to a woman on the job market but look decidedly unattractive to a male job seeker. As a result, due to the pay alone, more women are likely to apply for that female-dominated job. Also, pay and authority are not the only incentives and costs that jobs entail. Job seekers, too, often have a general idea of the sex composition and gendered connotation of a particular job. As they compare themselves with what they assume is the typical worker in a given job, they, too, are likely to assess their social fit in that workplace. As they do, they anticipate the social rewards and costs that fit entails: the ease and simplicity of being like the others or the daily struggle of being different.

Women, then, have a strong material interest in applying for men's jobs. Yet, not only their gender-biased self-assessments of their own abilities but also other aspects of the way gender affects the rewards and costs of jobs blunt the full effect of this material interest on their job-seeking behavior. For men, on the other hand, assessments of ability and the rewards and costs of jobs all point them in the same direction: toward men's jobs and away from women's jobs. Not surprisingly, then, studies show that the gender-biased choices of men and women workers, as revealed in the jobs they apply for, are a contributing factor in the sex-segregated structure of jobs. And when the sex composition of a job changes, it almost always does so by women entering men's jobs rather than men entering women's jobs (Reskin and Roos 1990).

A study by Roberto Fernandez and Colette Friedrich (2007) provides particularly clear evidence of the way cultural beliefs about gender bias the jobs for which men and women apply. This was a study of initial applications for jobs at a large call center. In many workplaces, hiring agents steer job seekers toward applying for some jobs and not others. This makes it difficult to tease out whether the job seekers' own initial preferences are biased toward same-sex jobs or they are just steered to those jobs.

The call center Fernandez and Friedrich studied used an unusual job application procedure that eliminated the possibility of steering. The call center required all job seekers to initiate their application by telephone through a computer-automated system that asked their interest in various jobs. After hearing a brief description of each job from the system, applicants were asked to rate it on a scale from not interested to "strong desire and ability to do this job." Among the jobs were some for which applicants were likely to have a gendered image, such as "receptionist," a typically female job, and "computer programmer," a typically male job. Despite the fact that the receptionist job paid half as much as the computer programmer job, 67% of women applicants, compared with only 38% of men, ranked themselves as higher in interest and ability for the receptionist job than for the computer programmer job. Two-thirds of those who expressed the highest level of "desire and ability" for the computer job were male.

The gender-biased job preferences of applicants, however, are not strong enough to fully account for the degree of sex segregation we see in jobs and occupations. Fernandez and Friedrich, for instance, found that, in the labor market of the area in which the call center was located, the jobs of receptionist and computer programmer were considerably more sex segregated than we would expect if their sex compositions were just a result of applicant preferences such as they found in their study. Rather, the sex segregation of jobs is jointly produced by the framing effects of gender stereotypes for both employers on the demand side and applicants on the supply side of the job matching process.

Workplace Dynamics

Once on the job, workplace actors' routine sex categorization of one another continues to prime gender as a discreet background identity that is ever available as an aid to making sense of and coordinating with others, particularly in work settings that have an element of uncertainty or ambiguity to them. Given its routine availability, many aspects of the workplace structure can trigger gender stereotypes to become effectively salient and subtly bias the performance expectations actors develop for themselves and others as they work together. The mixed-sex nature of an encounter, the gendered connotations of a job or assignment, or simply the need to find something in common with someone new you must work with can all make gender effectively salient.

As we saw in the last chapter, to the extent that gender shapes workplace actors' performance expectations for one another, it will subtly bias who speaks up and who holds back, how they evaluate each other's performances, who becomes influential, and who seems appropriate for leadership. These are all processes that are fundamental to the dynamics of the workplace. However, they are not the only ones by which the gender framing of people in the workplace shapes the emergence of gender differences in work outcomes. In addition to priming gender stereotypes, routine sex categorization in the workplace creates the basis for two further processes that also affect workplace dynamics. The first is a cluster of related processes associated with in-group biases, social networks, and perceptions of who can be trusted and counted on. The second concerns the development of gendered workplace cultures.

In-Group Biases, Networks, and Perceived Trust

Sex categorization makes sex a salient distinction among workers that sets in motion in-group, out-group, us-and-them dynamics. A great deal of psychological research has shown that salient group distinctions prime people's unconscious cognitive bias to favor their own group, others things being equal (Brewer and Brown 1998). In the workplace, in-group biases can shape whom people feel they can trust, rely on, and work easily with. As a result, these biases affect whom workplace actors seek to include in their social networks. And as a consequence of these biases, people have a tendency to act preferentially toward "people like us."

Sociologist Rosabeth Kanter (1977), in a classic study of corporate management, pointed out that in-group biases encourage those in authority to engage in what she called "homosocial reproduction." Faced with the inherent uncertainties of management, Kanter argued, authorities look for subordinates they can count on. In the process, authorities preferentially turn to people like themselves to carry out important tasks and sponsor them more strongly for promotion.

There is substantial evidence that this homosocial reproduction process does indeed occur in the contemporary workplace. For instance, in Elizabeth Gorman's (2005, 2006) studies of U.S. law firms that we discussed earlier, she found clear evidence of in-group bias effects, along with stereotype bias effects. She found not only that work uncertainty increased the number of males promoted (a stereotypic gender status bias) but also that this effect was stronger, the more male partners (i.e., managers) there were in the firm (an example of in-group bias) (Gorman 2006). Similarly, Gorman (2005) also found that the number of women employed in a firm, especially if they were employed as partners, increased the number of women hired, independent of other factors.

In-group biases implicitly encourage workers as well as managers to seek same-sex others to rely on. Yet workers also have an interest in forming network ties with high-status others who can provide valuable information and connections for getting ahead. In a workplace where high-status others are disproportionately men, these two interests work together to encourage men in the workplace to associate with other men (Cabrera and Thomas-Hunt 2007; Ibarra 1992). For women, however, these interests conflict. Most high-status others in the workplace will not be same-sex others. Also, their own lower gender status makes women less desirable to others as network partners. To break out of this and be included in the high-status networks that give them the opportunities to reach the top, research suggests that women, in addition to being highly competent, need to find a high-status, typically male person to vouch for them and lend them legitimacy as someone who can be counted on (Burt 1998). Such added backing is less critical for highly competent men. Yet for the very reasons Kanter describes, high-status sponsorship can be more difficult for women to find.

The salience of a group distinction like sex or race is especially high in the workplace when one group is only a small minority of the workers present. Among the corporate managers Kanter studied, for instance, women were rare enough to be tokens in the jobs they held. Under these circumstances, Kanter argued, the rarity and distinctiveness of the minority heighten their visibility and set in motion particular us-and-them dynamics in the workplace.

By putting those in the minority in the spotlight, visibility adds to the performance pressure they feel on the job. The effect of this pressure depends on whether the minority members are from a lower status group than the majority, as women in a male-dominated job are, or from a higher status group, as men in a women's job are. For Kanter's token women managers, their lower gender status triggered others' skepticism about their competence. The pressure of these negative performance expectations combined with their visibility to create distracting anxiety for the women managers, which made it even harder for them to succeed, compared with their male colleagues.

At the same time, the visibility of the minority makes the gender boundary more salient for the majority sex as well. The members of the majority start to think of themselves more in terms of their sex and may begin to introduce more gendered comments and jokes into their daily interactions in the workplace. This only accentuates the apparent difference between minority tokens and the majority and makes it more difficult for the tokens to fit into workplace events and interactions. This, too, affects the tokens' access to information about work strategies and opportunities and increases the difficulty of succeeding. Together, Kanter argues, these in-group, out-group dynamics systematically disadvantage tokens in their efforts to succeed in comparison with their majority colleagues.

Subsequent studies have generally confirmed Kanter's description of the dynamics women face when they are a small minority in men's jobs (Yoder 1991). Perhaps not surprisingly, then, working in a male-dominated occupation has been shown to increase the likelihood that women leave their jobs, independently of their skills, family characteristics, and other such factors (Maume 1999). A major problem with women in the sciences, for instance, is not only that fewer women train for scientific careers but also that more women drop out of jobs in science and engineering than do men with similar abilities and training (Valian 1999).

What happens when men enter women's jobs? The evidence suggests that men's higher gender status buffers them to some extent from the negative effects of the us-and-them dynamics that their gender difference evokes in the workplace. Christine Williams (1992) interviewed men who worked in traditionally female jobs, such as elementary school teacher, and found that they reported being sometimes left out of the "girls network" that surrounded them but were nevertheless respected for their competence and even favored by superiors for promotions to positions of authority. In a systematic study with national data, Michelle Budig (2002) found that men are just as advantaged in pay over similar women in women's jobs as in men's jobs. Men are advantaged for promotions in women's jobs, too, although, as we would expect, not as strongly advantaged as they are in men's jobs.

Gendered Workplace Cultures

In her early study, Kanter described how minority-majority dynamics can trigger the development of gendered workplace cultures in settings in which the sex composition is tilted toward one sex. Subsequent research has shown that many other aspects of the workplace can increase the salience for workers of their identities as men and women and, with that, the likelihood that they introduce gendered images, interests, and activities into the everyday culture of the workplace (e.g., J. Martin, Knopoff, and Beckman 1998; P. Martin 1996, 2003; Pierce 1995; Williams 1992). Two important factors are the extent to which the authority structure of the workplace is dominated by a given sex and the extent to which the work that actors are engaged in is stereotypically gender typed. Also, even in a work setting in which virtually all actors are of the same sex, workers may draw on gender as convenient basis of commonality through which to get to know and deal with their fellow workers. As they do so, they infuse their work conversations and informal work relations with topics, interests, and forms of behavior that are typically closer to the experience, knowledge, and stereotypical expectations of members of their own rather than the other sex.

Organizational scholar Joanne Martin (forthcoming) concludes from a review of studies that workplace cultures in organizations with male-dominated authority structures often emphasize the use of stereotypically masculine ways of interacting, such as aggressive arguments, tough negotiations, and self-promotion. Female-dominated work organizations are rarer (see Ferree and P. Martin 1995). Martin and colleagues, however, studied one of the largest, a major cosmetics company (J. Martin et al. 1998). In this company, the workplace culture had taken on a decidedly feminine tone that emphasized personal closeness among workers, self-disclosure of feelings and personal information, and sensitivity to family concerns.

While relatively benign for the members of the sex that dominates the organization, these gendered workplace cultures further infuse gender into workplace actors' understanding of the nature of the work they do and what it takes to do it well. In this way, gendered workplace cultures bias workers' as well as employers' images of the preferred worker for jobs. This, too, helps reproduce and maintain the sex segregation of the job. And of course, these gendered workplace cultures create obstacles for members of the other sex who do try to enter the job and struggle to fit in and succeed (e.g., J. Martin and Meyerson 1998; Pierce 1995). In a study of a large, male-dominated technology corporation, for instance, Joanne Martin and Debra Meyerson (1998) found that all the top female executives had encountered problems in socially integrating themselves into their workplace and feeling comfortably themselves there.

As our discussions of employer and worker preferences and workplace dynamics demonstrate, the subtly gendered biases that sex categorization sets in motion throughout so many of the social relations that make up the workplace create an often invisible web of effects that implicitly direct men and women into different and unequal positions in the world of paid work. In general, the effects of gender biases are modest in any given workplace situation, on the order of a few percentage points of difference. However, these small biases repeat and repeat over multiple settings. The effects accumulate over men and women's careers. As they accumulate, these effects create and re-create the gendered structure of work.

There are two locations in the world of work, however, where the typically small biases triggered by gender processes become more substantial and act as a significant barrier to women's equality in workplace outcomes. One of these, the glass ceiling, affects primarily elite women who seek to move into positions of highest authority in work organizations. The second, the maternal wall of obstacles women face in the workplace when they have primary responsibility for dependent children, is especially consequential for overall inequality because it affects most women workers at some point in their careers.

The Glass Ceiling

Women have increasingly made their way into the ranks of middle management in the contemporary work world, but their progress to the very top remains slow (Gorman and Kmec 2009; Reskin and Ross 1995; Smith 2002). Women are still rare as CEOs, top corporate officers, presidents, and directors of major firms and institutions. Several factors contribute to this slowdown at the top, including the availability of sufficiently experienced women candidates. There are reasons to believe, however, that the implicit biases women face accumulate to become especially burdensome at this level. The social relational processes in the workplace that we have discussed thus far— gender-biased preferred worker images, performance evaluations, self-assessments of ability, and workplace dynamics—all converge to construct a so-called glass ceiling for women at the very top (Gorman and Kmec 2009).

There is some controversy about whether this glass ceiling is just the final, additive result of the same level of biases that affect women at lower levels of organizations or an actual intensification of these biases at the top (Baxter and Wright 2000; Elliot and Smith 2004; Gorman and Kmec 2009). The evidence so far is mixed. A recent study, however, shows that at least in some organizational contexts (e.g., internal promotions in large organizations), higher levels of authority ratchet up the intensity of the biases that the gender frame evokes for women (Gorman and Kmec 2009).

Women confront several additional contextual contradictions as they approach the highest ranks of authority. To begin with, since top management continues to be dominated by white men, women, like people of color, face the special dynamics of tokenism when they begin to enter top positions. More problematically, however, women's assumption of great authority over others introduces a new level of incongruity between their behavior and the prescriptive requirements of gender stereotypes that presume a lower status position for women and expect communality from them as well. Recall that the most undesirable traits in women, and the ones most likely to trigger negative reactions from others, are attributes like domineering and arrogant that violate the presumption of women's lower status (Prentice and Carranza 2002; Rudman et al. 2009). As Laurie Rudman and Peter Glick (2001) have shown, in American culture, actions that display dominance or the assertion of authority over others are also perceived, at least in women, to be uncommunal and "not nice." Thus when women seek high authority over others, including men, they appear to illegitimately violate their status position relative to men and also undermine their required performance as warm, concerned women. When a woman actively pursues high authority, then, she is at risk of triggering resistance and hostility in those around her because her behavior contradicts the basic, rulelike structure of the gender beliefs that people implicitly rely on to make sense of their everyday interpersonal relations.

In the work world, of course, any woman who is in a position to try for the top is already a highly accomplished and experienced professional. Her professional achievements will be in the foreground and her gender in the background as people consider her for a top job. Yet people's routine sex categorization of her and others creates an implicit backdrop in which the social alarms that signal violations of the rules of the gender system are ever available to be tripped. When they are tripped, they alter the context in which her ambitions and achievements are judged, as research has shown (Rudman et al. 2009).

As we saw in the last chapter, women typically manage the risk of criticism they face as they reach for authority by balancing a strong representation of professional competence and agency with a softening display of social warmth and cooperative concern. As a woman rises higher and the gender contradictions intensify, this balancing act becomes more complicated. The risks increase that others' reactions to the woman's performance will fall to either side of the effective balance point and recast her within a limiting, gender-stereotypic image. She may end up perceived as highly competent but emotionally limited and cold and, therefore, not material for the very top. Or she may be seen as generous and reasonably able at her job but lacking the killer instinct necessary for top management (Heilman and Parks-Stamm 2007; Kanter 1977). Either construction makes it that much more difficult for her to make it.

Although the glass ceiling is a labyrinth of social pressures, it is not impenetrable (see Eagly and Carli 2007). Jobs at the top carry major rewards in power, status, and money that provide strong incentives for women despite the obstacles. Also, as more and more women reach middle management, the pool of women who have the training and experience to reasonably pursue top jobs continues to grow. It may be that the struggle to balance work achievement with the pressures of gender expectations encourages those women who do make it to develop relatively effective management styles.

Alice Eagly and colleagues conducted a meta-analysis of 45 studies of the leadership styles of men and women leaders in organizations (Eagly, Johannesen-Schmidt, and Van Engen 2003). They found that women leaders were modestly but reliably more likely than men to employ a "transformational" leadership style, in which leaders gain the trust and confidence of their followers by leading by example and offering a clear vision of goals and steps to achieve them. Research has shown a transformational style to be associated with superior leader effectiveness (see Eagly et al. 2003, p. 571).

As Eagly points out, transformational leadership combines agentic goal orientation with a more collective, collaborative approach. As a result, it may be more congenial than traditional, directive leader styles for women who are trying to balance their leader performance with their gender performance. If the winnowing pressures of balancing high achievement with the management of gender incongruity cause slightly more women than men who make it to have the skills of effective leadership, then this provides a wedge that has the potential to crack open the glass ceiling in the future. To the extent that women do achieve top leadership positions and prove effective in them, people's experiences of men and women will be altered in ways that puts pressure on gender stereotypes to change.

The Maternal Wall

There is a second context in which women also face intensified gender bias in the workplace. This is the relatively common context in which women either represent themselves or are taken by others to be not only *workers* but *mothers*, in the special sense of those that have primary responsibility for the everyday needs of dependent children. Several studies have shown that working mothers suffer a penalty in their wages of about 5% per child, compared with nonmothers, even after controlling for the factors that usually affect wages, such as education, work record, the effects of part-time or interrupted work, and job characteristics (Anderson, Binder, and Krause 2003; Budig and England 2001). In fact, as sociologist Jennifer Glass (2004) has observed, employed mothers as a group now account for most of the gender gap in wages.

Gender stereotypes about women's communal nature come to the fore when a woman is identified as a mother and clash in a distinctive way with the agentic image of the ideal, preferred worker. As sociologist Mary Blair-Loy (2003) has shown, there is an opposition in the contemporary United States between our cultural schemas of "family devotion" and "devotion to work" that becomes particularly acute for working mothers. Current cultural ideas suggest that good mothers should put family first and be "always there" for their children (Hays 1996). Yet, these ideas conflict with similar beliefs that ideal workers should be devoted to and ever available for work (Acker 1990; Ridgeway and Correll 2004a; Williams 2000). It is important to note that this conflict exists at the level of the broader culture, rather than necessarily in the minds of most working mothers who are committed to both their jobs and their children. Fathers do not face this contradiction in the same way because the culture associates their family role with that of provider rather than as the primary caretaker of their children's daily needs.

There is increasing evidence that in the workplace, the cultural opposition between the good mother and the ideal worker causes motherhood to be seen as an additional, gender-related status characteristic that is even more directly related to work performance than the simple fact of being a woman or a man (Correll, Benard, and Paik 2007; Ridgeway and Correll 2004a). Logically, work performance involves both effort and ability. The demands of motherhood are culturally presumed to particularly undermine the effort component of job performance (Ridgeway and Correll 2004a). Thus mothers, even in comparison with women who are not mothers, are presumed to be lower status, less valued, and less competent workers. As a result of their lower status, working mothers are held to a higher standard to prove commitment and ability at their jobs than are other women or men.

Sociologist Shelley Correll and colleagues (2007) conducted a study that provides especially clear evidence that a status bias against mothers in the workplace underlies the wage penalty they face. Her evidence suggests that this status bias also provides a basis for discrimination against working mothers in hiring and promotion. Correll's study had two components. The first was a controlled experiment in which study participants evaluated the otherwise similar resumes of white and African American women and men who were either parents or not parents and who had applied for a high-level marketing position. Results showed that simply adding the phrases "mother to Tom and Emily" and "PTA coordinator" to their files caused both white and African American mothers to be judged significantly more harshly than their counterparts without children. Mothers were rated as significantly less competent and committed than other women, required to have a higher score on a management exam to be considered hirable, and allowed fewer late days at work than nonmothers. The salary recommended for them was also $11,000 lower than for nonmothers, and they were less likely to be recommended for management training. In contrast, fathers, compared with men who were not fathers, were rated as more committed to their jobs, allowed more late days, and were recommended for higher salaries.

In the second component of Correll and her colleagues' study, versions of these same resumes were sent in application to real advertised marketing jobs to test the likelihood that employers would call the applicant for an interview. Results showed that actual employers were twice as likely to call the childless woman for an interview than the otherwise identical mother, a clearly significant difference. They were slightly more likely to call the fathers than men who were not fathers, but that difference was not significant.

There is good evidence, then, that when women give evidence of being mothers in a work context, they trigger an added gender bias that causes others to judge their job competence and commitment more harshly. This, in turn, reduces the likelihood that they will be hired, promoted, or paid well, compared with equally qualified women who are not mothers. Because bias against mothers in the workplace is evoked by a perceived clash between the time demands of motherhood and devotion to work, this bias should be especially strong for jobs that make intensive or rigid time demands on employees. These include high-powered 24/7 business and professional jobs and also working-class jobs that have mandatory overtime or very inflexible time schedules. Given the bias that motherhood evokes in intensive jobs, perhaps it is not surprising that women who succeed in high-level business and professional jobs are especially likely to be childless in comparison with other women (Goldin 1995).

Fathers, because they are assumed to be providers rather than primary caretakers, do not face a similar bias in the workplace and sometimes actually experience a benefit compared with other men. It may be, however, that if a father goes beyond the traditional father role to give evidence of being himself a "mother" (i.e., a primary caretaker), he, too, would experience discrimination in the workplace.

EMBEDDING GENDER INTO NEW PROCEDURES AND STRUCTURES

We have seen, then, that the gendered structures of work that are responsible for so much of the inequality between men and women's outcomes are actually enacted and maintained through an interlocking web of social relations among workers and employers and job applicants, all of whom, at various points and in varying degrees, draw on the gender frame to help coordinate their workplace actions. These same gendered social relations have an additional effect in the workplace as well. They have the potential to embed gendered assumptions into new workplace procedures and structures as these are created. While the primary, direct effects of the gender frame is on behavior and judgments in social relations, then, these social relations can have the secondary but important effect of embedding gender into the more enduring structures and procedures that workplace actors jointly create.

We have already seen a hint of how this occurs. When employers seek to hire for a given job, they implicitly enter into an imaginative social relation with the kind of person they expect to hire. Cultural beliefs about gender and existing gender structures in the labor market encourage employers to implicitly sex-categorize and gender the image they develop of their preferred worker. To the extent that this preferred worker image is communicated among hiring agents and written into job descriptions or ads, the image begins to take on a more objective character as an aspect of organizational procedure that, as we have seen, applicants as well rely on to coordinate their behavior with employers.

New images of preferred workers are created as changing technologies and ways of organization lead to new types of jobs. The development of the Internet, for instance, has led to a plethora of new jobs, such as Web site programmer. At these sites of change, individual workplace actors come together under the inherently uncertain conditions that accompany innovation. These are precisely the conditions under which people are likely to draw on the ever available frame of gender to clarify the nature of the new work and the nature of the new workers who will carry it out. Contingent circumstances—the sex composition of the local pool of interested prospective employees or something about the work itself that is easily linked to gendered expectations—are likely to shape the exact nature of the effects gender has on the newly forming image of the preferred worker. These processes in turn shape the sex composition of the initial workers in the job. Eventually, the job itself begins to acquire a more male or female image and to be shaped by the status and competence assumptions that accompany that image. In this way, the social relational processes of the workplace are always at risk of embedding gender into the preferred worker images that emerge for new jobs, too, as they develop at the edge of the changing economy.

Gendering the image of new jobs is not the only way that workplace social relations can create new gendered structures and procedures. Like new types of jobs, new practices and ways of doing things in organizations must be worked out by individual actors who are "at the table" when the decisions about these practices are made. When gender is effectively salient in these social relational settings, decision making will be implicitly biased by gender stereotypes and in-group dynamics. Acting on these implicitly biased judgments, the decision makers develop procedures that embody gender-stereotypic assumptions and the decision makers' own in-group interests. As a result, they inscribe gender assumptions and boundaries into the new arrangements they produce.

We have a documented example of this process in studies of the development of established job evaluation and wage-setting practices (Nelson and Bridges 1999; Steinberg 1995). In large organizations, as new jobs are created, formal procedures are used to evaluate the content of the job in order to assign a salary to it. The resulting salaries, existing as they do within the organizational structure, are often somewhat insulated from direct market forces (Nelson and Bridges 1999). Ronnie Steinberg (1995) studied the conditions under which one widely used job evaluation system, the Hays system, was created. It was developed in the middle of the last century before equal rights laws and cultural assumptions about women's equality in the labor force were fully established. Historical evidence suggests that in this environment, decision makers often explicitly drew on gendered assumptions about workers in devising job evaluations. As a result, Steinberg argues, they infused gender bias into the ostensibly objective evaluation criteria of the Hays system in ways that gave greater attention to job characteristics found in historically male work and more finely differentiated job complexity, which justifies wage increases, in men's jobs than in women's jobs. These evaluation criteria then became an established, institutionalized approach that has persisted and, Steinberg argues, continues to affect the wages assigned to men's and women's jobs today.

Robert Nelson and William Bridges (1999) studied the job evaluation and pay systems developed and used in several public- and private-sector organizations. They found that dominant organizational actors, largely white males, denied women and other lower status actors a powerful voice in the decision-making contexts in which pay-setting practices developed. These exclusions introduced in-group and gender status biases into the decision-making processes in which pay practices were established. As a consequence, the pay practices the organizations developed disadvantaged female-dominated jobs and tended to preserve male pay advantages. These biased pay structures then persisted through organizational inertia.

As these examples show, as organizational practices are created, the relational contexts among the decision makers involved can pull gender into the proceedings in explicit or, more often, implicit ways. The infusion of gender into new practices is not uncontested in this process, however. In the contemporary workplace, new procedures are typically developed with some organizational awareness of legal and social constraints to avoid gender and racial discrimination. In an effort to comply with equal opportunity laws and limit their legal liability, most organizations create special rules or processes that are explicitly intended to suppress or correct gender and race bias in personnel decisions. Common examples are diversity training programs for managers and employees and the institution of employee grievance procedures. Yet, ironically, the intended effects of these compliance procedures are frequently implicitly blunted in the social relational processes through which they are carried out. Although there are ways to make such procedures work, research has shown that it is quite common in practice for them to end up having very little effect on the actual diversity of the organization (Edelman and Petterson 1999; Kalev, Dobbin, and Kelly 2006). In this way, also, implicit gender and race processes in relations among workplace actors continue to reconstruct structures and practices that maintain gender and race inequalities in workplace outcomes.

SUMMARY AND CONCLUSIONS

As we have seen, the contemporary work world is a dynamic battleground in which the forces that undermine gender inequality and those that act to reproduce it play out. In the face of the leveling effects of bureaucratic rationalization, efficiency, legal constraints, and women's own interests in bettering their lives, the often hidden force that acts to reproduce and re-create gendered structures and procedures in the work world is the implicit use of gender as a framing device for workplace relations among people. The world of paid work is enacted through an intricate array of social relations. Workers train for and apply to jobs, employers read resumes and interview applicants, and, once hired, workers engage one another as they carry out the work process. Each of these goal-oriented social relations requires workplace actors to consider their own judgments and actions in relation to others to act effectively themselves, making paramount the problems of coordinating with others. The background gender frame offers a too convenient cultural device to assist in this process. Actors can implicitly draw on the gender status beliefs and beliefs about each sex's specialized traits that are repeatedly activated in the background throughout workplace relations to fill in the details of an uncertain work task, setting, or person; to provide a simplifying interpretation of complex circumstances; or to simply find something in common with people they must work with. In this way, the organization of work is gendered in varying degrees. In this chapter, we attempted to see how this gendering of work both reproduces existing organizational structures of gender difference and inequality in workplace outcomes and creates new ones.

We began with the obvious but critical observation that workplace relations take place within existing employment organizations and labor market structures that constrain and shape much of what workplace actors do. To understand the process by which work is gendered, then, we need to pay close attention to the interface between the implicit, background gender frame made available by routine sex categorization in work relations and the institutional frame within which individuals are acting. The existing institutional organization of work itself routinely activates the gender frame for workplace actors through the mixed-gender composition of those involved, the culturally gendered connotations of the work itself (e.g., manual labor or nursing), or the way it is organized in terms of status or authority. In so doing, the institutional frame also affects whether gender is just diffusely present for workplace actors (in a mixed-sex but gender-neutral context) or is a more powerful backdrop that becomes part of how the actors carry out their organizational duties (when work is gender typed).

In addition to affecting the implicit power of the gender frame over individual judgments, the institutional context also shapes the extent to which individuals are rigidly constrained by organizational rules or have the discretion to act on their own gender biases. Thus the direct effects of the gender frame on individuals' evaluations and behaviors are greater in workplace contexts that involve greater ambiguity, uncertainty, and discretionary behavior. This does not necessarily mean, however, that more bureaucratically constrained work contexts are less biased. Bureaucratic structures and rules themselves often embody implicit assumptions about the gendered nature and inequality of the workplace actors who are expected to carry them out. One of the more powerful effects of the gender frame is to infuse gendered meanings into new workplace practices, structure, and rules as these are developed by actors in the workplace. Once such gendered institutional procedures develop, they act to re-create gender inequality in workplace outcomes independently of the personal biases of individual workplace actors.

The institutional organization of paid work at present is deeply structured by gender. Most occupations and jobs are sex segregated. The types of jobs men and women are concentrated in generally reflect cultural beliefs about gender status inequality as well as gender differences (Charles and Grusky 2004). This gendered structure of jobs changes dynamically, typically as women move into men's jobs (but not vice versa) and the economy changes, but it is also created anew as newly developing jobs become labeled as men's or women's jobs. Most of the gender gap in wages and authority is due to the different jobs men and women occupy.

The sex segregation of jobs and occupations, which is so consequential for gender inequality, is an emergent product of the *job-matching* process by which, on the *supply* side, workers train for and seek jobs and, on the *demand* side, employers hire and promote workers. How does the gender frame shape the social relational process of job matching? The sex-segregated nature of a relevant labor market or the status or complexity associated with a job can pull cultural assumptions about gender status and sex-typed skills into the processes by which employers develop an image of the *preferred worker* that they would like to hire for the job. Employers' images of a good "manager," for instance, have been shown to overlap stereotypic images of men rather than women. Then, as employers review applications and interview candidates with the preferred worker image in mind, an element of stereotype fit can subtly bias the evaluation of applicants' competencies and suitability for the job. The better fitting sex is more likely to be hired or promoted, research suggests.

The choices of job applicants on the supply side of the job-matching process are also shaped by the gender frame and contribute to the emergence of the sex-segregated job structure. From childhood on, gender frames the social relations through which people try out or avoid different tasks, compare their performances with those of others, and decide where their own talents lie. Independent of actual performance, people are less likely to attribute ability to themselves for tasks that are gender typed for the other sex. And attributed ability affects the likelihood that people pursue training for occupations based on that ability. Women, however, also have material interests in pushing against the implicit biases that undercut their attraction to and performance at men's jobs since men's jobs pay better and carry more authority. Men do not have such incentives to resist gender biases to enter women's lower paying jobs.

Once employees are on the job, routine sex categorization keeps the gender frame ever available in the background for workers to draw on as an aid in making sense of and coordinating with others, particularly in ambiguous or gender-typed work contexts. This creates the framework for in-group, out-group dynamics and the development of gendered workplace cultures. In-group biases are particularly problematic for low-status minorities such as women or people of color in predominantly white male organizations, but they create lesser barriers for men in female workplaces, too. Particularly when the authority structure of a work organization is dominated by one sex or the other, the culture of routine interaction in the workplace tends to take on a stereotypically gendered tone that creates further obstacles for workers of the other sex.

In general, the effects of gender biases are quite modest in a single workplace context, but they repeat over and over and accumulate to shape men's and women's careers and the gendered structure of work itself. Also, there are two locations in the work world where the typically small biases triggered by the gender frame become more intense. The first of these is the glass ceiling that confronts elite women who seek top management. High authority is culturally incongruent with prescriptive gender beliefs that women should be nondominant and communal. Evidence suggests that the problems of managing this gender incongruity encourage some top women leaders to adopt a "transformative" leadership style that turns out to also be an effective management style.

A second location of intense bias is the maternal wall that confronts mothers of dependent children in the workplace. Since mothers are culturally expected to be always there for their children, the assumption is that they cannot be the ideal, committed worker. Research shows that others judge working mothers' job competence and commitment more harshly than similar nonmothers and, consequently, are more reluctant to hire them and pay them well. Mothers suffer a wage penalty in the labor force that contributes substantially to the gender gap in wages.

The direct effects of the gender frame are on behavior and judgments that make up the job-matching process and workplace social relations, but these gender-framed social relations have another equally important effect. We examined how decisions made in social relations that are implicitly biased by gender beliefs embed gendered meanings into the more enduring structures and practices that workplace actors jointly create as they carry out their organizational duties. These gender-infused arrangements (e.g., procedures for evaluating job pay) then persist through organizational inertia. Effects of the gender frame on workplace relations can also blunt the practical effect of other procedures that organizations adopt to suppress gender and race bias in personnel decisions and meet legal obligations for equal opportunity. Thus, the use of gender as a framing device for workplace relations among people not only reproduces existing structures of sex segregation and gender inequality in the work world but also projects sex segregation and inequality into the future by creating new versions of these gendered structures in the ever evolving social organization of paid work.

The investigations we have undertaken in this chapter, then, have brought us a bit closer to understanding how gender inequality persists in the modern world despite institutional, economic, and political processes that work to undermine it. By continuing to shape social relations that subtly direct men and women toward different and unequal positions in the world of paid work, the cultural beliefs that define gender as a status inequality continue to construct a fundamental material reality that, in turn, largely supports these beliefs. The work world is not the only critical battleground for the future of gender inequality in the modern world, however. We will see in the next chapter that the gender structure of the home is equally important not only in itself but also for the way it enables or constrains men and women's access to the money and power of the work world.

FIVE

Gender At Home

IN THE CONTEMPORARY United States, as in the past, "home"—that is, the family household—is not merely our home as individuals, it is also the home base for our cultural understandings of gender. Although our use of gender as a primary frame for relating to others may pull gender into the organization of paid work, gender is not merely pulled into the organization of the home—it *is* the organization of the home. The roots of gender as a cultural system for coordinating joint action with others on the basis of difference lie in the efforts of people to organize themselves into family units for sex, survival, and the raising of children. After all, people seek others for family ties precisely on the basis of their identities as males or females, and they relate to their kin on such terms as well. If gender is deeply rooted in the organization of the family household, then those households become potent arenas for the maintenance or change of our cultural beliefs about who men and women are and how they are (or potentially are not) unequal.

It is not only our cultural beliefs about men and women that are at stake in the family, however. The family household is also a crucial nexus for material exchange between men and women. As a result, the significance of the gender organization of the home for the future of gender inequality lies not just in the cultural representations of gender that it supports. As we will see, the gender organization of the home also plays a central role in constructing inequalities between men and women in material resources and power, both directly within the home and indirectly in the labor force. The gender organization of the home, then, is a wellspring for the system of cultural beliefs and material arrangements that sustain gender inequality.

Not surprisingly, then, the home, with the world of paid work, is the other major arena in which forces that work to undermine gender inequality contend with those that continue to reproduce it. Home and work, of course, are inherently interdependent. Jobs produce the resources that people use to create and sustain households. Households, in turn, help workers maintain their social and emotional well-being and raise the children that society depends on for citizens and future workers.

The most powerful forces currently working to undermine gender inequality—women's growing role in the labor force and economic and political pressures to treat people as workers and citizens rather than as men and women—operate primarily in the public world outside the family. Yet these forces also change the material terms on which men and women confront one another in the family. Women who earn as much as their husbands, for instance, have more bargaining power in family decisions than do women who are largely dependent on a husband's income. If changes in the public world put pressure on gender arrangements at home, by the same token, arrangements in the home push back against these economic and political forces. They do so by shaping men and women's availability for paid work and by helping maintain the cultural assumptions by which men and women are judged as workers.

For these reasons, the household division of labor—who does what to maintain the home and care for children—is a dynamic battleground in the contemporary United States that carries great consequences for the future of gender as a distinct system of difference and inequality in society. At present, the gender division of household labor remains strikingly unequal. Although women do less housework than in the past and men do more than they used to, women still do twice the housework that men do (Bianchi, Robinson, and Milkie 2006). Women also spend about twice as many hours caring for children as men do (Bianchi et al. 2006).

But it is not just the extra hours women put in that matter. Women are also culturally presumed to be the ones most directly and morally responsible for the care and well-being of children and the making of a home. In fact, our more general stereotypes of women as communal and men as agentic have a specific and powerful instantiation within our contemporary, cultural understandings of the family. In the context of family, women are cast more specifically as devoted caregivers and mothers, and men are cast as providers. Sociologist Mary Blair-Loy (2003) describes how the contending forces of industrialization and persisting cultural beliefs about gender have left us, at this point in U.S. history, with a widely shared, hegemonic cultural schema of the tie between women and the family that she calls *family devotion*. By this schema, a good woman should be, as a deep moral obligation, intensively committed to her family and to the care of those in it, especially children, and this commitment should take precedence over all others. This hegemonic cultural schema essentializes women's role in the family by suggesting that women are uniquely and innately able to care for children so that even a father's care is not fully equal to that of a mother. As several writers have observed, at this point in our history in which the work world has developed an image of the ideal worker as intensively committed to work, we have also honed a parallel image of intensified mothering (Crittendon 2001; Hays 1996; Williams 2000).

The schema of family devotion describes an ideal type that is widely recognized as a matter of public understanding and frequently represented in the media. It is not uncontested, however, nor necessarily fully embraced by all women or men. Because most women work, they also contend with and often embrace the ideal worker schema (Blair-Loy 2003; Stone 2007). When women enter into a heterosexual family relationship, however, and especially when they have children, the more intense and essentialized version of the female stereotype that is represented in the schema of family devotion is evoked for them and for others. It is then that these women must struggle with that schema, regardless of whether they embrace it. They must struggle with this schema's implication that they are, as the woman of the household, ultimately responsible for the housework and care work that a home entails. They must struggle as well with the problems of juggling their commitment to family with their commitment to paid employment.

When men enter into a heterosexual family relationship and have children, the parallel cultural schema that is evoked for them is that of provider. This schema, too, carries a powerful connotation of moral obligation. The provider schema implies that men satisfy their strongest responsibility to the family (i.e., the masculine version of family devotion) through work outside the family rather than through contributions to household labor. In comparison with the image of women as caretakers, however, the provider schema is less essentialized within the male sex category. Widely accepted gender status beliefs continue to imply that men are generally more competent providers than women. Yet cultural beliefs recognize that women, too, can be material providers and often are. Note that this shows once again how our cultural beliefs about gender construct a situation for individuals in which it is easier for them to behaviorally "mark," or signify the boundary between the sexes, by doing or not doing the feminine (caregiving) than by doing or not doing the masculine (providing). However, it also creates a situation in which men may feel vulnerable to censure for taking on major responsibility for core caregiving activities that have been culturally essentialized as feminine.

Like the general stereotypes of males and females, the more specific and moralized cultural schemas of men and women in the family describe gender differences in terms that create and justify gender inequality not only in the household division of labor but also in society more generally. Tellingly, although the schema of family devotion moralizes women's obligation to the home, housework and care work are nevertheless devalued as "women's work." A recent study of contemporary social stereotypes based on a representative sample of Americans found, as other studies have, that housewives are perceived to be in the bottom half of social groups in the United States in terms of social status, below groups such as blue-collar workers (Cuddy et al. 2007; Cuddy, personal communication; Fiske et al. 2002). Furthermore, although the work people do in their own homes is typically not waged, when we examine what it costs to hire someone else to do housework and care work, we see that it is quite poorly paid for the effort and responsibility that it entails. In 2007, for instance, data from the Bureau of Labor Statistics showed that the average hourly wages of child care workers were comparable to those of parking lot attendants and bell hops (Center for the Child Care Workforce 2009). Equally telling of the value our society attaches to care work, Paula England and colleagues found that occupations that involve care work are paid 5% to 10% less than jobs that are otherwise equivalent in their demands (England, Budig, and Folbre 2002).

By investing primary responsibility for child care in women, the parallel schemas of family devotion and provider also cause women, rather than men, to disproportionately bear the personal costs of raising children. Especially in a society with little public provision of child care, the time and effort of raising children competes with the time parents have for market work and for the money and power that market work brings. In the face of this dilemma, hegemonic cultural schemas impel women to sacrifice and men to maximize their market work, feeding disparity in their earnings and in the positions of power and respect they can earn outside the family. Adding to this disparity is the fact that, as we saw in the last chapter, mothers, when they do market work (and most do), are disadvantaged by biases created by the same schema of family devotion. These biases create a further wage penalty for motherhood.

Children, of course, are a public good for society. We all need children to be the citizens and workers of tomorrow, and we all benefit from children who have received the care they needed to become productive members of society. Yet by assigning women primary responsibility for children, as our cultural schemas do, we lay the burdens of producing this public good disproportionately on the shoulders of individual mothers rather than sharing it among us all.

Since children typically remain their mother's responsibility whether she is married or not, both single and married mothers face the wage penalty of motherhood (Budig and England 2001). Between reduced time for market work and biases in the workplace for their work, the family devotion and provider schemas contribute substantially to wage and power inequalities between men and women. In so doing, these cultural schemas increase women's material dependence on men. Because, as we saw in the first chapter, material dependence creates power, these schemas alter men and women's bargaining power in family relationships.

The contemporary American home, then, is a fluid nexus of moralized cultural schemas of family men and women juxtaposed with the changing material exigencies of the people who join together to form households and raise children. Our purpose in this chapter is to examine how people's use of gender as a primary frame for coordinating family behavior mediates this interplay between cultural schemas and material pressures. We will see how the evocation of cultural schemas in social relations among family members constructs the household division of labor. We will see as well how these cultural beliefs become the lens through which material changes in men's and women's circumstances have their effects on the household division of labor. The effect, as we will see, is often to slow the potentially equalizing impact on household work of women's growing involvement in the labor force. But we will also see that cultural beliefs do not completely blunt the impact on family organization of material changes in men's and women's lives.

Our discussion will focus on heterosexual couples who live together in the same household, both married and not, and with and without children. Heterosexual couples, in my own view, are not worthier than other family types. I focus on them because of their centrality to our hegemonic cultural understandings of gender and also because these households have been the object of most empirical studies.

The proportion of U.S. households that are heterosexual couples has declined substantially in recent decades, but they are still the most common form of living arrangement. In 2009, 50% of households were married opposite-sex couples, and another 6% were unmarried opposite-sex couples. Next most common are people living alone (27% of households), and single-parent households, same-sex couples, and other groups of related and unrelated people make up the remaining 17% of households (U.S. Census Bureau 2009). It is worth noting that the declining dominance of heterosexual-couple households is loosening the moorings of our more abstract, general stereotypes of men and women from their historical roots in more specific, hegemonic, and moralized understandings of families. At present, however, these moralized schemas of family men and women remain a powerful, if contested, cultural influence.

As I consider the division of labor in heterosexual households, I will, to the extent that evidence is available, attend to differences among these households and to differences between them and other household types. Quantitative studies of the division of labor in heterosexual households have paid some attention to differences among these families by class, although there has been less attention to differences by race. Where I can, however, I will comment on such differences. I will also make some reference to household work in other types of households, specifically single and single-parent households and gay and lesbian households, as useful contrasts to the division of labor in the households of heterosexual couples. In what follows, I develop a more specific model of how the framing device of gender shapes social relations in the family and then use this model to examine evidence about the household division of labor in the contemporary American home.

THE GENDER FRAME IN FAMILY RELATIONS

In the home, just as outside it, people cannot relate without sex-categorizing one another and priming cultural beliefs about gender. But two distinctive aspects of the home alter the way this process plays out in that context compared with the public, more impersonal world of work. First of all, cultural beliefs about the social institution of the family define it as a quintessentially gendered context. That is, it is a context whose goals and activities are tightly linked by cultural beliefs to the stereotypic skills and attributes of both sexes. As a result, in contrast to the workplace, where gender is often only diffusely salient for actors, gender at home is virtually always both clearly salient and relevant to what takes place. As a result, we should expect gendered expectations on the part of both self and others to be rather powerful determinants of behavior in the home.

A second distinctive aspect of social relations in the home alters the way these gendered expectations work their effects on behavior in the family, compared with more impersonal contexts. The cultural beliefs about gender that sex categorization activates are by definition stereotypes. In the home, however, people form long-term ties that allow them to develop intimate, highly individualized impressions of one another. How do stereotypic beliefs continue to have an impact on their behavior toward one another?

Recall that when we first form an impression of another, our initial sex categorization of them causes the subsequent knowledge we acquire about them to be nested within our prior understanding of them as male or female (Brewer 1988; Fiske et al. 1999). While this is true of all we encounter, it is especially the case with those we get to know in the context of seeking a sexual and domestic partner. We are interested in such persons because of their sex, among other things, so that from the beginning, the cultural meaning of their gender identity is foregrounded for us and becomes a powerful backdrop against which we judge the meaning of all that we come to know about them. Jason is perceived to be a very sensitive person, especially for a man. Jennifer is strong-minded for a woman. Each is understood against the cultural standard for their sex. Thus, although we relate to family partners in terms of nuanced personal identities, those identities are understood in a way that has been systematically infused with cultural assumptions about men and women. In this way, gender as a stereotyped cultural identity is also a background identity in the home, but one that provides an ever-present referent by which we judge ourselves, as well our family members.

Depending on the circumstances, slightly different sets of cultural beliefs about gender can provide the referent by which family members judge one another in the home. Our generic, hegemonic stereotypes about men and women are ever available to frame our understandings of self and other in the home. In addition, to the extent that couples form committed, heterosexual ties, the more specific cultural schemas of family devotion and provider become an increasingly salient referent. Especially when couples have children, these family gender schemas come to the fore for family members themselves and for others who relate to them.

It is also possible that couples will hold alternative gender beliefs in addition to their cultural knowledge of hegemonic stereotypes. As we argued in chapter 3, people are most likely to use alternative beliefs as a referent for their behavior in social relationships with similar, like-minded others. Because similarity is related to attraction, people are more likely to form intimate ties with those who are socially similar to them and share many of their beliefs. People are especially likely to marry others from their own social class and racial or ethnic group and, to a lesser extent, those with similar political views (McPherson et al. 2001). If people hold alternative gender beliefs, then, it is entirely possible that the family will provide a context in which they have greater freedom to use those beliefs as a referent for their own and their family members' behavior. In these families, alternative gender beliefs are likely to affect the household division of labor. Holding alternative views does not mean that the pressure of hegemonic gender beliefs disappears entirely, however, since these beliefs may still linger implicitly in the background of family members' expectations for one another in the home.

One obvious source of alternative gender beliefs, of course, is people's commitment to egalitarian rather than status-unequal gender relations. With this may come a sense that not only women but also men can be primary caretakers, just as women can be providers (Coltrane 1996). Another source, however, may be membership in a racial or ethnic minority that holds slightly different beliefs about who men and women are and how they should behave (Kane 2000). As we have commented before, African Americans tend to hold slightly less polarized, more moderate gender beliefs that see little contradiction between care work in the home and paid work (Collins 1991; Dugger 1988). To the extent that this is true, we would expect to see a smaller gender gap in house and care work in African American families.

Everyday social relations in the family, then, although based on sharply defined personal identities, take place in continual reference to a variable set of cultural beliefs about gender. As family members struggle to accomplish the necessary tasks of family life—cooking, cleaning, shopping, laundry, child care, home maintenance, paying the bills—always before them are the organizational problems of which member has responsibility for what and how their efforts should be coordinated. The implicit referential backdrop of taken-for-granted gender beliefs provides a set of metarules for solving these organizational problems. When juggling the hectic demands of family life, even committed gender egalitarians may find themselves unconsciously falling back on hegemonic cultural assumptions to assign tasks and get things done.

The tendency to fall back on stereotypic gender assumptions to solve the organizational problems of the household division of labor is further reinforced by three additional factors. First, since people themselves are raised as gendered members of households, they are more likely to have acquired skills and experience for household tasks that are traditionally associated with their gender (Cunningham 2001). Women often have more experience cooking on the stove, for instance. Men are often more experienced at cooking on the barbecue. It is always quicker to do what you already know well.

Second, since gender beliefs are a continual referent for people's own behavior and sense of identity in the home, and because household tasks themselves carry a gendered connotation, the performance or nonperformance of those tasks can be a symbolic gender display for the person. As a number of gender scholars have observed, performing particular, gender-linked household tasks offers an opportunity to experience oneself as a culturally competent and therefore acceptably good member of one's sex category and to simultaneously demonstrate this competence to others as well (Berk 1985; Brines 1994; Coltrane 1989; Fenstermaker 1996; West and Fenstermaker 1993). The mundane task of cooking, for instance, may sometimes become for a woman an expressive act of caring for her family that represents her womanly nature to herself and to her family. Mowing the lawn or firing up the backyard barbecue may give a man a satisfying sense of manly competence and pride in helping his family. To the extent that the performance of household tasks becomes a gender display, it transforms routine household work into a symbolic enactment of cultural ideas of not only gender difference but also the status and power inequality that the difference connotes.

Third, the potential for household tasks to be perceived as a display of gender competence creates a disincentive for performing tasks stereotypically assigned to the other sex. It is one thing to occasionally pinch hit by performing the other sex's tasks because there is a real need to get them done and the other is unavailable. Mom mows the lawn when Dad is out of town, and Dad cooks when Mom has a late business meeting. But to take on routine responsibility for tasks linked to the other sex when the other is available to do them is to risk criticism from others and even from oneself for gender deviance (Rudman and Fairchild 2004). The risk is especially great for men who take primary responsibility for caregiving since this is essentialized as a core task of femininity by dominant cultural schemas of the family. Committed gender egalitarians may intentionally defy this risk, but they cannot fail to confront it (Coltrane 1996; Risman 1998).

The effect of stereotypic gender beliefs operating in the background of social relationships in the family, then, is to create a convergence of factors that encourage family members to gradually settle on a division of household labor that corresponds to those cultural beliefs. There is the practical ease of relying on a pregiven organizational blueprint that roughly accords with family members' developed skills. There is also the social ease of an arrangement that avoids the risks of gender deviance while providing opportunities to gain expressive rewards from culturally approved gender displays.

Family members themselves are not the only audience for the household division of labor in the home. Family members' relationships with people outside the family also create pressures to organize household work in accord with cultural schemas. Relatives visit and comment on how things are done. Neighbors observe and implicitly judge. Coworkers and bosses make gendered assumptions about family members' responsibilities and express their approval or disapproval. In contrast to family members, who may share alternative gender beliefs, outsiders are especially likely to enforce conventional gender schemas. With less at stake personally, outsiders are likely to fall back on easily available gender schemas to frame their reactions to a family's division of labor. The moral dimension of the cultural schemas of family devotion and provider particularly empowers outside observers to criticize unconventional arrangements. A husband who is unemployed and takes care of the house encounters hostility from the neighbors. A wife who travels with her job, leaving daily child care to the husband, raises eyebrows among the relatives.

Despite the differing contingencies that families face and the variety of individual personalities they contain, then, they nearly all encounter a powerful convergence of social relational processes both inside and outside the family that pushes them toward a household division of labor that corresponds to stereotypic cultural assumptions. Couples who share alternative gender beliefs have some buffer from these pressures, but even they feel the push of hegemonic gender schemas in the reactions of outsiders and in the implicit effects of these schemas on their own behavior. The resultant effect of these overlapping social relational effects is that the household division of labor becomes a structural feature that is overwhelmingly driven by gender. The cultural schemas, both hegemonic and alternative, that the framing device of gender makes repeatedly salient in family relations become an interpretive lens that moderates the effects of material resources on the household division of labor and provides a frame within which class and race effects are nested as well.

THE HOUSEHOLD DIVISION OF LABOR IN THE CONTEMPORARY UNITED STATES

Now that I have outlined an account of the gender frame in family relations, the next task is to compare the implications of this account with empirical evidence about how American families actually organize the tasks of maintaining a household. The framing account suggests that the household division of labor in contemporary American families will have several distinctive characteristics. First, it will be organized much more powerfully by gender than by any other distinctive characteristic of family members, such as their labor force involvement and earnings or even their race and class. This gender organization should be apparent both in the total hours men and women put into household work and in the specialization of tasks that they take on. Second, within the overarching gender organization of household work, the framing account also suggests that groups that hold alternative gender beliefs, such as committed egalitarians and some racial and ethnic groups, may have more moderate (or extreme) gender divisions of work in the home. Third, since the formation of a committed heterosexual tie makes salient not merely general gender stereotypes, but the family-based schemas of family devotion and provider, marriage and cohabitation should change the amount of housework men and women do. The salience and relevance of family-based gender schemas really skyrocket, however, with the birth of a child. Since the content of these schemas obligates women particularly in regard to child care, we should, fourth, expect parental status to have especially strong effects on women, affecting their work in the home, as well as their market work. The intense activation of family schemas triggered by the birth of a child should affect mothers' and fathers' social relations with others as well, modifying their social networks. Fifth, we expect to see that interactions with others outside the family also shape the gender organization of the household division.

Before investigating these questions, it is useful to acquire a little information on how the household division of labor has been studied in recent years. The best data come from time diary studies that ask a representative sample of men and women in households to report the specific housework and child care activities that they engaged in over a 24-hour period (see Bianchi et al. 2006, chapter 2; U.S. Bureau of Labor Statistics 2010). The shortcoming of time diary studies, however, is that the detail of the home work data they gather often limits the other information that can be gathered about the respondents. More general surveys of U.S. households ask questions about household work along with a rich variety of other questions. These studies, however, simply ask men and women to estimate the hours they spend each week on household tasks, which is likely to be less accurate. Despite their differences, however, the two methods produce similar results about the comparative number of hours men and women spend on housework and care work. Each shows that contemporary U.S. women do about twice the hours of both housework and child care that men do (Bianchi et al. 2006; Coltrane 2000). These quantitative studies of household work are supplemented by qualitative studies that observe and interview smaller samples of families about their household arrangements. We will draw on all three types of studies in our examination.

These studies vary in the detail they ask about the specific household tasks that men and women do. Almost all studies, however, distinguish between housework and child care. Most studies of housework focus on the core tasks of cooking, washing the dishes, house cleaning, laundry, and sometimes shopping. These are the housework tasks that are less discretionary in their timing in that they must be performed frequently on a routine schedule to maintain the household. Other tasks such as yard work and home repair need to be done less frequently. Child care is usually measured as the total hours taking care of children, but this is sometimes broken down into routine child care and time spent in interactive enrichment activities, such as reading to a child (Bianchi et al. 2006).

The Power of Gender in Household Labor

It seems almost trivial to ask the extent to which the household division of labor is organized by gender. The question seems trivial, however, only because it is so obvious and taken for granted in our society that responsibility for household tasks will be assigned on the basis of sex category. When we step back from our unquestioned assumptions, we can view the household as simply a set of jobs to be accomplished. From this perspective, we can ask, just as we did about the work world, how powerful is gender as a *force* in organizing the household division of labor? My account of the framing effects of gender in family relations suggests that it should be a very powerful force indeed, even more powerful than gender is in the structure of paid work. Furthermore, because of the way the framing device of gender causes people to draw on widely shared cultural schemas as implicit referents for their behavior in the family, gender should act as a relatively homogenizing force on the household division of labor across diverse families. In other words, families who differ in many ways are still likely to have roughly similar divisions of household labor.

As we know, people have many identities other than their sex category. They belong to a race or ethnic group and have a certain education, occupation, and income. One way to see the power of gender as an organizing force in the household division of labor is to examine the extent to which people's sex category alone predicts the amount and nature of the household work they do in comparison to their other identities. Over the past two decades, a large number of detailed studies have examined the factors that predict the total hours and relative contributions men and women make to household labor. As reviews of this literature show, a variety of factors such as hours in the paid labor force, earnings, education, gender role attitudes, race, and the presence of children affect women's and men's hours of household labor in varying degrees. But none of these factors trumps simply being a male or female as a predictor of how much household labor a person does. The unequivocal finding of studies in this area is that, controlling for all of these social and ideological factors, women still to do substantially more hours of household work than do men (Bianchi et al. 2000; Kroska 2004; Shelton and John 1996). The gender gap in household labor is not primordial and unchanging. As we would expect from other improvements in women's status, it has narrowed significantly in recent years (Bianchi et al. 2000, 2006). Yet despite these changes, it remains the case that of all the identities and contingencies that affect the time people devote to household labor, the one that most powerfully shapes and coordinates their contributions is their identity as male or female.

According to a qualitative study by Christopher Carrington (1999), the power of the gender frame in organizing household work can be seen even in lesbian and gay households. When both members of a couple are of the same sex, sex difference is not available as a basis for the household division of labor, and Carrington observes that these households typically have explicitly egalitarian views of how work in the home should be divided. Yet, as we have seen, hegemonic cultural schemas of gender and the family cause the doing of household labor itself to have a gendered connotation. Such is the power of these hegemonic schemas that, according to Carrington, even these homosexual couples cannot fully escape the status inequality and gender identity implications that household work connotes. Because of housework's implicit connotation as lower status, feminine work, the partner who earns more often "buys out" of it, leaving the other partner to do more, despite their egalitarian views. The resultant inequality of domestic work creates a degree of gender contradiction for the gay male partner who does more and the lesbian partner who does less. Carrington argues that these couples often manage this contradiction by representing their arrangements to others outside the household in a way that protects the identities of the partner whose housework could be interpreted as gender deviant. In gay male couples, the domestic efforts of the partner who does more are often de-emphasized, Carrington claims, and in lesbian households, those of the partner who does less are highlighted.

We can see the organizing power of cultural beliefs about gender not only in the amount of household work men and women do but also in the specialized nature of the tasks they take on in the home. Cultural beliefs about men and women in the family assign the work of maintaining a home primarily to women. Not surprisingly, then, studies show that the core housework tasks that must be repeated most frequently— cooking, washing dishes, cleaning, and laundry—are also the tasks that are performed disproportionately by women. Men specialize in the less frequent tasks that can be scheduled more flexibly, such as yard work. Suzanne Bianchi and colleagues (2000) examined detailed time diary data collected on a representative sample of adults in 1995 and found that while women did twice as much housework as men overall, they spent about four times more time doing core housework tasks than men. Men, on the other hand, spent twice as much time as women doing the less frequent tasks of outdoor chores, repairs, and bills.

A related picture emerges from recent studies of the gender division of child care tasks. In recent years, married fathers have become much more involved in child care than in the past and now put in about a third of the total child care hours, compared with mothers' two-thirds (Bianchi et al. 2006). But time diary data from 2000 show that fathers do not do a full third of the routine tasks of child care, focusing instead on doing more than a third of the more attractive, interactive tasks like reading or playing with a child (Bianchi et al. 2006, p. 64).

There are several ways, then, that the gender division of labor shows how family members are implicitly relying on cultural beliefs about gender status and difference as they organize household work. Work in the home, as in the paid labor force, is gender segregated. Sociologists Sampson Blair and Daniel Lichter (1991) adapted the same measure that is used to estimate the gender segregation of jobs and occupations to calculate the segregation of household tasks. They found that based on the tasks men and women reported doing in a 1988 national survey, the average man would have to reallocate 61% of his family labor to different tasks to achieve proportionate equality between men and women in the way they distribute their time across domestic tasks. Recall that the similar measure of the segregation of jobs indicates that more than 40% of women would have to change occupations to achieve a proportionate distribution of men and women across occupations. The comparison of these two findings suggests that the division of household labor is even more gender segregated than the division of paid labor. Like the division of paid labor, the gender segregation of household tasks in the United States has declined since the 1960s, but the decline has leveled off since the 1990s, according to Jennifer Hook's (2010) recent analysis.

Sociologists Joan Twiggs, Julia McQuillian, and Myra Marx Ferree (1999) looked more carefully at husbands' and wives' participation in the core housework tasks that are most closely associated with women. These tasks, they found, formed a clear hierarchy in how female typed they were and, therefore, how likely husbands were to participate in them. Doing dishes was the least sex typed and served as an entry-level task for husbands who were beginning to help beyond the traditional masculine tasks. Preparing meals was the most feminine task, and only husbands who did more housework overall, including the other core housework tasks, were willing to take it on. That these tasks showed such a clear pattern of gender typing over different families demonstrates again the power of widely shared cultural schemas in organizing household work.

How Do Employment and Earnings Affect Household Work?

If the use of gender as a primary frame for organizing social relations in the family causes cultural schemas to so powerfully shape household labor, then those same schemas are likely to act as a lens through which family members interpret the implications of their employment and earnings for the housework and child care that they do. In 2007, 73% of prime working-age women and 86% of prime working-age men were in the paid labor force (Cotter, Hermsen, and Vanneman 2010). Men's intense involvement in paid work is fully consistent with cultural schemas of their provider role in the family. It is women's growing commitment to market work that creates pressures for change in family gender schemas and the household division of labor. As women's hours of paid employment increasingly resemble men's, the time they have available for work in the home also is increasingly much the same as men's. Furthermore, while women's paychecks are still less than men's on average, their earnings contribute a growing proportion of the total income available to sustain the home. These changes, then, have fundamentally altered the material foundation that supported the traditional gender division of household labor. The result is a growing tension between the changing material terms on which men and women confront one another in the home and the existing gendered schemas of their family roles. This tension has transformed the home into a crucial battleground over the future of gender inequality.

How does this confrontation between material circumstances and deeply held cultural assumptions play out? The framing argument suggests that because cultural beliefs about gender are used to coordinate and organize household labor, these beliefs will also provide framing assumptions through which the implications of women's changing employment circumstances will be interpreted. As a result, women's employment and earnings will indeed have equalizing effects on the household division of labor, but the power of these effects will be blunted to some extent by the cultural schemas through which men and women frame their accommodations to them.

Most studies of the effects of employment and earnings focus on married or cohabiting heterosexual couples. Not surprisingly, these studies show that the more hours women put into paid work, the fewer hours they spend on household work. Men's and women's reactions to the constraints imposed by women's employment nevertheless show the effects of gender schemas. Women employed full-time still do considerably more household work than their husbands do (Coltrane 2000; Shelton and John 1996). Although most studies show that husbands contribute more work in the home as their wives are employed more hours, the effect is modest and doesn't replace the hours of housework that the wives have cut back (Bianchi et al. 2000; Coltrane 2000; Shelton and John 1996). Husbands, then, do not fully fill in for their wives at home when their wives work for pay. As a result, while women's employment does significantly reduce the gender gap in household labor, its most powerful effect is to reduce the total hours of household labor that are performed overall (Bianchi et al. 2000, 2006; Hook 2010).

Men's employment hours have much smaller effects on household labor than do women's employment hours. This, too, suggests the effects of cultural beliefs that housework is primarily women's responsibility. In general, the more hours men put into paid labor (an activity consistent with their cultural role as provider), the less housework they do and, to a lesser extent, the more housework their wives do (Bianchi et al. 2000; Coltrane 2000). In their study of the sex segregation of household tasks, Blair and Lichter (1991) also found that the more hours men worked for pay, the more they tended to concentrate their housework activities in the discretionary men's tasks of home repair and yard work, further exacerbating the gendered nature of the household division of labor. A more recent study confirms that men's employment hours particularly reduce the time they contribute to nondiscretionary tasks like cooking (Hook 2010).

Employment hours affect men's and women's time for household work, but the value of the earnings they bring home, scholars have argued, further affects their power to bargain over how much household work they will do (Brines 1994; England 2006). The argument is that while household work may sometimes be rewarding for the gender display it allows and for the concern it shows for family members, it is nevertheless relatively routine work that is devalued by our society in comparison to work for pay. As a result, by this argument, domestic partners who bring more money to the family use this resource to tacitly bargain down the amount of household work they do. Those who earn less compensate by doing more household work. Note that this argument is gender neutral in that it simply suggests that housework is done by domestic partners who earn less.

The large number of studies that have used this approach to examine the impact of earnings on housework have found that money does indeed talk in the household division of labor, but it talks in a decidedly gendered voice. Relative earnings are associated with the hours of housework that husbands and wives put in (Bianchi et al. 2000; Bittman et al. 2003; Brines 1994; Evertsson and Nermo 2004; Greenstein 2000; Shelton and John 1996). However, much like the effects of employment hours, women's housework is much more sensitive to differences in their relative earnings than is men's.

Recently, Sanjiv Gupta (2007) examined the effect of earnings more closely and showed that it is really women's absolute earnings, not their earnings relative to their husbands', that affect how much housework they do. The more women earn, the less housework they do. Controlling for their own income, their husband's income has little effect on how much housework women do. Furthermore, when high-earning women do less housework, it is not necessarily the case that their husbands, who are often also high earners, do a great deal more. Rather, consistent with cultural gender schemas, families seem to act from an implicit presumption that it is the wife's responsibility to see that the housework is done, not the husband's. The wife can either do most of it herself or, if she personally earns enough, she can pay to have it done—buying take-out, hiring a house cleaner, paying for child care, sending out the laundry.

It is the wife's money, studies suggest, not her husband's, that primarily determines whether her housework load is reduced by such expenditures (see Gupta 2007, p. 400). When a wife hires others to do the housework, those others, too, are almost always women and thus do not challenge the gendered structure of work in the home. Given the low wages, they are also often immigrant or minority women, adding a class and race dynamic to the gendered nature of the work (Coltrane 2000; Romero 1992). This is an example of how gender interests intersect with race and class interests in many settings. In this case, well-off women act to solve their gender problem in the home in a way that takes advantage of their dominant class and race position relative to other women.

Men's housework varies much less than women's and is less affected by differences in relative earnings. Nevertheless, most studies do show that husbands do more housework when their wives' earnings approximate or exceed their own (Bianchi et al. 2000; Coltrane 2000). The smallest gender gaps in housework are in families in which husbands and wives have similar incomes (Coltrane 2000).

What happens to husbands' housework in deviant families in which the wife contributes almost all the family income and the husband very little? Sociologist Julie Brines (1994) noticed that in families like this, husbands' housework actually declined from the levels found in families in which men's earnings were only modestly less than their wives'. Brines suggests that perhaps these men who earn very little feel the pressure of violating the cultural schema of provider and resist compounding their gender deviance by taking on the feminine tasks of housework. Further analyses have shown that it is only a small percentage (e.g., 3%) of very extreme households that show this effect, so it is not a consistent social pattern (Bittman et al. 2003; Gupta 1999). In a qualitative study of married couples in which the wife earned at least 50% more than her husband, Tichenor (2005) found, however, that such couples did implicitly feel the pressure of their gender deviance. Most often, wives continued to do more housework and child care than their husbands. Both worked together to represent their efforts to others as properly fulfilling the roles of homemaker and provider, despite their unusual income situation. In the few cases in which the husband stayed home, he often did take on more housework but struggled to explain his efforts to friends and others.

The new material contingencies created by women's increased labor force involvement and income, then, do indeed put pressure on the traditional gender division of household labor (e.g., Sullivan 2006). The framing gender schemas that people rely on to organize work at home, however, still have a powerful pull. Reflecting taken-for-granted assumptions that women are responsible for homemaking and that it is relatively devalued work, men do not respond to women's greater labor force involvement and earnings by taking on a lot more housework, even though women do less. The gendered lens through which couples experience the new material realities, then, blunts the force with which these material circumstances undermine gender inequality in household work. Blunted or not, however, the net effect of these changes in women's work and income is to reduce the gender gap in housework. Changes in housework, in turn, put growing pressure on traditional cultural schemas of gender and the family.

Alternative Beliefs: Race and Gender Ideology

Clearly, cultural beliefs about men and women in the family serve as powerful, if often implicit, referents for behavior in family relations. Given this, it matters what cultural beliefs family members hold. I have argued that while virtually everyone knows the mainstream, hegemonic cultural schemas of men's and women's roles in the family, not everyone endorses these beliefs, and some hold well-developed alternative beliefs. Because people tend to form families with those who are similar to them, people with alternative beliefs may often marry others who share those beliefs. When couples share alternative beliefs, these alternative beliefs should have an impact on their household division of labor.

One major reason that people may hold alternative beliefs is that they belong to a racial or ethnic minority that has developed a cultural perspective on gender that is more or less traditional than the current hegemonic perspective. There is evidence that African Americans often hold more moderate gender beliefs than the mainstream white population, while Hispanics and possibly Asians have more traditional beliefs than the mainstream (Collins 1991; Dugger 1988; Kane 2000). Another reason for alternative beliefs is education, which is often used as an indicator of social class and tends to be associated with more egalitarian ideologies about gender (Shelton and John 1996).

We do not have the detailed studies of how the household division of labor differs by race that are needed to fully address the question of the impact of alternative gender beliefs. Nevertheless, the studies that exist suggest that race does matter in just the way we would expect. A recent analysis of time diary data collected in 2003 and 2004 from a national sample of dual-earner married couples compared the household division of labor among African Americans, Asians, Hispanics, and whites (Wight, Bianchi, and Hunt 2009). Consistent with what we would expect from racial differences in gender beliefs, they found that the gender gap in time spent on housework was significantly greater among Hispanics and Asians than among whites and African Americans and that the gender gap was smallest among African Americans.

A study by Terri Orbuch and Sandra Eyster (1997) shows particularly clearly how alternative gender beliefs mediate racial differences in the household division of labor. These sociologists studied a sample of 143 white and 121 black couples over the first three years of their marriage. In addition to measuring the housework men and women in the couples performed, the researchers also measured their gender beliefs about men's and women's family and work roles. They found that African American couples reported significantly more egalitarian gender beliefs than the white couples. They also found that African American husbands participated more than white husbands in core housework tasks that are traditionally feminine typed. Furthermore, in a statistical analysis that controlled for employment and other factors, the researchers found that differences in African American and white couples' gender norms fully accounted for remaining race differences in the household division of labor. This last finding is especially interesting for us here because it suggests that racial differences in gender beliefs really are associated with differences in the household division of labor.

As we have seen, cultural beliefs about gender are the prism through which couples react to the material constraints of employment and earnings. Consequently, it is possible that alternative beliefs might cause material factors such as employment and earnings to affect the household division of labor slightly differently in different racial or ethnic groups. Although Orbuch and Eyster (1997) did not find such differences, Wightand colleagues (2009) report some preliminary evidence of such differences.

In contrast to the paucity of studies of racial differences in the household division of labor, a large number of studies have examined educational differences. These studies consistently find that education reduces women's housework and increases men's, reducing the gender gap overall (Bianchi et al. 2000; Shelton 2000; South and Spitze 1994). As Beth Shelton (2000, p. 350) observes, education is strongly correlated with personal gender attitudes, so that a likely explanation for this effect is that educated people are more likely to have acquired alternative, more egalitarian gender beliefs, which in turn moderate their gendered division of work in the home. Overall, though, the moderating or exacerbating effects of people's gender ideologies on their housework are modest. Also, reflecting men's higher status in hegemonic gender beliefs (and also in some alternative beliefs), men's personal gender ideologies tend to have a bigger effect on the household division of labor than women's (Coltrane 2000). Even those who hold alternative gender beliefs, then, seem not to be fully free of the impact of hegemonic cultural assumptions on their household divisions of labor.

Marital Status

Since housework is a highly gendered task in U.S. culture, cultural beliefs about gender are likely to be salient for men and women even in single-headed or, as we have seen, in same-sex households. It is likely, then, that people rarely are able to approach housework as just a set of technical tasks that must be accomplished. There is always a gender frame that affects how much and what they do. Not surprisingly, then, when sociologists Scott South and Glenna Spitze (1994) examined the hours of housework men and women reported doing in a national sample of households, they found that even among single people living on their own, women did more housework than men.

When a household is built around a heterosexual couple, however, the specific cultural schemas of men and women in the family are evoked with greatest clarity. The evocation is particularly strong if the couple is married. When people move into such households, the intensified salience of family devotion and provider schemas is likely to increase the hours women spend in housework, to decrease the time that men contribute, and to increase the gender segregation of the tasks they do. In their study, South and Spitze (1994) did indeed find that the gender gap in housework hours was greater in cohabiting couples than in single households and was greatest among married couples. It is possible, however, that the differences South and Spitze found were not due to people changing their housework levels as they moved into heterosexual unions but rather to differences in the types of people who live alone, cohabit, or marry.

Our framing perspective suggests that people should actually change their housework behavior when they move in and out of heterosexual unions because of the changing salience of cultural schemas of the family. Therefore, a better demonstration of our argument comes from a study by Sanjiv Gupta (1999). Gupta examined data from a national sample of households in which the same men and women reported their housework activities at two time intervals five years apart. He found that, controlling for other life changes such as employment or the birth of children, men decrease their housework hours when they enter cohabiting or marital relationships. They particularly decrease the time they put into female-typed housework (i.e., the core tasks of cooking, dishes, housecleaning, and shopping). On the other hand, when men leave marriages through divorce, separation, or widowhood, they increase the total housework and female-typed tasks they do.

The results for women are nearly the mirror opposite of men's. When never-married women enter cohabiting and marital relationships, they significantly increase the amount of housework they do, controlling for employment and other factors, and they spend more of their time doing female-typed housework tasks. When women leave a marriage, both their total housework and their female-typed housework decrease. Interestingly, Gupta found that the time men and women put into female-typed housework was even more sensitive to their change in marital status than their total hours of housework. These results suggest that the power of the gender frame in organizing household work does indeed intensify when people move into the specifically gendered context of a heterosexual union. In this context, referential cultural schemas about the homemaker and provider roles work to exacerbate gender inequality in the total housework people do, as well as the sex segregation in the type of household work they do.

Parental Status

The event that really crystallizes the gendered organization of household work is the transition to parenthood. The arrival of a child dramatically increases the time demands for work in the home at the same time that it activates in people's minds the most powerful, essential, and moral components of our cultural schemas about gender in the home. While the family devotion schema may encourage women to do housework, it obligates them to take on primary responsibility for child care. Similarly, the provider schema acquires new moral force when children join the family. The moral tone that gender schemas take on in the context of parenthood intensifies their power as an evaluative standard by which men and women judge their own and each other's actions in the family. It intensifies the reactions of outsiders to a family's household division of labor as well.

The arrival of a child immediately presents the parents with an organizational problem: how to arrange their schedules to provide the time necessary for the baby's care. In the contemporary United States, married women who are childless put as many hours into the paid labor force as do childless married men, and the women also do more housework (Bianchi et al. 2006, p. 55). Adding a child in this situation creates a crisis over the allocation of time to work in the home. Parents react to this pressing time allocation crisis through the moral prism of family gender schemas that have powerful consequences for gender inequality. Following the dictates of the family devotion and provider schemas and the gender status differences embedded within them, families solve the crisis primarily by mothers, not fathers, changing their allocation of time between home and labor force.

Laura Sanchez and Elizabeth Thompson (1997) used data that surveyed a national sample of households at two time intervals to examine the impact of the transition to parenthood on men's and women's employment hours and on their hours of housework and child care. Sanchez and Thompson found that parenthood did not reduce and sometimes increased fathers' hours of employment, and it did not change the housework fathers did. Other data also show that in 2000, about 90% of fathers were employed for more than 40 hours a week, regardless of the number of children they had at home (Bianchi et al. 2006, p. 46). Interestingly, Sanchez and Thompson also found that parenthood caused men who differed in their own personal gender ideologies to become more similar to one another in the amount of household work they did. It is as if the intensified salience of hegemonic gender schemas in these fathers' relationships both within and without the family overwhelmed their own idiosyncratic gender attitudes.

Not surprisingly, Sanchez and Thompson (1997) found that the arrival of children caused women to significantly curtail their employment hours and increase their housework. Of course, both mothers and fathers took on new child care duties, but women performed about two-thirds of these. In married couples, then, the addition of children causes the division of household labor and the allocation of time between family and market work to become even more strongly organized on gendered lines and to become more unequal.

What is the net effect of the changes men and women make in the allocation of their time when they become parents? Recent data show that the total hours of market work and family work that married mothers and fathers contribute is roughly similar, but women do two-thirds of the family work and men do two-thirds of the market work (Bianchi et al. 2006). Although the total hours are similar, of course, resources, status, and power flow more directly from market work than from family work. Thus, the way the gender frame solves the time crunch of providing for children creates a family division of labor that establishes a powerful foundation for gender inequality not only in the family but also in the larger society.

The decision of couples to reduce the mother's rather than the father's hours of employment is not just a rational decision based on who makes the higher wages. Sociologist Mary Blair-Loy (2003) studied couples in which the wives were highly paid finance executives who made much more than their husbands. Despite these wives' enormous earnings, Blair-Loy found that these couples frequently didn't even consider the possibility that the husband rather than the wife might reduce his work time to care for a child. Not only do mothers feel the moral obligation to personally care for their child but also fathers at such a time resist cutting back on their newly salient role as provider. The fact that these families made such choices despite the financial costs shows the power of the gender schemas that framed their decisions.

Of course, statistics that show that, on average, married women curtail their employment hours when they become parents cover over a wide diversity of decisions by different individual mothers. Some mothers continue to work full-time, others drop out of the labor force, and many others work part-time. In 2000, 78% of mothers with children under age 18 in the house were employed, and of those, 77% were employed full-time (Bianchi et al. 2006, p. 46). Of mothers with at least one child under age one year, however, only 46% were in the labor force. By the time their kids were older than six, 73% were in the labor force. Although there has been a popular discussion recently about whether educated mothers are increasingly opting out of the labor force to care for their children, recent studies contest this (Stone 2007). Most educated mothers continue to be highly involved in the labor force. Those who do drop out for a period to take care of their children typically report doing so because of the prejudice and inflexibility they as mothers encounter from their employers rather than from their own positive choice to stay at home (Stone 2007).

The arrival of children not only changes the gender organization within the family but also substantially alters men's and women's social networks outside the family (Munch, McPherson, and Smith-Lovin 1997). Taking on the home- and child-centered tasks of motherhood reduces the size of women's social networks when their children are pre-school age and reduces their frequency of contact with those they know outside the family. Cultural assumptions about the duties of motherhood, then, enclose women within the family and reduce their contacts in the outside world. The arrival of children does not reduce the size of men's networks. It does, however, increase men's contact with kin. These changes, then, draw both men and women into a more domestic social pattern while their children are small, but women's access to contacts outside the domestic sphere are restricted in ways that men's are not.

Outside network contacts bring people information, opportunities, and material resources. Also, the contemporary organization of the work world is one in which the childbearing years coincide with the critical years of career building. As a result, the restrictive impact of childbearing on women's but not men's networks disproportionately disadvantages women's career contacts at a critical juncture. The effect can be a lifetime disadvantage in earnings and career success. In assigning them primary responsibility for child rearing, then, gender schemas alter women's social contacts with others in ways that reinforce gender inequality in the work world. We see again, then, the interdependence between gender inequality in the division of household labor and gender inequality in the world of work.

SUMMARY AND CONCLUSIONS

I began this chapter by saying that the social institution of the family is in many ways the "home" of gender as a cultural frame for coordinating social relations. After all, the roots of the gender frame lie in people's efforts to organize family units for sex, survival, and children. The social organization of the family household is, as a result, a powerful wellspring for the system of cultural beliefs and material arrangements that sustain gender inequality in society. Both material exchanges between men and women and cultural beliefs about who men and women are and why they are or are not unequal are at stake in how households are organized into a division of labor—who does what to maintain the home and care for children. Consequently, if we are to understand how gender inequality persists in the contemporary United States and how the use of gender as a primary frame for social relations contributes to this persistence, we need to consider how the framing process plays out in the household division of labor. This is what we have attempted to do in this chapter.

The first task was to develop a specific account of how the gender frame works in the family context and specify its implications for the household division of labor. The context of the family has several distinctive aspects that affect how the gender frame shapes people's expectations and behavior in the home. As a social institution in American society, the family carries with it hegemonic cultural schemas of men's and women's expected roles within it that are more specific, moralized instantiations of general stereotypes of women as communal and men as agentic. For women, these moral schemas prescribe *family devotion* that is linked to essentialized assumptions about women's capacities as mothers and caregivers. The comparable moral schema for men is that of a *provider* who satisfies his greatest responsibility to his family through work outside the family rather than within it.

In the home, the framing perspective suggests that gendered expectations, shaped by both general stereotypes and moral schemas of family gender roles, will play a powerful role in shaping behavior. This is because the intensely gendered nature of the family context makes cultural beliefs about gender highly salient to family members and directly relevant to their activities. (Note how this differs from the workplace, where gender is often only diffusely salient for participants.) Furthermore, hegemonic gender beliefs work their effects on behavior in the home not only through the expectations of family members for themselves and each other but also through the expectations of relatives, neighbors, and other outsiders who interact with the family members.

Another distinctive aspect of the family that affects how the gender frame works in that context is the intimacy of the ties that members form. Through close ties, family members develop detailed, highly individualized impressions of each other that go far beyond cultural stereotypes. Yet, these personalized impressions are nested from the beginning in family members' initial understandings of each other as male or female. Furthermore, the gendered context of the family keeps the background frame of cultural beliefs about gender ever salient. This process infuses gendered meanings into the nuanced family identities that develop. It also maintains cultural beliefs about gender as an ever-present referent by which family members judge themselves and each other.

The combination of gender beliefs that act as daily referents for behavior in the home depends on the specific family context. General gender stereotypes are ever available as a referent in all families. When the household is based on committed heterosexual ties, the more specific schemas of family devotion and provider grow in salience, and this salience further intensifies with the addition of children. Also, to the extent that family members may share alternative gender beliefs, these, too, should measurably affect their behavior in the family.

This account of how the gender frame shapes expectations and behavior in the family makes several predictions. First, the household division of labor, both in terms of the total hours men and women contribute and the specialization of the tasks they perform, should be organized more powerfully by gender than by any other characteristic of family members, such as their labor force participation, earnings, social class, or race. Second, within this overall gender organization of labor, couples who hold alternative gender beliefs should have more moderate or extreme gender divisions of work in the home, depending on those beliefs. Third, entering into a committed heterosexual tie, evidenced by cohabitation or marriage, should change the amount and type of household work men and women do, making their activities correspond more closely to the family devotion and provider schemas. Fourth, this effect on the household division of labor among heterosexual couples should intensify with the arrival of children.

Our next task was to compare these implications to the evidence, both as a kind of test of the validity of the framing perspective and to understand the contribution of framing effects in the home to the persistence of inequality. First, the data clearly confirm that being male or female is by far the most important predictor of who does what in the household and how much he or she does. Women do twice as many hours of housework and child care as do men. The tasks men and women do in the home are more gender segregated than are jobs in the work world, with women specializing in core tasks of cooking and cleaning that must be performed regularly. A woman's own earnings, rather than her male partner's, determine whether she does the household work herself or purchases outside help to assist her. When women substantially increase their employment hours, the strongest effect is to reduce the total hours of household work that is done in their home, even though men's contribution to that work does increase somewhat. Second, based on studies of racial groups and couples with higher levels of education, alternative gender beliefs do have a moderating effect on the household division of labor, as expected.

Third, entering into a committed heterosexual tie, particularly through marriage, increases the amount of household work that women do and reduces the amount that men do. It also causes the work that they do to become more gender typed. Thus, referential cultural schemas about the devoted family woman and the provider man appear, as expected, to be triggered by marriage and act to exacerbate both gender inequality and sex segregation in household work.

Fourth, the transition to parenthood further crystallizes the gendered organization of household work, as expected. Faced with the time demands of parenthood, it is mothers rather than fathers who reallocate more of their time to the home and less to the labor force. This, in turn, increases earnings differences and inequalities in long-term career outcomes for mothers and fathers, which further exacerbates gender inequality both within the family and in the larger society.

All in all, then, the data on the household division of labor in contemporary American families correspond rather closely to our predictions about how the gender frame shapes behavior and reproduces gender inequality in the context of the family. It does indeed appear that the repeated, implicit evocation of cultural gender beliefs and schemas in family relations powerfully frames the decisions and actions through which family members construct their division of household labor. These gender beliefs become the lenses through which material changes in men's and women's circumstances, such as women's increased employment, have their effects on the household division of labor, partially blunting the potential of those effects to undermine the beliefs themselves.

The contribution of these effects in the home to the overall maintenance of gender inequality in the contemporary United States is difficult to overstate. Persistent inequality and sex typing of household labor adds a powerful source of daily confirmation for family members of hegemonic cultural beliefs that women are, in their natures, communal caregivers while men are more agentic and better providers. Persistent gender inequality in household responsibilities also feeds gender inequality in access to money and power outside the home. Together, these effects of the ways people draw on gender beliefs to coordinate their activities in the home act as powerful sustaining forces for the system of cultural beliefs and material arrangements that maintain gender inequality in the contemporary world.

SIX

The Persistence Of Inequality

INTRODUCTION

It is time now to return to the question with which we started. How does gender inequality persist in the modern world? How does it persist in the face of ongoing social and economic changes that are undermining the material arrangements upon which it has seemed only recently to depend, such as women's lesser involvement in the paid labor force compared with men? As a system of inequality, gender, as we have seen, is not directly or simply a matter of which sex is richer or has more power. Gender is at root a status inequality—that is, a system of inequality that is founded on cultural beliefs about status differences between types of people—men and women. Yet recall that, to persist over time, the shared cultural beliefs that confer greater status on one category of people than on another must be supported by average differences between these types of people in the material resources and power that they command.

In complex societies like the contemporary United States, differences in the resources and power that people command are largely a result of inequalities in the positions they hold in the organizations and groups that make up society. Thus, the contemporary question becomes: How does gender inequality persist in the face of social and institutional changes that undercut it as a basis for the distribution of people into positions of resources and power in society's most significant organizations and groups? A further issue makes this question even more complicated. Technological innovations, shifting economic forces, and the continual interests of women and men in bettering their lives create ongoing pressures that alter the very structures of the social organizations—such as the workplace or the heterosexual union—in which positions of resources and power are embedded in our society. How does gender continually re-create itself as a system of inequality in such a changing landscape and despite countervailing forces that undercut it?

We have seen the beginnings of an answer to the persistence question in previous chapters. People's continual use of gender as a primary frame for organizing social relations results in the background activation of gender status beliefs throughout both workplace relations and activities at home. These beliefs in turn implicitly shape behavior and evaluations in ways that reproduce gender inequality over time in the workplace and home and blunt the impact of forces for change.

Yet the framing effects of cultural beliefs about gender that we have examined so far mostly tell us how the gender system reproduces itself within existing economic arrangements and accepted assumptions about the organization of close heterosexual bonds. What about sites at the edge of social and technological change where substantially new forms of work and new forms of heterosexual unions are being innovated? Small start-ups take advantage of technological developments to pioneer new industries, such as the dot-coms and biotech firms of recent years. These new industries reorganize the economic structure of society for the future. In a similar way, the changing social terms on which young women and men come together to form intimate bonds have the potential to create new forms of heterosexual unions.

This leading edge of change is of great consequence to the gender system. These are the sites in which substantially new distributions of power and material resources between men and women might come about and might, in turn, undermine gender status beliefs. Or these sites might be the locations in which gender status differences are reinscribed into new forms of social organization—in effect, reinventing gender inequality for a new era. What happens to gender as a principle of social organization and inequality at these sites of change, then, is central to the persistence question. As a result, these sites of change will be a major focus of our analysis in this chapter.

Forces for Change

Before turning to a specific analysis of the persistence question, it is useful first to remind ourselves of the contemporary forces that challenge the persistence of gender inequality. These are the forces that work against the continuing use of gender as a principle for distributing people into unequal positions of power and resources in contemporary society. There are three broad sets of such forces. First is a set of institutional forces that have been documented by Robert Max Jackson (1998). As we discussed in the first chapter, these consist of pressures on economic and political organizations to rationalize their procedures in pursuit of profits and power by treating people as "workers" or "citizens" rather than in terms of traditional distinctions such as gender. Working in concert with these pressures for rational efficiency is a growing cultural logic of individual or "human" rights that is expressed in laws prohibiting gender or racial discrimination in education and employment. A second set of forces for change we have already alluded to. These consist of ongoing technological and social innovations such as the development of the Internet or techniques of genetic analysis or the emergence of globalized markets. These innovations force change in old organizational solutions to problems of economic efficiency and social life and create opportunities to do things differently—to organize social relations in a new way. A third and final set of forces that work against gender inequality are the interests of women and committed egalitarians of both sexes in improving women's lot in life through everyday choices in work, personal relations, and politics.

Explaining Persistence

Together, these forces create a broad sweep of processes at both institutional and individual levels that work to undermine differences between men and women in the positions of power and resources that they attain in the organizations and groups that make up society. And yet, as we have commented in previous chapters, the slowing and even stalling of the pace of change in gender inequality in recent years suggests that these forces for change coexist with other processes that continue to reconstruct gender inequality not only in established contexts but also in new contexts. It is notable that studies of gender wage inequality in the "new economy" (i.e., jobs produced by technological changes and economic restructuring) show that, although the results are complex, women have not fared much better in the new economy overall (McCall 2001).

One factor that has undoubtedly slowed progress toward gender equality is that, with the exception of women's own interests, the forces for change operate primarily in the public sphere of economic and political organizations and affect the family only indirectly. The lack of deep change in the structure of the family has been a powerful force that pushes back against gender change in the public sphere by affecting women's and men's availability for positions of power and resources in work and politics. Pointing to gender inequality in the family as the factor that continues to re-create gender inequality in resources and power more generally, however, begs the question of the persistence of inequality in the home.

How, then, does gender inequality persist in the face of ongoing social and economic change and forces that work to undermine it? I argue that the central, underlying factor that allows inequality to persist is the way that changes in cultural beliefs about gender *lag* changes in material arrangements based on gender. The concept of cultural lag is well known in the social sciences (Brinkman and Brinkman 1997; Ogburn 1957). It refers to the idea that changes in nonmaterial culture (e.g., shared cultural beliefs) frequently lag behind changes in material culture. I argue that cultural lag occurs with regard to shared beliefs about gender and plays a key role in the persistence of gender inequality over transformations in material arrangements based on gender.

More specifically, I will argue that shared gender stereotypes, which are what people think "most people" assume about gender, change more slowly than people's own behavior in response to new opportunities. People's gender stereotypes also change more slowly than their perceptions about their own gendered characteristics. Yet, it is their assumptions about what most people think that people use to coordinate their behavior with others on the basis of gender. The result is that when people at sites of social change come together to construct some new form of business or new type of relationship and sex-categorize one another in the process, the cultural beliefs about gender that are activated in the background are more traditional than the innovative circumstances they confront. To the extent that they draw on these beliefs to help define and organize their new, uncertain project, they implicitly inscribe trailing assumptions about gender into the procedures and social forms that they create. As they do so, the new gendered arrangements may not leave cultural assumptions about men and women unchanged. However, they are likely to reestablish in new organizational forms the core principles that lie at the heart of gender stereotypes—the principles of gender difference and male status dominance. To the extent that people do reestablish in new material form the core principles of gender difference and male status dominance, they create arrangements that also satisfy people's conservative individual interests in maintaining a basic stability in gender as a primary system of meaning for making sense of self and other. The cost of stability in shared gender meanings, however, is the maintenance of the status privilege for men that is currently embedded in them.

Examining the Argument

In this chapter, I will develop these arguments about the persistence of gender inequality in greater detail. To do so, we need to start by considering why changes in gender stereotypes should lag behind changes in material arrangements between men and women. We will see that there are reasons to expect that the content of these stereotypes is likely to be particularly slow to change with respect to their core principles of meaning for organizing social relations. These are gender difference and male status dominance.

We next need to examine the evidence about the extent to which cultural beliefs about gender actually have changed. What does this evidence indicate about the relationship between changes in gender beliefs and recent changes in material circumstances between men and women—women's growing involvement in the paid labor force, for instance, or their representation in traditionally male professions such as law or medicine? There are two sides to this question that we need to consider. Like others, I have argued that cultural beliefs about gender and material arrangements between men and women are interdependent so that changes in one should affect the other. Consequently, we would expect to see some evidence of change in gender beliefs in response to the major changes in women's work roles in the past several decades. On the other hand, I am claiming that changes in gender beliefs lag behind material changes. We would see evidence for this lag argument if the changes that have occurred in gender beliefs are relatively slight, compared with material changes, and if consensual gender stereotypes—what we assume most people think—have changed the least.

After examining changes in gender beliefs, the next major task will be to go to social sites at the edge of change in contemporary society to examine how and why lagging cultural beliefs about gender would be pulled into them. We need to be particularly sensitive to the circumstances in which gender change happens in such sites and those in which it does not. To examine sites of social innovation in the public world of work, we will consider studies of start-up companies in the information technology and biotechnology fields. To consider a site of innovation in close personal relations, we will examine the changing patterns of behavior through which college students form heterosexual unions and intimate relationships.

WHY SHOULD GENDER STEREOTYPES LAG BEHIND?

I have argued from the beginning that gender stereotypes are the cultural rules for enacting the material structure of gender difference and inequality in our society. This necessarily suggests a reciprocal link between the material arrangements that organize men's and women's lives and the content of their gender stereotypes. If there is a reciprocal link between them, why would change in gender stereotypes lag behind changes in those material arrangements? The answer lies in two related processes that buffer stereotypes from the immediate impact of potentially disconfirming gender experiences. The power of both of these buffering processes is driven by the importance of gender to people as a primary frame for making sense of self and others and organizing social relations.

The first set of processes operates at the level of individual cognition. Individuals have powerful, largely unconscious tendencies to perceive and interpret people and events in terms that confirm their prior expectations (Fiske, Lin, and Neuberg 1999). Social cognition research has shown that these confirmation biases make people more likely to notice, attend to, and remember events and experiences that confirm what they expect or want to see and to overlook, ignore, or discount things that disconfirm their expectations. The deeper people's cognitive or emotional commitments are to their prior expectations, the more powerfully people unconsciously distort what they see and remember to fit what they expect.

The deep commitment most people have to gender as a primary frame for understanding self and other fuels powerful confirmation biases that help sustain gender stereotypes in the face of disconfirming experiences. Studies show that people find it easier to recognize, think about, and remember information that is consistent with gender-stereotypic expectations (Von Hippel, Sekaquaptewa, and Vargas 1995). People also spontaneously fill in unspecified details of male and female behavior to make an experience consistent with gender expectations (Dunning and Sherman 1997). Thus people often fail to see disconfirming information or, if they do see it, often implicitly reinterpret it in stereotype-confirming ways. As a result, when changing social circumstances cause people to have more gender-atypical experiences, the impact of these experiences on their gender stereotypes is blunted by the fact that people often do not recognize these experiences for what they are.

Even when people do clearly recognize an experience as disconfirming their cultural stereotypes, their first reaction is to treat the disconfirming event or person as an "exception," with few implications for what can be expected in most situations (Hewstone 1994). If, over time, continuing social change causes people to have more and more of these exceptional experiences, pressure to change their stereotypes of what most people are like will build. But because persistent change only slowly seeps through people's confirmation biases, the content of their perceptions of what the typical man or woman is like will lag behind actual changes in others' and their own material experiences.

The second process that buffers people's gender stereotypes from disconfirming experiences is more social. It derives from people's taken-for-granted presumption that gender stereotypes are common knowledge and widely accepted in society (Prentice and Carranza 2004; Zelditch and Floyd 1998). It is the presumption that gender stereotypes are widely shared that allows people to use gender as a frame for coordinating their behavior with others. Doing so, however, also creates as a side effect social processes that inhibit the public expression of stereotype-disconfirming behavior or information.

Precisely because they assume that others accept widely held stereotypes, people fall back on communicating stereotype-consistent information to others as a way of forging common ground between them and facilitating their relationship. Anna Clark and Yoshihisa Kashima (2007) demonstrated this in a pair of experiments that showed that when people have access to information that is gender stereotype consistent and also information that is inconsistent, they spontaneously communicate more consistent information as a way of connecting and coordinating with the other. As the researchers showed, people do this specifically because they assume, as people do about gender stereotypes, that the stereotypes are widely accepted in the community. As a result of this communicative bias, even when people's changing experiences give them access to information that contradicts gender stereotypes, they tend not to pass it on to others, blunting its impact. Instead, others continue to hear a reaffirmation of the stereotypes.

Another side effect of people's presumption that gender stereotypes are common knowledge is that people expect that others will treat them according to those stereotypic beliefs. As a result, even when people no longer personally endorse gender stereotypes, they still must take those stereotypes into account in deciding how to act themselves, particularly in public settings. Research has shown that the perception that most others hold a stereotype has a major effect on a person's tendency to act on, or refrain from acting on, that stereotype (Sechrist and Stangor 2001). Thus, the presumption that gender stereotypes are widely shared encourages people to act in accord with the stereotypes, particularly with strangers or in public places, even when their own views and perhaps those of their friends do begin to change.

Such public conformity is further encouraged by the fact that violations of the prescriptive requirements of gender stereotypes (that women be communal rather dominant, that men be forcefully agentic rather than weakly emotional) actually elicit negative, sanctioning reactions from others (Prentice and Carranza 2004; Rudman et al. 2009). Laurie Rudman and Kimberly Fairchild (2004) have shown that people anticipate the negative reactions such gender violations incur and try to avoid them. The resulting public gender conformity sustains everybody's continuing acceptance that gender stereotypes are what most people believe by reducing the number of disconfirming events that people witness around them, even when their own personal experiences seem increasingly contradictory.

Neither individual confirmation biases nor the social processes that conserve gender stereotypes fully protect people's gender beliefs from the eventual impact of men's and women's changing material circumstances. As economic and technological changes increasingly lead more and more men and women into contexts and experiences that contradict traditional cultural beliefs about gender, these experiences begin to filter through the cognitive and social processes that initially hide them. As people increasingly come to recognize that not only is their experience changing but also so is that of most people, the content of their gender beliefs begins to change. This change, however, systematically lags behind change in their material experiences.

In thinking about the extent to which gender beliefs might lag behind material change, it is useful to distinguish among three types or levels of gender beliefs. Two of these are aspects of gender stereotypes and thus are held by individuals as cultural beliefs that they assume are shared. The third type of gender belief is more personal: how individuals perceive themselves in terms of the attributes contained in gender stereotypes.

As we know, gender stereotypes, which are beliefs about the attributes that most people would attribute to the typical man or woman, contain both prescriptive and descriptive attributes. The prescriptive elements of stereotypes are traits that are seen as more desirable in one sex than in the other and reflect assumptions about what men and women *should* (or should not) be. The descriptive attributes of stereotypes simply assess how men and women are thought to actually be. Not surprisingly, there is a great deal of overlap in the traits that people report as desirable for men and women and those they report as typical of them (e.g., Prentice and Carranza 2002). Nevertheless, beliefs about how men and women should be represent the most powerfully normative elements in the cultural rules by which people coordinate their behavior with one another on the basis of gender. As we have seen, people are especially likely to avoid publicly violating the prescriptive aspects of gender stereotypes because of the sanctions they may evoke. This public avoidance, however, means that the prescriptive elements of gender stereotypes should be especially resistant to disconfirmation and change in the face of changing material relations between men and women. The merely typical, descriptive aspects of stereotypes are also greatly buffered from change by the presumption that they are commonly accepted by most people, but they are likely to be a bit more susceptible to change than are prescriptive beliefs.

In contrast to the prescriptive and descriptive elements of cultural stereotypes, gendered self-perceptions are assumptions about the self rather than about the beliefs and attributes of others. It is at the individual level that people most directly experience the gender contradictions and disconfirmations that changing material circumstances create. Although they often are not privy to the contradictions that others experience, they do have access to their own disconfirming experiences that filter through their confirmation biases. Because people have greater access to contradictory gender information at the personal level, gendered self-reports are likely to form the leading edge of change in a society's gender beliefs. Even they, however, are likely to lag material changes to some degree. The social importance of the gender frame gives individuals a powerful incentive to perceive and interpret their personal attributes as broadly consistent with widely accepted cultural beliefs about gender. As a result, lagging cultural beliefs about gender slow down changes even in gendered self-perceptions.

We should expect, then, to see some lag between material changes in women's and men's lives and corresponding changes in all three types of gender beliefs. The lag, however, should be greatest for gender stereotypes, particularly the prescriptive aspects of these stereotypes.

Gendered self-perceptions should be the most responsive to material changes. How do these expectations correspond to the empirical evidence about changes in gender beliefs over recent decades, during which there have been substantial changes in women's material circumstances relative to men? This is the next question we need to examine.

PERSISTENCE AND CHANGE IN CULTURAL BELIEFS ABOUT GENDER

Efforts to assess actual change in gender stereotypes and beliefs have produced complicated and sometimes controversial results (e.g., Eagly and Diekman 2003; Lueptow, Garovic-Szabo, and Lueptow 2001). Much of the confusion stems from methodological issues. A wide variety of measures have been used in studies of gender beliefs, and these often tap different aspects or levels of those beliefs. Also, the groups of people to whom the measures have been administered have typically been nonrepresentative samples of convenience. Despite all this, some broad patterns emerge from the findings of these studies, especially if one is careful to attend to differences among prescriptive stereotypes, descriptive stereotypes, and self-perceptions.

Gendered Self-Perceptions

Let's start with people's descriptions of themselves. Here there is clear evidence that changes in women's status and roles over the last several decades have indeed resulted in systematic changes in the gendered attributes that women attribute to themselves. These changes are just what we would expect, given the nature of the changes in women's roles relative to men. Furthermore, there is evidence that even these self-descriptions, which should be most responsive to material changes, have lagged some years behind those material changes.

Jean Twenge (2001) used the statistical technique of meta-analysis to combine the results of 158 samples of American college students and 10 samples of high school students who had completed self-descriptive measures of assertiveness or dominance in the years between 1931 and 1993. Using a number of indicators of women's status, such as women's educational attainment, their representation in the professions, and their age at first marriage, Twenge shows that women's occupation of high-status roles increased in the period before and during World War II (1931–1945), declined again in the immediate postwar, baby boom era (1946–1967), and then increased substantially in the most recent period (1968–1993). Twenge then compared this pattern of status change with changes in the assertiveness women attributed to themselves and found a close correspondence. The average assertiveness reported by women increased in the prewar period, declined somewhat in the postwar period, and then increased again in the last period. Given the general association in our society of high-status roles with the appearance of assertiveness (see chapter 3), this is just what we would expect.

So changes in women's self-described assertiveness generally tracked changes in the status of the roles that American women occupied at given periods. But looking more closely, did changes in assertiveness precede or lag changes in women's roles? Twenge examined whether college women's self-reported assertiveness was best predicted by the indicators of women's status in society up to 10 years earlier or up to 10 years after their assertiveness was measured. She found that the women's self-reported assertiveness most clearly reflected the material conditions of women in society 10 years earlier, when these college women were children. Changes in women's gendered self-descriptions, then, tracked but lagged societal changes in women's positions of power and resources.

What about men's assertiveness? Since our gender stereotypes link men with greater agency and assertiveness than women, it is not surprising that the men in the studies Twenge examined generally rated themselves as more assertive than women rated themselves. In contrast to women, men's occupation of high-status roles in American society did not change dramatically over the period of time Twenge examined. Not surprisingly, then, men's self-described assertiveness also did not change in any consistent, reliable fashion over this period either.

If women's self-reported assertiveness changed over time but men's did not, that means that the gender gap in self-perceived assertiveness has decreased since the late 1960s. In the data she examined, Twenge (2001) found that while women used to rate themselves as considerably less assertive than men rated themselves, by the early 1990s, they scored about the same as men on self-reported assertiveness. Janet Spence and Camille Buckner (2000) found similar evidence of a reduced gender gap in self-perceptions of agency. In 1996, they asked two substantial samples of college students to rate themselves in terms of a series of gendered attributes. The women in these samples scored significantly lower than men on only about half of the items measuring "instrumental" (i.e., agentic or assertive) traits. Here, then, is a clear sign of change in gendered self-perceptions. As men's and women's educational and occupational roles have become more similar, their self-described personalities, on traits most closely associated with work roles, have become more similar.

Nevertheless, it is interesting to note the instrumental traits on which men's and women's self-reports still differed in Spence and Buckner's study. These were traits like feels superior, stands up to pressure, competitive, decisive, aggressive, dominant, forceful, and has leadership abilities. In contrast to the attributes on which men and women rated themselves similarly (independent, active, self-reliant, individualistic, ambitious), the instrumental traits on which men's self-ratings remained higher than women's are those associated with social dominance and forcefulness. Although the gender gap has narrowed in self-perceived agency, then, certain core differences in traits related to men's status dominance remain.

The students Spence and Buckner (2000) studied also rated themselves on "expressive" traits that tap the communal side of cultural beliefs about gender. Since men's and women's family roles have changed much less than women's work roles have, we should expect to still see strong gender differences in self-rated communality. This is indeed what Spence and Buckner found. Women's self-ratings were significantly and substantially higher than men's on virtually all expressive items, including devoted and helpful to others, emotional, understanding, warm, compassionate, sympathetic, and affectionate. In contrast to change in the agency dimension of gender, then, there is little evidence that the gender gap in self-perceived communality has declined.

Gender Stereotypes

My argument about persistence, however, depends more on gender stereotypes than on self-perceptions because stereotypes represent shared common knowledge about gender that people use to coordinate their social relations with others. Unfortunately, measures of gender stereotypes have not been systematically administered over the years in the way that personality measures of assertiveness have. As a result, there is no study equivalent to Twenge's that systematically tracks changes in gender stereotypes over the years. However, it is possible to compare the results of some recent studies with ones from the 1970s.

Janet Spence and Camille Buckner (2000) asked the college students in their 1996 samples to rate the typical male and typical female college student on the same instrumental and expressive traits that they had used to rate themselves. This provided a measure of the descriptive gender stereotypes that students held. Men in the sample rated the typical man as substantially higher than the typical woman on all 22 instrumental traits. Women similarly rated the typical man as higher on 21 of the 22 instrumental traits. The one difference was that women, unlike men, did not think that the sexes typically differed in being analytic. Both men and women also agreed that the typical woman was much higher than the typical man on all 16 expressive items. Spence and Buckner note that these ratings are almost unchanged from those Spence collected from college students in the 1970s. In contrast to self-perceptions, then, Spence and Buckner found little change in descriptive gender stereotypes. Another study that examined college students' ratings of the typical man and woman on agentic and communal traits from the 1970s to the present similarly reports little change in descriptive stereotypes, other than an actual intensification of perceived gender differences in communality (Lueptow, Garovich-Szabo, and Lueptow 2001).

It seems clear, then, that descriptive gender stereotypes have lagged well behind changes in women's roles in the work world and also behind changes in women's own self-perceptions of their agentic qualities. Amanda Diekman and Alice Eagly (2000) have found that people do anticipate that the typical traits of men and women will eventually change if women's work roles become increasingly similar to men's. But has there been absolutely no actual change in descriptive stereotypes so far? While Spence and Buckner (2000) and Lueptow and colleagues (2001) found very little, other studies hint of a recent narrowing in the perceived differences between typical men and women on the "softer" aspects of agency.

Alice Eagly and various colleagues have conducted a number of studies that asked people to rate how the typical man or woman is viewed by society on traits tapping not only communality and assertive agency, as the studies just discussed primarily did, but also underlying cognitive ability, like reasoning, problem solving, and analytical ability (Cejka and Eagly 1999; Diekman and Eagly 2000; Koenig and Eagly 2006). As we know, cognitive competence is typically associated with agentic behavior because people tend to infer that those who act forcefully about something probably know something about it (Ridgeway, Berger, and

Smith 1985). But still, underlying ability is a little different from the forceful, agentic behaviors necessary to apply that ability to accomplish a goal or perform well. It is also a little different from the forceful agency associated with social dominance. Thus, cognitive competence represents that softer edge of agency that plausibly could be the first point at which widely shared descriptive stereotypes might begin to change in response to women's changed work roles.

Like other researchers, Eagly and her colleagues found that the typical man is still viewed as significantly more forcefully agentic (e.g., competitive, aggressive, arrogant, or dominant) than the typical woman, and the typical woman is still seen as much more communal (e.g., warm, kind, nurturing) than the typical man. Yet they also found that women were seen as only slightly less cognitively competent than men (Cejka and Eagly 1999; Diekman and Eagly 2000; Koenig and Eagly 2006). A strength of these studies by Eagly and her colleagues is that they employed not only samples of college students but also non-student samples of people questioned at random in public places such as airports and fairs. Furthermore, since the researchers asked people to rate how the typical man or woman is viewed "by society," they measured perceptions of "most people's" gender beliefs. Reassuringly, students and nonstudents generally agreed about the nature of current descriptive gender beliefs—which is as we would expect if these beliefs are indeed widely shared in society.

Since we don't have good comparative data from earlier eras, we cannot be certain that the narrow gap in cognitive competence we see in contemporary gender stereotypes represents a clear change in those stereotypes from the past, but it is at least plausible to suggest that it does. Although the evidence is not conclusive, it is possible, then, that change in widely held descriptive stereotypes about men and women finally may be beginning to occur. Nevertheless, traditional gender stereotypes are still largely intact. Even at the descriptive level, then, change in gender stereotypes has substantially lagged behind change in women's work roles.

Prescriptive Beliefs

If there is a possibility of some slight change in the descriptive aspects of gender stereotypes, there is no evidence of change in prescriptive gender beliefs. Deborah Prentice and Erica Carranza (2002, 2004) asked a group of contemporary college students to rate how desirable a wide variety of traits are in a man or in a woman in American society.

Thus these were measures of the perceptions of most people's beliefs about the traits men and women should possess. Studies since the 1970s have similarly asked respondents to rate these traits' desirability for men and women.

Prentice and Carranza (2002) found that strong prescriptive gender beliefs continue to exist and remain similar to those of the past. Warmth and communality were still seen as especially desirable in a woman, and social dominance (arrogant, controlling, rebellious) was still believed to be especially undesirable in a woman. For a man, assertive agency (aggressive, forceful, leaderlike, competitive) was particularly desirable, and submissive emotionality (yielding, emotional) was particularly undesirable. These results show that the prescriptive elements of traditional gender stereotypes are still very much with us. Both the core hierarchical (men should be dominant, women should not) and difference (women should be communal, men should be independent and competitive) dimensions of gender stereotypes continue to carry a prescriptive edge in cultural beliefs about how men and women should be.

Where Are We Now?

We have clear empirical evidence, then, that changes in gender stereotypes have lagged substantially behind changes in material arrangements between men and women. What hints of changes we see in contemporary stereotypes are those we would expect, given the nature of the changes that have occurred in men's and women's everyday material lives. Women's own self-perceptions, rather than their presumptions of most people's views, have particularly responded to changes in their status and workplace roles. Together, this evidence provides strong support for our argument that while the content of cultural beliefs about gender generally reflects the material resources and power that men and women command in society, changes in these cultural beliefs lag behind changes in the underlying material arrangements based on gender.

In the main, contemporary Americans continue to presume that most people hold remarkably traditional gender beliefs, particularly about how men and women should be. The core prescriptive traits that embody gender hierarchy and gender difference are especially unchanged. These dimensions of hierarchy and difference, in turn, are central to the use of gender as a primary frame for making sense of self and other and coordinating behavior on the basis of that understanding.

There are, however, some suggestions of change in the nature of the status beliefs that make up the hierarchical dimension of gender stereotypes. Gender status beliefs attach greater status worthiness and competence at "what counts" to men rather than women. Competence logically involves both underlying ability and the forceful capacity or effort to bring that ability successfully to bear on a task or problem (Koenig and Eagly 2006; Ridgeway and Correll 2004a). There is suggestive evidence that the presumed gap between the typical man's and woman's underlying ability has narrowed in descriptive, if not prescriptive, stereotypes, plausibly in response to women's growing labor force involvement. Consequently, the hierarchical dimension of gender status and competence increasingly turns on cultural perceptions that men and women continue to differ substantially in the forceful agency or dominance necessary to successful accomplishment. As we know, however, inequality requires the perception of difference. It is therefore equally significant that both descriptive and prescriptive contemporary stereotypes continue to represent strong gender differences in communality as well as forceful agency.

As contemporary men and women confront social situations at the edge of social change in the United States, then, the cultural stereotypes they have to draw on to frame their encounters with one another will be considerably more traditional than the innovative circumstances they face. The next question we need to consider, then, is the extent to which these trailing gender beliefs will cause them to reinscribe gender inequality into the new industries and social forms that they innovate.

GENDERING SITES OF INNOVATION

People routinely encounter material opportunities and pressures to do things differently than they have before. Most of these encounters with changing material circumstances occur within the framework of established workplace, community, or political organizations or established institutions such as the family. As we have seen, behavior in these established institutional contexts is framed by the backdrop of lagging cultural beliefs about gender, as well as the foreground of institutional schemas, rules, and procedures that are themselves implicitly gendered. Perhaps it is no surprise, then, that people's responses to material change in these established contexts frequently reframe the new possibilities into social patterns that continue to represent the core principles of gender difference and hierarchy, even if in slightly altered form.

Not all encounters with new material circumstances occur in established institutional contexts, however. People do innovate new forms of economic activity and develop new forms of social union. These sites at the edge of change, where people come together to innovate new ways of doing things, are typically small, interpersonal settings outside the direct control of a more encompassing organization. The garage that was the birthplace of an early computer company is an example. People come together in such settings with the explicit goal of pursuing an innovative idea for a new type of business or a new way of relating in intimate unions. Yet how do they deal with the inherent uncertainty of their task? How do they organize and coordinate their efforts to pursue their goal?

In an interpersonal setting like this, we know that the participants will cognitively categorize one another according to U.S. culture's primary person schemas, including sex/gender. We also know that this will implicitly prime lagging gender stereotypes and the stereotypes of other primary person categories, such as race. Thus participants in sites of innovation always have a background person frame, anchored in the primary frame of gender, to draw on to coordinate their behavior. This background frame, however, offers little specific guidance for pursuing the participants' goals in the setting. As a result, to organize their new context, participants also borrow more specifically from established institutional schemas that they are familiar with from related activities and settings. They may draw, for instance, on familiar ideas of how to divide work tasks or establish responsibility. Or they may draw on established schemas of heterosexual unions even in contexts where the explicit goal is to be free of such schemas in order to innovate.

People confront innovative settings, then, with a combination of a background framework of primary person categories and a foreground framework of borrowed institutional schemas for organizing behavior. In contrast to established settings, however, the normally powerful institutional schemas in the foreground are weakened as guides for behavior. The participants' goal in the setting, after all, is to innovate, to find new ways of doing things. This goal necessarily entails revising in some way the usual ways of doing things that are inscribed in the borrowed institutional schemas.

The relative weakening of the usual institutional frameworks for organizing behavior in innovative settings clears the way for the background person frame to have stronger effects on behavior, judgments, and emergent patterns of relationships. The inherent uncertainty of the innovative task, in the context of weakened institutional framing, creates greater ambiguity in the judgment of competence, performance, and value in the setting. These conditions of ambiguity enlarge the scope for implicit gender stereotype bias in the judgments and decisions that are made in the initial organization of these settings. Of course, the participants' goals of innovation, of doing things differently, may sometimes make them consciously resist gender stereotypes in their behavior. They may value diversity as an aid to innovation, for instance, or even intentionally pursue gender equality. Yet, the goals of innovation are not likely to undermine the impact of the background frame of gender as much as they do the foreground of institutional procedures. The gender frame not only is deeply rooted in people's basic habits of sense making in social situations but also shapes behavior unconsciously when people are not closely monitoring their actions.

The precise implications of the gender frame for patterns of relationships and gender inequality in the innovative site will depend on the context, as we will see. Furthermore, as we will also see, the contextually specific implications of the gender frame interact with the borrowed institutional logic in their effects on the relations that emerge between women and men in the new setting. To the extent, in turn, that the emergent relations between men and women embody gender inequality, those relations will affect whose interests are most directly represented in the new organizational blueprint of routines, procedures, and rules that the participants develop to pursue their goals. And to the extent that the innovative site becomes a model for an emerging new industry or new form of intimate union, that blueprint and the gender inequality inscribed in it will spread. In this way, the core principle of gender hierarchy will be transmitted in varying degrees forward into new forms of economic and social organization.

Stated abstractly, then, that is my analysis of how gender inequality persists in varying degrees even in sites of innovation. The basic analysis applies to how people confront the innovation of social unions, as well as new forms of work. I will start, however, by fleshing out the analysis with examples from the world of work. Gender in the workplace, as we know, is of central importance for the future of gender inequality because it is the principal arena through which men and women gain access to material rewards and positions of power in society. It is also the organizational arena in which there has been the greatest change in gender relations in recent years. The interdependent and self-reinforcing nature of gender patterns across various arenas of social life suggests that change in these patterns will come iteratively. That is, change will be greatest where it can build on earlier changes. The work world, then, is not only important for the future of gender inequality but also an arena in which there is a substantial possibility of change. To what extent does gender inequality persist even at innovative sites in the work world? To address this question, we examine research on small, pioneering firms in two key sites of innovation in the new economy: the biotech industry and the information technology industry. After looking at these innovative work sites, we will turn to a site of innovation in personal intimate unions among college students.

Innovative Workplaces in Biotech

Fundamental advances in the life sciences set the stage in the 1970s and 1980s for the emergence of a new type of industrial firm: the small, science-focused firm dedicated to the development of basic innovations in biotechnology (Smith-Doerr 2004). The size, structure, and dedication to scientific innovation characteristic of these firms distinguished them from the large, established pharmaceutical corporations that have always created products based on research in the life sciences. These pioneering small firms were the cutting edge of an emerging new industry that would become increasingly important in the economy.

The period of the 1970s and 1980s also coincided with a period in which women greatly increased their attainment of advanced educational degrees, including in some formerly male fields like the life sciences (England et al. 2007). In comparison to the physical sciences and engineering, women are much better represented in the life sciences, currently constituting about 30% of PhDs in the biological sciences (Smith-Doerr 2004, p. 103). Related to women's inroads into the life sciences, biology, unlike the physical sciences and engineering, is not a field that is strongly linked in American culture to the special skills of one sex rather than the other.

The mixed-gender composition of the available workforce and the relative gender neutrality of biology as a task create a context that shapes the nature of the biases that we would expect the gender frame to introduce into these small, innovative biotech firms. The substantial mix of women among life scientists is likely to make gender status beliefs effectively salient among the founders and workers in these firms, but only diffusely so. Gender's relevance to perceptions of competence will be reduced by the gender neutrality of the biological task. As a result, implicit performance expectations will only weakly favor men over similar women for core scientific work, although they should favor men more strongly for positions of substantial authority.

This background gender frame, however, will work its effects in the context of the organizational structures and procedures the founders of these firms draw on to organize the work. As sociologist Laurel Smith-Doerr (2004) describes in her intensive study of these biotech firms, most have drawn on an emerging new organizational logic referred to as the network form of organization. This form organizes research and development tasks as team projects, but the firm itself only specializes in key, cutting-edge aspects of these projects. To carry various projects to completion, the firm forms partnerships with a network of other firms that flexibly combine and recombine their specialties in joint teams to complete shared projects. The emphasis is on collective team accomplishment, flexible movement of scientists among teams as needed, team diversity as an aid to innovation, and a relatively flat hierarchy of control.

This form, as Smith-Doerr (2004) points out, offers a number of structural assets for women scientists who seek equal outcomes with their male colleagues. The flat hierarchy and team structure spread resources, information, and opportunities broadly, so that even socially different or marginalized scientists potentially have relatively equal access. The flexible teams also allow women scientists to agentically pursue their own success by moving as needed among teams and avoiding "bad actors" who might be biased against them. It similarly makes it more difficult for others, including those bad actors, to informally consolidate power in ways that allow them to block the women's advancement.

The informality of this distinctive organizational form and the way it is structured in terms of interpersonal networks also has a potential dark side, however, that we need to keep in mind. Its flexible, interpersonal nature potentially allows substantial scope for the gender frame to affect judgments and behavior. We should expect, then, that the extent to which women achieve equality with men in this new organizational form will depend on the extent to which the background frame of gender allows them to take advantage of the structural assets that the form offers.

As we have seen, the gender frame in the life sciences is only modestly disadvantaging to women. As a result, women should find it only slightly more difficult than similar men to prove their credibility as scientists in these firms. This baseline credibility, especially in combination with the organizational value placed on team diversity, should allow women to act effectively in the firm to take advantage of the structural opportunities it provides. Thus, we should expect women to do fairly well in these small biotech firms. Gender status beliefs still give men a slight advantage, however, so even here, in this best case organizational form, we should see some lingering gender inequality. This should be greatest in terms of positions of substantial authority.

What, then, do we find about the gender structures that emerge in these innovative biotech firms? Smith-Doerr (2004) shows that women in fact do rather well in them and better than similar women life scientists do in established hierarchical organizational settings, such as the university or large pharmaceutical firms. With the innovative firms' emphasis on diversity among their employees, women are hired into these firms in equal proportions to men relative to their representation in the pool of available PhDs. As for achievement once hired, an important coin of the realm in knowledge-producing firms is being named on a patent for a new discovery. Sociologist Kjersten Whittington, working with Smith-Doerr (2008), found that women scientists in these network biotech firms were just as likely as men to have at least one patent to their names. However, we see the remaining advantage the gender frame gives men in the fact that men nevertheless held significantly more patents on average than did similar women in these firms.

Promotion is also an important indicator of gender inequality. The flat hierarchies of network firms mean fewer and presumably weaker supervisory positions. Women, however, have a much greater chance of gaining one of these supervisory positions in network firms than in university or pharmaceutical settings, where supervisory positions are heavily male dominated (Smith-Doerr 2004). Women scientists still face a powerful glass ceiling at the next level, however, when they attempt to attract the venture capital necessary to found their own biotech start-ups (Smith-Doerr 2004). Lagging gender stereotypes about men's greater forceful agency and appropriateness for authority contribute to the fact that the founders of funded biotech start-ups are virtually all male.

What we see in small, innovative biotech firms, then, is pretty much what we would expect from the joint effects of the gender frame in that context and the organizational model of the network form. The gender frame rewrites some degree of gender inequality into workplace outcomes even in this potentially advantageous organizational frame. This provides a good illustration of how the persistence process works. Yet persistence is not all that happens in these firms. Change is forged as well. Because the gender frame only modestly disadvantages women in the biotech context, they are able to take advantage of the structural opportunities the network form offers them to come closer to equality with their male colleagues than do women life scientists in the established organizational contexts of universities and pharmaceutical corporations. The reduced but not eliminated gender inequality in innovative biotech firms in turn is likely to affect the procedures and routines these firms adopt. These implicitly more egalitarian routines increase the likelihood that the incorporation of women will persist as the firm develops. In the case of biotech, then, we see how gender inequality both persists over social and technological innovation and can be modified in the process by the forces of change.

Innovative Workplaces in Information Technology

Another key site of innovation and change in the economy is in the area of information technology (IT), broadly defined to cover the computer, software, telecommunications, and Internet industries. The leading edge of change in information technology is also the small, innovative research and development firm. Many of these small IT firms, too, have drawn on the network form to organize their activities. The consequences of this organizational form for gender inequality, however, have been quite different in the IT industry (McIlwee and Robinson 1992; Smith-Doerr 2004; Whittington 2007). The reason, I argue, is that the implications of the background gender frame for the expected competence and credibility of women engineers and scientists in the IT context are considerably more disadvantaging than in the biotech context.

Information technology is a field based on the physical sciences, mathematics, and engineering, all of which are strongly linked in American culture with the stereotypic skills of men. Relatedly, the gender composition of the pool of workers with advanced degrees in this area is considerably more male dominated than that of the life sciences. By our analysis, then, the gender-typed nature of the work should make gender status beliefs implicitly salient and task relevant for participants in these innovative IT firms. As a consequence, these status beliefs will strongly bias expectations for competence and performance in favor of men.

For women scientists and engineers, implicit biases against their competence turn the flexibility and informality of the network form from a strategic asset to a disadvantage. Burdened by the implicit biases of employers and coworkers, we would expect women to face an uphill battle proving their credibility and value as project team members. Without substantial credibility, they will have difficulty taking advantage of the structural flexibility to move effectively around obstacles and successfully pursue promising opportunities. Furthermore, the gender typing of the work and the skewed gender composition of the workers may lead to in-group biases and the development of a masculine workplace culture (Martin forthcoming). In this context, an old boy network could implicitly take over the flexible structure and dominate opportunities for achievement. Fed by lagging stereotypes that act through the background frame of gender, then, gender inequality could be powerfully reinscribed into the routines and practices of the innovative IT firm.

Given this analysis, perhaps we should not be surprised to learn that when Kjersten Whittington (2007) studied patenting among industry scientists, she found that women physical scientists and engineers were no less disadvantaged in small, less hierarchical research firms than they were in large corporations. In both contexts, women held significantly fewer patents on average than otherwise similar male colleagues. Furthermore, unlike in the biotech industry, women in small, less hierarchical IT firms were less likely to hold even one patent than men and were no better off in this way than women physical scientists and engineers in large corporations.

Further evidence that the informality and flexibility of the flat hierarchy, network form of organization does not pay off for women scientists in IT comes from a classic study by Judith McIlwee and Gregg Robinson (1992). The researchers compared women engineers in a small, decentralized computer start-up with those in a large, established aerospace corporation. Women, they found, were much less likely to be promoted to senior engineers or management in the start-up than in the rule based corporation. As we have seen before, when informal stereotype bias is likely to be especially disadvantaging to women, formal rules and procedures can level the playing field a bit. In a situation in which informal bias is substantial, the leveling effects of formal rules can be relatively advantageous to women, even when these rules themselves are not entirely without bias in their effects.

The best evidence of how the background frame of gender especially disadvantages women in small, innovative IT firms comes from a study of high-tech start-up firms in Silicon Valley (Baron et al. 2007). The great majority of these start-ups were IT firms, although some biotech firms were also included. Founders and CEOs of these firms were asked to describe the organizational model or blueprint they had in mind when they first started the firm. The researchers classified these founding blueprints into five different organizational logics, but a particular contrast can be made between the interpersonally oriented "commitment" model and the rule-based "bureaucracy" model. The commitment model emphasizes company culture, fitting in, and informal peer group control instead of the specialized roles and formal control of bureaucracy. In the context of the masculinized culture of most of these high-tech firms, this commitment logic is likely to be especially problematic for women because it allows a fuller scope for stereotypic gender bias to operate in the background.

As we would expect, then, when the researchers examined the proportion of women incorporated into core scientific roles in these start-ups, they found that that proportion grew significantly faster in start-ups that followed a bureaucratic logic rather than other logic. Start-ups based on a commitment logic were especially slow to incorporate women scientists (Baron et al. 2007).

The researchers in this study were aware that although formal rules reduce the scope for individual stereotype bias, the rules can at the same time incorporate and objectify that bias in the way they are implemented. As we saw in chapter 4, the stereotype biases operating in the interpersonal contexts in which rules and the procedures for applying them are first developed can write subtle gender biases into the procedures themselves. The researchers, in fact, found that when a bureaucratic logic was adopted in the early, interpersonally oriented days of the start-up, it tended not to have a lasting positive effect on the incorporation of women scientists into the firm, probably because bias itself was subtly built into the rules and procedures. Formal rules and procedures had the strongest positive effect on the gender mix of scientists in the firm when they were adopted a little later, as a corrective to the informal, interpersonally structured days at the beginning (Baron et al. 2007).

Although bureaucratic rules offer a modest corrective to the powerful inscribing of gender inequality into innovative IT firms, there is a final irony here. Among the Silicon Valley start-ups included in the study, the researchers found that those organized on the commitment model were among those most likely to be well received by the market and were the least likely to fail over the period of study (Baron et al. 2007). Thus, the best received IT start-ups tended to be the ones that followed an organizational blueprint that was least hospitable to women scientists and most vulnerable to producing a boys' club–oriented company culture. Here we see a powerful effect of the way lagging cultural beliefs about gender continue to link IT work to the expertise of men. Working through the background frame of gender in social relations, these trailing cultural beliefs inscribe gender inequality into the very fabric of the most successful IT start-ups.

The Persistence of Gendered Logics

Baron and his colleagues' studies of high-tech start-ups show not only how the founding blueprints of these firms can be infused with gender implications, but also how these organizational blueprints can have lasting implications for how men and women fare within the firm. The blueprints established by founders, the researchers discovered, continued to shape the firm's basic organizational procedures well after the founders themselves left the firms (Baron et al. 2002). As these procedures persisted, so did the gendered logics that they implied.

Furthermore, as small, innovative start-ups pioneer new industries at the edge of change in the economy, the gendered regimes embodied in the organizational practices and procedures that they develop are likely to spread to other new firms that develop in the industry. Organizational behavior scholar Damon Phillips (2005) provides a good example of how this occurs in his study of the "organizational genealogies" of Silicon Valley law firms. Phillips linked the founders of new firms with the parent firms in which they had previously worked. He found that the extent to which women were institutionalized as leaders (i.e., as partners) rather than just as subordinates (associates) in the parent firm predicted the opportunities for advancement women experienced in the new firm that the founder created. Phillips's evidence suggests that this did not occur simply because the parent firm gave the founder personal experience with women in leadership. Personal experience was not the most important factor. Instead, it seemed that founders transferred the parent firm's organizational routines (i.e., blueprints) to their new firms. As they did so, they unintentionally transferred to the new firms the implicit gender hierarchy embedded in those routines. The more similarly work was organized in the new firm to the way it was in the parent firm, the more powerfully gender hierarchy in the parent firm predicted gender inequality in the new firms.

The way the background frame of gender infuses gender inequality into the organizational routines of small, pioneering firms, then, potentially has long-range consequences for the future of gender inequality in the workplace as the economy changes and new industries emerge. As members of early firms found new ones, these emerging organizational blueprints spread. Some eventually become dominant templates for the industry. As they do, the gender hierarchy embedded in these templates comes to characterize the emerging industry.

The effects of the spread of emerging organizational routines cut two ways in regard to the persistence of gender inequality. As we saw in the case of small, network-organized biotech firms, under some circumstances, pioneering firms can become social laboratories in which modified organizational routines develop that foster less gender inequality than in more established, less innovative organizations in the same field. Presumably, the spread of these routines to new firms in the field will spread with it improved opportunities for women's advancement. Given that change in the gender system is typically iterative, it is not surprising that these improvements have occurred in the life sciences, where they build on previous advances for women, compared with other scientific fields.

The case of small, innovative information technology firms is quite different, however. This is a context in which lagging cultural beliefs about gender powerfully disadvantage women. As a consequence, the background frame of gender causes even the apparently promising network form of organization to play out in a manner that results in substantial gender inequality among the scientists and engineers in these firms. As this inequality subtly infuses the organizational practices of these firms, the spread of these practices to new firms reconstructs the material structure of gender hierarchy for the new economy.

Innovative Intimate Unions: The College Hook-up

Sites of change in the work world are important for the future of gender inequality because of the direct impact they have on men's and women's access to material resources and power and because, as sites in which much gender change has already occurred, they are likely sites for additional change. Intimate heterosexual unions, however, are also terrifically important for the future of gender inequality. As we have seen, they not only provide their own sources of interpersonal power and access to material resources but also powerfully affect the availability of men and women for positions of power and resources in the public worlds of work and politics. Much is at stake as well, then, at sites of change in the intimate, heterosexual unions that people form. How do lagging gender stereotypes affect the change or persistence of inequality at these sites?

More lasting heterosexual unions typically emerge from a more casual sorting process in which men and women meet one another and engage in exploratory personal and sexual contacts. For the past few decades, the traditional structure of this sorting process was the casual date, in which a man asked a woman to accompany him for some social event. Recently on college campuses, however, this traditional dating process has become a site of change and social innovation, as several researchers have documented (see Hamilton and Armstrong 2009).

Changing material circumstances over the past several decades have set the stage for this social innovation (England, Shafer, and Fogarty 2008; Hamilton and Armstrong 2009). A sexual revolution, spurred by the increasing availability of the birth control pill from the 1960s on, has led to more permissive norms about premarital sex among women as well as men. Accompanying this sexual revolution has been the post-1970 gender revolution, in which women have flooded into higher education and taken on increasingly successful work careers. More women than men now graduate from college, and these women increasingly anticipate careers similar to their male peers (Englandand Li 2006). As part of this anticipation, college women, especially middle-class ones, often expect to delay marriage and commitment until after college (Hamilton and Armstrong 2009). These patterns of change have altered the material terms on which young men and women in college encounter one another and explore the formation of intimate unions. In a world in which college women feel freer, sexually, and more empowered, socially, than in past decades, the old dating script, in which men asked and women waited to be asked, was ripe for revision.

As women and men on college campuses have begun to pioneer alternatives to the casual date, what would we expect to see from the perspective of the argument we have been pursuing in this chapter? First, it is clear that the background frame of gender will be highly salient to participants and strongly relevant to their behavior and judgments. Forming a heterosexual bond is a quintessentially gendered goal. The institutional frame of the traditional dating and romantic courtship script will also be salient, but its impact will be greatly weakened by the participants' explicit goal of doing things differently. Thus, participants will pursue their intended goals of egalitarian relations in which women are active sexual agents like men against the powerful but implicit backdrop of lagging gender stereotypes about gender difference and male status dominance. As they try to make sense of their uncertain new circumstances, we should expect that they will unconsciously draw on those old stereotypes and, as they do, rewrite inequality and male status dominance into the new cultural blueprints they forge for casual intimate encounters.

Between 2004 and 2007, sociologist Paula England and her colleagues surveyed more than 4,000 undergraduates at five large state and private universities and conducted personal interviews with a smaller group of these students (England et al. 2008). Since 2007, England and additional colleagues expanded the survey to more than 10,000 additional students at many more college campuses across the country (England, personal communication). Their findings have confirmed that the casual date has been replaced by the hook-up as the primary means of making an initial intimate heterosexual connection on college campuses. Hook-ups occur when a man and a woman encounter one another in a casual, mixed-sex social setting, such as hanging out at a pizza place or at a party, and end up splitting off for sexual contact of some sort that might or might not include intercourse. Hook-ups imply no affectional commitment or necessary interest in future contact. Like the casual date it has replaced, however, hook-ups do sometimes lead to repeat hook-ups and eventual relationships.

In some respects, the hook-up is a considerably freer and less constrained format for initial intimate contacts than the stylized date. Men and women socialize and attend events in looser, less exclusive, and more casual mixed-sex groups. Intimacy and sexual contact then emerge out of that socializing process based on individual interest. We should not be surprised to learn, however, that in other respects, the gender structure of hook-ups remains constraining and unequal.

The students England and her colleagues (2008; England, personal communication) studied reported that women were only a bit less likely than men to initiate the intimate talking and dyadic focus that began the hook-up process. After that, however, things become considerably more stereotypically gendered and unequal. Men were reported as the ones who typically initiated the move to sexual interaction. Interestingly, women were especially likely to see men as the sexual initiators. This suggests that men interpreted some sexual contacts differently than the women did, possibly in response to gender stereotypes, or that these same stereotypes made women more reluctant to report their own initiation of sexual activity. The most dramatic evidence of the persistence of male status dominance, however, can be seen in the nature of the sexual interaction that students reported. The researchers found that the focus of the sexual activities both male and female students reported was more often oriented toward the male's sexual pleasure than the female's pleasure. Perhaps as a result, men were twice as likely as women to experience orgasm from any given type of sexual contact. An intensive qualitative study of the hook-up experiences of women in a Midwestern college dormitory found very similar results (Hamilton and Armstrong 2009).

The continuing impact of male status dominance and lingering ideas of men's and women's stereotypic natures can also be seen in the social reputations that male and female students acquire for engaging in hook-ups (England et al. 2008; Hamilton and Armstrong 2009). Although some hooking-up is accepted practice, men and women who are thought to have hook-ups with too many people or to have sex too casually acquire distinctive reputations. These reputations are judged by a familiar double standard that clearly shows the impact of lagging gender stereotypes on students' judgments. Both male and female students referred to women who hooked up too often as "sluts." Similar men were sometimes criticized by women as "man whores" but were also often praised as "studs," especially by other men. Reputations of this sort create a structure of norms and sanctions among students that reinforce a surprisingly traditional structure of gender inequality in sexual relations between men and women on campus.

The hook-up is an innovative new social form at the edge of change in intimate heterosexual unions. It is changing the path by which young men and women, at least on college campuses, forge intimate ties that move them toward more lasting relationships. Yet the implicit effects of lagging gender stereotypes on students' behavior and judgments of one another have reinscribed gender hierarchy into the shared normative blueprints that have emerged to structure this new social form. As the hook-up form becomes increasingly mainstream on college campuses and perhaps spreads more broadly among young adults, the structure of inequality that it implies spreads as well. In this way, the hook-up form reestablishes gender hierarchy in intimate social relations for a new era. Despite the changing and increasingly egalitarian material terms on which young men and women encounter one another, then, lagging cultural beliefs about gender continue to cause substantial inequality to persist in close heterosexual bonds.

SUMMARY AND CONCLUSIONS

How then does gender inequality persist in the modern world despite the ongoing stream of social, political, and economic changes that alter the very material arrangements on which it seems, at any given time, to depend? In this chapter, we returned to this question armed with the insights we have gained from our previous investigations of how gender functions as a primary frame for coordinating social relations; how, through this coordination process, cultural beliefs about gender shape behavior and judgments; how this process plays out in the workplace and the home; and how it infuses gendered meanings into the structures and practices by which work and home are organized. These previous investigations had already given us an important piece of the answer to the persistence puzzle. In chapters 4 and 5, we saw how the background activation of gender status beliefs within existing economic arrangements and accepted cultural conceptions of close heterosexual bonds shapes behavior and evaluations in those contexts in ways that reproduce gender inequality and blunt the impact of forces for change. Thus gender inequality persists partly because everyday reliance on the gender frame in social relations has embedded beliefs about gender status and difference in established institutions of work and family that powerfully control access to resources and power.

The leading edge of change in society, however, consists of sites outside established social institutions where new forms of work or new types of heterosexual union are innovated. These sites of innovation often become templates for the future, and so the future of gender as a principle of social organization and inequality depends on them. Answering the persistence question requires us to look closely at how the gender frame works at these sites of change.

Above all, however, answering the persistence question requires us to look more deeply into the relationship between the cultural beliefs about gender status in which gender inequality is rooted in contemporary society and the material distributions of resources and power between men and women. The nature of this relationship is key to how the persistence process works throughout society but especially at sites of economic and social innovation. In this chapter, I have argued that change in cultural beliefs about gender *lag* changes in material circumstances between men and women and that this lag is the central factor that allows gender inequality to persist in the face of social and economic forces that work to undermine it. As a consequence, when people come together at sites of innovation, the cultural beliefs about gender that are activated in the background for them are more traditional than their new circumstances. To the extent that they draw on these beliefs to help organize their uncertain new project, they implicitly inscribe trailing assumptions about gender status into the new practices and social forms that they create. This is the heart of the persistence process. In this chapter, we analyzed it in detail.

The first step was to examine the argument that cultural gender beliefs lag changes in material arrangements between men and women. Research has documented two related processes that buffer gender stereotypes from the immediate impact of disconfirming gender experiences. At the level of individual cognition, the commitment most people have to gender as a primary frame for understanding self and other fuels largely unconscious tendencies to perceive and interpret events and people in terms that confirm gender stereotypic expectations. In addition, the presumption that gender stereotypes are common knowledge inhibits the public expression of stereotype-disconfirming behavior or information. Based on these buffering processes, we expected that the core prescriptive elements of gender stereotypes (hierarchy and difference) that carry inhibiting sanctions should be slowest to change, followed by the descriptive aspects of gender stereotypes. People's individual perceptions about their own gendered traits may change more easily, but due to confirmation biases, even these will lag material change.

We next turned to empirical evidence about how changes in gender beliefs have corresponded to material changes in women's position in society. There is strong evidence that changes in gendered self-perceptions have tracked changes in women's status and roles over the last several decades so that women have closed the gender gap with men in how assertive they describe themselves to be. Yet, these changes in self-perceived assertiveness have lagged about 10 years behind changes in women's positions in society.

We expected less change in gender stereotypes than in self-perceptions, and the evidence confirmed this as well. Perceived differences between typical men and women on the softer aspects of agency associated with cognitive ability have narrowed recently, but there has been little change on forceful agentic traits (men are still rated higher) or on communal traits (women are still rated much higher). Despite these few changes in descriptive stereotypes, there has been almost no change in prescriptive stereotypes. Both the core hierarchical (men should be dominant, women should not) and difference (women should be communal, men independent) dimensions retain a clear prescriptive edge in contemporary stereotypes. The evidence indicates, then, that cultural beliefs about gender do slowly respond to changes in women's and men's material circumstances, but changes in gender beliefs clearly lag behind material changes.

We next considered how trailing gender beliefs affect behaviors and judgments at sites of innovation. These sites are typically small, interpersonal settings in which the impact of borrowed institutional frameworks for organizing behavior are weakened by the goals of innovation and in which there is inherent uncertainty about how to proceed. These factors increase the likelihood that actors will implicitly draw on the background frame of gender to help organize their new activities, but the exact effects depend on contextual factors that affect the salience and relevance of gender to the new setting. We examined how this works at two sites of economic innovation, biotechnology and information technology start-up firms, and a site of innovation in personal intimate unions among college students.

Since the life sciences are no longer strongly gender typed, the background gender frame is salient in biotech start-ups, but only diffusely so, and it creates only modest disadvantages for women scientists in expectations for competence. The physical sciences and engineering remain strongly male typed so that the gender frame in IT firms is more powerfully relevant and more strongly disadvantages women scientists in expectations for competence. We examined evidence of how these effects play out in the context of the informal, team-oriented structure of work by which many high-tech firms are organized. Studies show that in biotech, women end up nearly (although not quite) as successful as their male colleagues and more successful than women in traditional, established life science firms. In IT firms, however, strongly disadvantaging expectations make the informal structure problematic for women's success. The IT firms that are organized according to a commitment blueprint that emphasizes informal fitting in are especially problematic for women scientists and engineers.

These studies show that the background gender frame continues to infuse gender inequality into the organizational routines of small pioneering firms at the edge of economic change. The result is both persistence and change. In biotech firms, the interaction between the less disadvantaging gender frame and the flexible structure allows these firms to develop modified organizational routines that foster less gender inequality than established institutions. In IT firms, however, the more powerfully problematic gender frame results in organizational routines that embed substantial inequality into the templates of a new industry. The organizational practices and routines these start-ups develop are consequential because they not only have persistent effects over the life of the firm but also spread to other start-ups in the field, carrying their implications for gender inequality with them.

Lagging gender stereotypes also affect the persistence or change of inequality in intimate heterosexual unions. Studies show that among college students, the traditional date has been increasingly replaced by the hook-up, a new, more casual form of intimate sexual encounter with an explicitly egalitarian ethos. Yet, lagging gender stereotypes have structured the norms and practices of this new intimate form in ways that result in substantial inequality in sexual outcomes.

At sites of innovation in forms of both work and social union, then, we see clear evidence of the persistence process in action. The contextually specific implications of trailing gender beliefs interact with the developing organizational logic of the innovative setting to shape the relations that emerge between men and women there. Those relations and the inequality they embody affect whose interests are most directly represented in the new organizational blueprint that comes to define the innovative setting. To the extent that the innovative site becomes a model for a new industry or form of intimate union, that blueprint and the gender inequality inscribed in it spread. In this way, the core principle of gender hierarchy is transmitted forward into new forms of economic and social organization. The extent of the hierarchy embedded in the new form, however, is sometimes less than that of established institutions. Since change in the gender system is iterative, it is greatest where it can build on earlier progress toward equality. Not surprisingly, then, emergent new blueprints for social forms are more likely to embody reduced gender inequality in the world of work than in intimate relations, where there has been less change overall, and especially in work settings that have become less gender typed.

SEVEN

Implications For Change

IN THIS BOOK, I have tried to reveal the often unrecognized forces that perpetuate gender inequality even in the modern context. It is only natural, however, to ask what the implications of these forces are for the ultimate achievement of gender equality. Contemporary levels of gender inequality represent a dynamic, changing balance between forces that act to undermine gender as a principle of inequality and those forces that have been our focus here—the ones that act to continually reconstruct it. Given this dynamic relationship, in addressing the persistence question, we have from the beginning necessarily also discussed the countervailing processes by which change comes about. In the last chapter in particular, we looked closely at the two-sided processes of change and persistence in cultural beliefs about gender and in the processes by which gendered assumptions are reinscribed into new forms of social and economic organization. Thus, we have already said quite a lot about how social, economic, and technological processes—and, especially, women's own interests in bettering their lives—alter the material terms on which men and women encounter one another and, in so doing, put pressure on cultural beliefs about gender to change in response. My purpose in this final chapter is not simply to revisit those arguments. Instead, my intent is to take up in brief form some lingering, deeper questions about the implications for inequality of people's use of gender as a primary frame for organizing social relations. If people use gender as a primary frame for relating to others, does that in itself make gender inequality virtually unstoppable?

To understand what this question entails, we need to go back to some basic points that I made at the very beginning of this book. Notice that I am asking whether gender inequality, once it exists, as it does now, becomes unstoppable because of the effects of the gender frame on social relations. Thus I am not now, as I was not at the beginning, asking questions about the historical origins or ultimate causes of gender inequality. Recall that the social relational processes through which the gender frame works mediate the persistence of inequality independently of ultimate causes. As I commented early on, however, I personally am unconvinced that there are any ultimate, determinative biological causes that make male dominance inevitable in the modern context. This assumption will be reflected in the background of my comments here. What I am asking now, however, is something different. I am asking whether the mediational use of gender as a cultural frame for social relations itself makes gender inequality virtually impossible to defeat—independent of discussions of biological or other ultimate causes.

There are three aspects of the gender-framing argument that might raise questions about whether gender hierarchy can be overcome. First, is it feasible that the use of sex/gender as a primary cultural frame for relating to others can be eliminated? Second, if it is not likely that people will stop using sex/gender as a primary frame for social relations, does this mean that gender inequality (if not necessarily male dominance) is virtually inevitable? Third, I have argued that change in the common knowledge cultural beliefs that make up the gender frame lags behind change in material arrangements between men and women. This, I have argued, is central to the processes by which gender hierarchy persists in the face of social and economic transformations. But do lagging cultural beliefs about gender also mean that gender inequality is unstoppable because beliefs never catch up with egalitarian forces? These are questions that I will briefly address in this chapter. As I do so, I will consider along the way where egalitarian change is most likely and most needed in the gender system.

AN END TO THE GENDER FRAME?

Gender works as a primary frame for social relations through two mutually reinforcing social processes. First, we learn from early childhood to automatically sex-categorize any person we attempt to relate to in any concrete way. Second, we also learn early on to associate the categories of male and female with widely shared gender stereotypes that define how the sexes are expected to behave. When we sex-categorize another in an effort to relate, these stereotypes are cognitively primed and made available to shape our impression of the other, even though, as we have seen, the extent to which they do so varies substantially with the context.

Automatic sex categorization, then, is the insidious process that transforms the gender frame into something that we apply to virtually everyone in every situation as we initiate the process of coordinating our behavior with others. To really end gender as we know it—that is, to end it as a distinct system of social practices for constituting males and females as different and for organizing social relations on the basis of that difference—we would need to stop automatically sex-categorizing everyone (Ridgeway and Correll 2000). Given its relevance to sex and reproduction, it is implausible to imagine that people will not learn to sex-categorize others. But could sex categorization become more discretionary and less automatic? Could people come to simply not notice the sex of others they deal with in contexts without any relevance to sex or reproduction? If this happened, gender would lose its status as a primary frame, and its role in organizing inequality would necessarily be greatly diminished.

Yet is this feasible? Personally, I doubt it. Sex categorization is the first social identity we learn for making sense of self and other (Zemore et al. 2000). From early childhood, our reliance on sex-categorizing others is deeply rooted in the very processes by which we learn to form and carry out social relationships (Maccoby 1998). And not only does routine sex categorization have deep roots in our fundamental understandings of how we coordinate our behavior with others but also it is equally fundamental to our understandings of our selves.

As one of the three or so identities that are most important to make sense of self and other in society, gender is central to the process by which people render themselves comprehensible to themselves in terms that are socially valid in their society. The sense of social confusion and even anxiety that many experience when they must deal with a sex-unclassifiable person is not just due to their confusion about who the other is. It is also due to the way an unclassifiable person challenges the stability and validity of their own identity as a man or woman. The depth of people's emotional investment in their social (not just physical) identities as male or female gives them a potentially powerful interest in continuing to enact sex/gender as a primary identity frame for social relations. For this reason, I doubt that people would willingly or easily unlearn their habits of routine sex categorization, even if they are capable of doing so (which I personally believe they are). In my view, then, the use of sex/gender as a primary frame for social relations is not likely to end anytime soon. If people ever do reduce their tendency to automatically sex-categorize, I suspect that it will be as a consequence, not as an antecedent cause, of substantial gender equality.

DOES THE GENDER FRAME MAKE INEQUALITY VIRTUALLY INEVITABLE?

As a frame for coordinating behavior, the gender frame is rooted in accepted beliefs about gender difference. Yet, as I argued in chapter 2, difference easily becomes inequality, especially among categories of people, like men and women, who must regularly cooperate with one another to achieve what they want and need in life. Given that people are not likely to stop using sex/gender as a primary frame for social relations, does this mean that the transformation of beliefs about gender difference into beliefs about gender status inequality is virtually inevitable? Does that, in turn, mean that it will be almost impossible to defeat contemporary gender status beliefs because they will simply be re-created in new form?

There is no denying that the use of sex/gender as a primary frame does continually expose beliefs about gender difference to the risk of becoming gender status beliefs. Recall from chapter 2 why this is the case. When people work together on a shared goal, hierarchies of status and influence tend to develop as the participants organize their efforts to achieve the goal. When these people also have categorized each other as different on a social distinction such as sex, there is always a chance that they will associate their status and influence in the local setting with their social difference and begin to form a status belief about that social difference (Ridgeway 1991; Ridgeway and Erickson 2000). Other factors must be present for such fleeting, initial status beliefs to consolidate and spread to become widely held gender status beliefs, but still, there is always a risk that this could happen (Mark, Smith-Lovin, and Ridgeway 2009; Ridgeway et al. 2009). Although the status beliefs that develop in this way could logically favor either women or men, in the context of a history of male status superiority, the strain will be to reestablish status beliefs favoring men.

The use of sex/gender as a primary frame, then, does create an ongoing risk of repeatedly re-creating gender status inequality. Indeed, this has been a major part of my argument in this book. Yet there are good reasons to believe that this risk can be overcome. As a consequence, although it may not be easy to defeat gender inequality, I do not believe that the gender frame makes this goal effectively impossible. In my view, the risk of continually regenerating gender inequality plausibly could be overcome through two interrelated processes: reducing gender status beliefs and reducing the range of contexts in which gender is culturally perceived as sufficiently relevant to measurably shape influence and status.

Reducing Gender Status Beliefs

The enduring source of gender inequality in the modern context is the widespread acceptance of *diffuse* status beliefs about gender that are embedded in gender stereotypes. Recall that diffuse status beliefs associate men with greater *general* competence (i.e., performance capacity), as well as superior specific skills at the tasks that count most in society. It is not unreasonable to expect that the diffuse nature of gender status beliefs could be eroded. The essential first step would be to undermine beliefs in overall, general competence differences between men and women. The evidence suggests that this is already happening to some extent. As we saw in chapter 6, women's increasingly similar involvement in the workforce compared with men and the gains women have made in positions of power throughout society have begun to be reflected in stereotypes of competence differences between the sexes. Typical women are no longer assumed to be less intelligent or analytical than men. Instead, the presumption of men's greater overall performance capacity increasingly is vested only in assumptions about their greater forceful agency (Cejka and Eagly 1999; Diekman and Eagly 2000; Koenig and Eagly 2006). To the extent that women continue to make gains in the instrumental world of work and power, it seems reasonable that assumptions about differences in forceful agency could decline as well.

Clearly, then, the gap is narrowing in beliefs about general competence differences between the sexes. As this gap closes, cultural beliefs about gender could fracture into a collection of *specific* status beliefs that advantage men in some settings and women in others. In the absence of beliefs about general competence differences between men and women, it is logically possible that this collection of specific gender status beliefs could create no clear-cut, overall status advantage for either sex. This is one way that the risks for inequality posed by using gender as a primary frame could be managed without entailing substantial gender inequality. Recall from chapter 2 that this state of affairs may in fact have characterized some small foraging societies that have been relatively gender egalitarian.

In the contemporary U.S. context, however, there is a problem with this prospect of gender as a set of specific status beliefs. The tasks at which men are believed to be more skilled are currently more valued than those at which women are thought to especially excel. In the present situation, then, specific gender status beliefs would still give men an overall status advantage. Consequently, to truly erode diffuse status beliefs that advantage men over women, the gap must be closed not only in beliefs about general competence but also between the value of feminine- and masculine-typed tasks. In the modern context, this effectively means that caregiving, which is stereotyped as the most essential feminine task, must come to be valued more like agentic, stereotypically masculine tasks.

The most likely way for caregiving to acquire a value in cultural beliefs that is more equal to that associated with agentic tasks is for men to take on a greater share of these tasks. If men, through their involvement, lend their higher status to these tasks, the value of the tasks will rise (and the status of men decline). This, of course, brings us back to the household division of labor. As we saw in chapter 5, the household division of labor has been one of the most obdurate features of the gender structure of contemporary America. It feeds gender inequality in the workforce as well. Bringing men into major responsibility for routine, familial caregiving is clearly essential for the achievement of gender equality in contemporary society.

Because caregiving is culturally understood as the essence of the feminine, a major reassignment of family caregiving tasks may create gender anxieties for both men and women. Not only might some men feel defensive about taking on a great deal of routine caregiving but also some women might feel they are giving up something unique and special. Even so, given the inherent rewards of some aspects of caregiving, bringing men into these tasks in a more major way does not seem an impossible goal. Similarly, women have clearly shown that the attractions of paid work and achievement are sufficient to draw them beyond an exclusive focus on caregiving. Thus, while closing the gap in the value placed on stereotypically masculine and feminine tasks is a formidable task, it does not seem to be an impossible one.

Even though people continue to use gender as a primary frame to make sense of social relations, its implications for inequality could also be reduced if cultural assumptions about gender's perceived relevance for some social tasks were to decline. This is equivalent to broadening the range of tasks that are culturally understood to be gender neutral rather than linked to the specific skills of one sex rather than the other. If cultural beliefs about the gendered connotations of tasks were to weaken, it would reduce the number of contexts in which gender acts as a specific, directly relevant status characteristic that substantially biases judgments and behavior.

Recall that although sex categorization cognitively primes gender stereotypes, the net impact of these stereotypes on inequality in a specific context depends on the extent to which gender is culturally linked to the context and on the extent to which other advantaging or disadvantaging factors present overwhelm the effects of gender. Gender, after all, is a background identity that always works its effects in combination with other contextually salient identities. Indeed, the way this exposes gender assumptions to other contextually created inequalities, such as that between a (woman) boss and (male) subordinate, is precisely what allows changing distributions of resources and power between men and women to gradually change gender beliefs. This same process can be exploited to reduce the cultural associations between gender and performance at various tasks.

To the extent that changing material circumstances create more and more situations in which the effects of gender stereotypes on expectations are overwhelmed by the impact of other, more contextually powerful factors, people have more and more experiences in which gender is not very diagnostic about who best can accomplish the task at hand. In these situations, the background identity of gender is effectively pushed more deeply into the background, and the task begins to take on a more gender-neutral connotation. Situations like this are most likely to occur in the work world both because women increasingly participate in this world on similar terms as men and because work institutions have structures of power and resources that are based on many factors other than gender. As we have seen before, change in the gender system occurs through iterative processes so that future change comes most easily in sites like the work world where previous progress has already been made.

We saw an example of such a shift in the gender typing of work tasks in our discussion in chapter 6 of women life scientists working in biotechnology start-up firms. Recall that with the growing number of women gaining advanced degrees in the life sciences in the last few decades, the formerly masculine connotation of this field has dissipated. This in turn has reduced the relevance of the gender frame in life science workplaces, weakening implicit gender biases and making it easier for women to succeed in those contexts. In the biotech start-ups we examined, women were able to exploit the opportunities made available by a weakened gender frame to achieve near parity with their male colleagues. Successes such as this by women in innovative sectors of the life sciences field further weaken the power of the gender frame in workplaces organized around the life sciences. Thus, it is certainly feasible that a wider range of workplace tasks could come to be perceived by those involved as relatively gender neutral in connotation.

Several significant cautions, however, must be kept in mind in considering this scenario for limiting inequality by reducing gender's perceived relevance for workplace tasks. Most important, workplace tasks will shift from gendered to more neutral only if men and women work on those tasks in the same jobs or teams rather than in sex-segregated positions and if the sex compositions of the jobs remain gender integrated rather than tip to the other sex (Kalev 2009). Many tasks and jobs, after all, have shifted from masculine to feminine in connotation (e.g., residential real estate sales), but this does not reduce the relevance of the gender frame in those work contexts (Reskin and Roos 1990).

Also, to truly reduce the relevance of the gender frame in the workplace, it is not just the case that women must take on men's typically more desirable tasks and jobs. Men must take on women's tasks and jobs, and these are usually less rewarded. Thus the problem of reducing gender's relevance in the workplace is also tied up with the issue of revaluing tasks associated with women.

A final caution to keep in mind is that even when the implications of gender for inequality in the context are weakened because the task takes on a more neutral association, the impact of gender status will not be completely diminished unless cultural beliefs about general competence differences also dissipate. Recall that we saw the lingering effects of these diffusely relevant gender beliefs even in those biotech start-ups where women otherwise did so well. The most likely scenario, then, would be that reductions in the perceived relevance of gender to various workplace tasks will develop in a mutually reinforcing process with declining beliefs in general competence differences between the sexes and declining differences in the value attached to male and female tasks. To the extent that diffuse gender status beliefs are eroded and more workplace tasks become gender neutral, people in these settings will still sex-categorize each other as way of jump-starting their understanding of one another, but the effective implications for inequality will be slight.

Nevertheless, there remains one important social context in which the prospects for reducing the relevance of the gender frame are slight. This, of course, is the heterosexual couple and households based on such couples. Given that such unions are based on sex difference, sex/gender will necessarily be salient for people in these unions and only too handy as basis for the household division of labor. It is not likely, then, that the impact of the gender frame on inequality in the heterosexual family can be overcome by pushing it into the deep background of how family members relate to one another. If the gender frame cannot be ignored in the heterosexual family, then its implications for inequality must be addressed more directly. Again, the only real solution will be to draw men even more fully into caregiving and responsibility for household work. This is a bedrock problem around which the achievement of gender equality turns.

DO LAGGING GENDER BELIEFS MAKE INEQUALITY IMPOSSIBLE?

I have argued that the use of gender as a primary frame for social relations does indeed pose risks for the perpetuation of gender inequality but that it is not impossible that these risks could be overcome in the modern context. Much of what I have suggested about how this could occur involves modifying gender status beliefs through changes in the workplace and in the household division of labor. Yet there is a lingering question here. I have also shown that changes in cultural beliefs about gender lag substantially behind changes in the material circumstances of men's and women's lives. The core dimensions of the beliefs that represent gender status hierarchy in addition to difference seem especially slow to change. Does this make equality unachievable because lagging beliefs will always blunt the impact of egalitarian material changes and reestablish material inequality in new forms?

The logical answer to this is no, at least if considered over the long run. In speaking of the processes by which material conditions erode and reshape cultural beliefs about gender, I have often used the image of waves moving a sandbar (Ridgeway and Correll 2000).

A single wave seems to have little effect, but a repeating, pounding pattern of waves utterly transforms the sandbar. The key, however, is that the waves of material change keep pounding despite the resistance of lagging beliefs. If the pressures for change keep up long enough and remain strong enough, even lagging diffuse gender status beliefs could eventually be worn down to a point where they are rendered essentially ineffective.

It seems unlikely that the current drivers of change toward greater equality will weaken in the foreseeable future. If the past is any guide, women's own efforts to better their lives, both through everyday choices and through political action, are not going to diminish. Indeed, women's growing sense of personal agency, which we saw in chapter 6, seems likely to inspire more such efforts. And at the societal level, the processes by which economic and technological developments undermine existing organizations and foster the emergence of new ones seem only to be accelerating. As we saw with the biotech start-ups, each of these transitions creates at least the possibility that more gender-egalitarian organizational practices and structures will develop and put further pressure on gender status beliefs. Pressures for economic efficiency and cultural and legal pressures for universalism add to the likelihood that this will happen.

Waves of material change are likely to keep coming, then, but will they prove strong enough over the long run to effectively overwhelm gender status beliefs? That is much harder to predict. There is a reservoir of resistance in people's deep investment in sex/gender as a category of social meaning for the self. For women, this conservative investment in existing gender beliefs that define difference in terms that imply status inequality is counterweighted by their interests in improving their position in society. Men, at least simply in their identities as men, have fewer direct interests in overcoming the current gender system. To the extent that diffuse gender status beliefs are eroded, the conservative interests that such beliefs create for men and women will also lessen. But in the meantime, this reservoir of resistance could potentially motivate actions that undercut the egalitarian effects of pressures for change.

Although lagging cultural beliefs about gender do not make equality unattainable, then, they do suggest that the achievement of equality is not assured and will not come about without the concerted efforts of people. Furthermore, change toward equality is likely to be an uneven process that proceeds in a two steps forward, one step backward fashion. The social dislocations produced by periods of rapid progress toward gender equality may often lead to periods of stasis and even partial retrenchment.

FINAL THOUGHTS

It appears that we are in just such a period of relative stasis right now in American society. After rapid and substantial erosions of gender inequality through the 1970s and 1980s, progress began to stall in the 1990s (Cotter et al. 2004) and has not clearly resumed since. Just as the earlier progress came from women's dramatic gains in the work world, this is where the stall has occurred. Progress toward equality in labor force participation and wages and the gender desegregation of jobs seem all to have leveled off. In discussing this slowdown with others, I have occasionally heard some voice the opinion that perhaps our society has reached its "carrying capacity" in terms of the labor force involvement of women. That is, if children are to be cared for as society requires, by this perspective, perhaps women cannot go much further in their commitments to success in the workplace.

This argument about carrying capacity, of course, reveals unthinking acceptance of traditional gender beliefs that essentialize child care as a unique capacity and responsibility of women and that justify substantial inequality on the basis of this assumption. Nevertheless, the argument also reveals the standoff we have come to in the contemporary American gender system. Great gains have been made, but to go dramatically further, we now need to make substantial changes in the household division of labor, which has thus far changed much less. As we saw in chapter 5, even though family forms have greatly diversified in recent years, the heterosexual family unit continues to be a potent arena for our most deeply held beliefs about gender difference and inequality.

The contemporary heterosexual family, then, finds itself in a kind of ground zero in the current struggle over change and persistence in gender inequality. For both men and women in these families, the material incentives for women to increase their achievement in the labor force are only increasing. Yet to really release women to realize their full potential in the labor force while giving children the care they need requires changes in both the household division of labor and the world of work that challenge traditional beliefs about gender difference and gender prerogatives. Men must take over a more equal share of duties at home, and workplaces must become more family friendly.

Thus far, we have seen resistance to such changes, but we can also see that cracks are appearing in that resistance. Bit by bit, men are slowly taking on more routine child care and other household duties. Family-friendly workplace policies are also becoming more common. In my own view, then, the current period of stasis will yield to further progress despite the difficulties that change entails in a deeply held system like gender.

References

Acker, Joan. 1990. "Hierarchies, Jobs, and Bodies: A Theory of Gendered Organizations." *Gender & Society* 4:139–158.

———. 2006. *Class Questions: Feminist Answers*. Lanham, MD: Rowman and Littlefield.

Agars, Mark D. 2004. "Reconsidering the Impact of Gender Stereotypes on the Advancement of Women in Organizations." *Psychology of Women Quarterly* 2:103–111.

Anderson, Deborah, Melissa Binder, and Kate Krause. 2003. "Motherhood Wage Penalty Revisited: Experience, Heterogeneity, Work Effort and Work-Schedule Flexibility." *Industrial and Labor Relations Review* 56:273–294.

Anderson, Lynn R., and P. Nick Blanchard. 1982. "Sex Differences in Task and Social-Emotional Behavior." *Basic and Applied Social Psychology* 3:109–139.

Aries, Elizabeth. 1996. *Men and Women in Interaction: Reconsidering the Differences*. New York: Oxford University Press.

Bales, Robert F. 1950. *Interaction Process Analysis: A Method for the Study of Small Groups*. Cambridge, MA: Addison-Wesley.

———. 1970. *Personality and Interpersonal Behavior*. New York: Holt, Rinehart, and Winston.

Balkwell, James W., and Joseph Berger. 1996. "Gender, Status and Behavior in Task Situations." *Social Psychology Quarterly* 59:273–283.

Banaji, Mahzarin R., and Curtis D. Hardin. 1996. "Automatic Stereotyping." *Psychological Science* 7:136–141.

Barnett, William P., James N. Baron, and Toby E. Stuart. 2000. "Avenues of Attainment: Occupational Demography and Organizational Careers in the California Civil Service." *American Journal of Sociology* 106:88–144.

Baron, James N., Michael T. Hannan, Greta Hsu, and Ozgecan Kocak. 2002. "Gender and the Organization-Building Process in Young, High-Tech Firms." Pp. 245–273 in *The New Economic Sociology: Developments in an Emerging Field*, edited by M. F. Guillén, R. Collins, P. England, and M. Meyer. New York: Russell Sage.

————. 2007. "In the Company of Women: Gender Inequality and the Logic of Bureaucracy in Start-Up Firms." *Work and Occupations* 34:35–66.

Baxter, Janeen, and Erick Olin Wright. 2000. "The Glass Ceiling Hypothesis: A Comparative Study of the United States, Sweden, and Australia." *Gender & Society* 14:275–294.

Beisel, Nicola, and Tamara Kay. 2004. "Abortion, Race, and Gender in Nineteenth-Century America." *American Sociological Review* 69:498–518.

Berger, Joseph, Thomas L. Conner, and M. Hamit Fisek. 1974. *Expectation States Theory: A Theoretical Research Program*. Cambridge, MA: Winthrop.

Berger, Joseph, Hamit Fisek, Robert Norman, and Morris Zelditch. 1977. *Status Characteristics and Social Interaction*. New York: Elsevier.

Berger, Joseph, Robert Z. Norman, James W. Balkwell, and Roy F. Smith. 1992. "Status Inconsistency in Task Situations: A Test of Four Status Processing Principles." *American Sociological Review* 57:843–855.

Berger, Joseph, Cecilia L. Ridgeway, M. Hamit Fisek, and Robert Z. Norman. 1998. "The Legitimation and Delegitimation of Power and Prestige Orders." *American Sociological Review* 63:379–405.

Berger, Joseph, Cecilia L. Ridgeway, and Morris Zelditch. 2002. "Construction of Status and Referential Structures." *Sociological Theory* 20(2):157–179.

Berger, Joseph, Susan J. Rosenholz, and Morris Zeldtich Jr. 1980. "Status Organizing Processes." *Annual Review of Sociology* 6:479–508.

Berger, Peter L., and Thomas Luckmann. 1967. *The Social Construction of Reality: A Treatise in the Sociology of Knowledge*. Garden City, NY: Anchor.

Berk, Sarah. 1985. *The Gender Factory: The Appointment of Work in American Households*. New York: Plenum.

Bettenhausen, Kenneth, and Keith J. Murnighan. 1985. "The Emergence of Norms in Competitive Decision-Making Groups." *Administrative Science Quarterly* 30:350–372.

Bianchi, Suzanne M., Melissa A. Milkie, Liana C. Sayer, and John P. Robinson. 2000. "Is Anyone Doing the Housework? Trends in the Gender Division of Household Labor." *Social Forces* 79:191–228.

Bianchi, Suzanne M., John P. Robinson, and Melissa Milkie. 2006. *Changing Rhythms of American Family Life*. New York: Russell Sage Foundation.

Biernat, Monica, and Diane Kobrynowicz. 1997. "Gender- and Race-Based Standards of Competence: Lower Minimum Standards but Higher Ability Standards for Devalued Groups." *Journal of Personality and Social Psychology* 72(3):544–557.

Bittman, Michael, Paula England, Liana Sayer, Nancy Folbre, and George Matheson. 2003. "When Does Gender Trump Money? Bargaining and Time in Household Work." *American Journal of Sociology* 109:186–214.

Blair, Irene V., and Mahzarin R. Banaji. 1996. "Automatic and Controlled Processes in Stereotype Priming." *Journal of Personality and Social Psychology* 70:1142–1163.

Blair, Sampson, and Daniel Lichter. 1991. "Measuring the Division of Household Labor." *Journal of Family Issues* 12:91–113.

Blair-Loy, Mary. 2003. *Competing Devotions: Career and Family among Women Executives*. Cambridge, MA: Harvard University Press.

Brewer, Marilynn B. 1988. "A Dual Process Model of Impression Formation." Pp. 1–36 in *Advances in Social Cognition*, Vol. 1, edited by T. Srull and R. S. Wyer Jr. Hillsdale, NJ: Lawence Erlbaum.

———. 1997. "On the Social Origins of Human Nature." Pp. 54–62 in *The Message of Social Psychology: Perspectives on the Mind in Society*, edited by C. McGarty and S. A. Haslam. Cambridge, MA: Blackwell.

Brewer, Marilynn B., and Rupert J. Brown. 1998. "Intergroup Relations." Pp. 554–594 in *The Handbook of Social Psychology*, 4th ed., edited by D. T. Gilbert, S. T. Fiske, and G. Lindzey. New York: McGraw-Hill.

Brewer, Marilynn B., and Layton N. Lui. 1989. "The Primacy of Age and Sex in the Structure of Person Categories." *Social Cognition* 7:262–274.

Brines, Julie. 1994. "Economic Dependency, Gender, and the Division of Labor at Home." *American Journal of Sociology* 100:652–688.

Brinkman, Richard L., and June E. Brinkman. 1997. "Cultural Lag: Conception and Theory." *International Journal of Social Economics* 24:609–627.

Broverman, Inge K., Susan R. Vogel, Donald M. Broverman, Frank E. Clarkson, and Paul S. Rosenkrantz. 1972. "Sex-Role Stereotypes: A Reappraisal." *Journal of Social Issues* 28:59–78.

Budig, Michelle J. 2002. "Male Advantage and the Gender Composition of Jobs: Who Rides the Glass Escalator?" *Social Problems* 49:258–277.

Budig, Michelle J., and Paula England. 2001. "The Wage Penalty for Motherhood." *American Sociological Review* 66:204–225.

Burleson, Brant R., and Adrianne W. Kunkel. 2006. "Revisiting the Different Cultures Thesis: An Assessment of Sex Differences and Similarities in Supportive Communication." Pp. 137–159 in *Sex Differences and Similarities in Communication*, 2nd ed., edited by K. Dindia and D. J. Canary. Mahwah, NJ: Lawrence Erlbaum.

Burt, Ronald S. 1998. "The Gender of Social Capital." *Rationality and Society* 10:5–46.

Buss, David M., and Doug T. Kenrick. 1998. "Evolutionary Social Psychology." Pp. 982–1026 in *The Handbook of Social Psychology*, edited by D. Gilbert, S. Fiske, and G. Lindzey. New York: Random House.

Cabrera, Susan F., and Melissa C. Thomas-Hunt. 2007. "'Street Cred' and the Executive Woman: The Effects of Gender Differences in Social Networks on Career Advancement." Pp. 123–147 in *The Social Psychology of Gender, Advances in Group Processes*, Vol. 24, edited by S. J. Correll. San Diego, CA: Elsevier Science.

Carley, Kathleen. 1991. "A Theory of Group Stability." *American Sociological Review* 56(3):331–354.

Carli, Linda L. 1989. "Gender Differences in Interaction Style and Influence." *Journal of Personality and Social Psychology* 56:565–576.

———. 1990. "Gender, Language and Influence." *Journal of Personality and Social Psychology* 59:941–951.

———. 1991. "Gender, Status, and Influence." Pp. 89–113 in *Advances in Group Processes*, Vol. 8, edited by E. J. Lawler, B. Markovsky, C. L. Ridgeway, and H. Walker. Greenwich, CT: JAI.

———. 2001. "Gender and Social Influence." *Journal of Social Issues* 57:725–742.

Carrington, Christopher. 1999. *No Place Like Home: Relationships and Family Life among Lesbians and Gay Men*. Chicago: University of Chicago Press.

Catalyst. 2008. "2008 Catalyst Census of Women Board of Directors of the Fortune 500." Retrieved June 3, 2010 (http://www.leadingwomenexecutives.net/LWE-landscape-for-advancement.html).

Cejka, Mary Ann, and Alice H. Eagly. 1999. "Gender-Stereotypic Images of Occupations Correspond to the Sex Segregation of Employment." *Personality and Social Psychology Bulletin* 25:413–423.

Center for the Child Care Workforce. 2009. "Wage Data Fact Sheet (2009 Edition)." Retrieved April 4, 2010 (http://www.ccw.org/index.php?option=com_content&task=view&id=19&Itemid=48).

Charles, Maria, and Karen Bradley. 2009. "Indulging Our Gendered Selves? Sex Segregation by Field of Study in 44 Countries." *American Journal of Sociology* 114:924–976.

Charles, Maria, and David Grusky. 2004. *Occupational Ghettos: The Worldwide Segregation of Women and Men*. Stanford, CA: Stanford University Press.

Chwe, Michael S. 2001. *Rational Ritual: Culture, Coordination, and Common Knowledge*. Princeton, NJ: Princeton University Press.

Clark, Anna E., and Yoshihisa Kashima. 2007. "Stereotypes Help People Connect with Others in the Community: A Situated Functional Analysis of the Stereotype Consistency Bias in Communication." *Journal of Personality and Social Psychology* 93:1028–1039.

Cohen, Elizabeth G., and Rachel A. Lotan. 1997. *Working for Equity in Heterogeneous Classrooms: Sociological Theory in Practice*. New York: Teacher's College Press.

Collins, Patricia Hill. 1991. *Black Feminist Thought: Knowledge, Consciousness, and the Politics of Empowerment*. New York: Routledge.

Collinson, David L., and Jeff Hearn (Eds.). 1996. *Men as Managers, Managers as Men*. London: Sage.

Coltrane, Scott. 1989. "Household Labor and the Routine Production of Gender." *Social Problems* 36:473–490.

———. 1996. *Family Man: Fatherhood, Housework, and Gender Equity*. New York: Oxford University Press.

———. 2000. "Research on Household Labor: Modeling and Measuring the Social Embeddedness of Routine Family Work." *Journal of Marriage and Family* 62:1208–1233.

Conway, Michael M., Teresa Pizzamiglio, and Lauren Mount. 1996. "Status, Communality, and Agency: Implications for Stereotypes of Gender and Other Groups." *Journal of Personality and Social Psychology* 71:25–38.

Cook, Karen S., Coye Cheshire, and Alexandra Gerbasi. 2006. "Power, Dependence, and Social Exchange." Pp. 194–216 in *Contemporary Social Psychological Theories*, edited by Peter J. Burke. Stanford, CA: Stanford University Press.

Correll, Shelley J. 2001. "Gender and the Career Choice Process: The Role of Biased Self-Assessments." *American Journal of Sociology* 106:1691–1730.

———. 2004. "Constraints into Preferences: Gender, Status, and Emerging Career Aspirations." *American Sociological Review* 69:93–113.

Correll, Shelley J., Stephen Benard, and In Paik. 2007. "Getting a Job: Is There a Motherhood Penalty?" *American Journal of Sociology* 112:1297–1338.

Correll, Shelley J., and Cecilia L. Ridgeway. 2003. "Expectation States Theory." Pp. 29–51 in *The Handbook of Social Psychology*, edited by J. Delamater. New York: Kluwer Academic/Plenum.

Cota, Albert, and Kenneth Dion. 1986. "Salience of Gender and Sex Composition of Ad Hoc Groups: An Experimental Test of Distinctiveness Theory." *Journal of Personality and Social Psychology* 50:770–776.

Cotter, David A., Joan M. Hermsen, and Reeve Vanneman. 2004. "Gender Inequality at Work." Pp. 107–138 in *The American People Census 2000*, edited by Reynolds Farley and John Haaga. New York: Russell Sage Foundation and Population Reference Bureau.

———. 2010. "End of the Gender Revolution? Employment by Gender: CPS, 25–54, 1962–2007." Retrieved June 29, 2010 (http://www.bsos.umd.edu/socy/vanneman/endofgr/cpsemp.html).

Crawford, Charles B., and Catherine Salmon. 2004. *Evolutionary Psychology, Public Policy, and Personal Decisions*. Mahwah, NJ: Lawrence Erlbaum.

Crittendon, Ann. 2001. *The Price of Motherhood: Why the Most Important Job in the World Is Still the Least Valued*. New York: Metropolitan.

Cuddy, Amy J., Susan T. Fiske, and Peter Glick. 2007. "The BIAS Map: Behaviors from Intergroup Affect and Stereotypes." *Journal of Personality and Social Psychology* 92:631–648.

Cunningham, Mick. 2001. "Parental Influence on the Gendered Division of Housework." *American Sociological Review* 66:184–203.

Davidson, Marilyn, and Ronald J. Burke. 2000. *Women in Management: Current Research Issues*, Vol. 2. London: Sage.

Deaux, Kay, and Mary E. Kite. 1993. *Psychology of Women: A Handbook of Issues and Theories*. Westport, CT: Greenwood.

Deaux, Kay and Marianne LaFrance. 1998. "Gender." Pp. 788–827 in *Handbook of Social Psychology*, edited by D. T. Gilbert, S. T. Fiske, and G. Lindzey. New York: McGraw-Hill.

Deaux, Kay, and Brenda Major. 1987. "Putting Gender into Context: An Interactive Model of Gender-Related Behavior." *Psychological Review* 94:369–389.

Diekman, Amanda B., and Alice H. Eagly. 2000. "Stereotypes as Dynamic Constructs: Women and Men of the Past, Present, and Future." *Personality and Social Psychology Bulletin* 26:1171–1188.

———. 2008. "Of Women, Men, and Motivation: A Role Congruity Account." Pp. 434–447 in *Handbook of Motivational Science*, edited by J. Y. Shah and W. L. Gardner. New York: Guilford.

Dovidio, John F., Clifford E. Brown, Karen Heltman, Steve L. Ellyson, and Caroline F. Keating. 1988. "Power Displays between Women and Men in Discussions of Gender Linked Tasks: A Multichannel Study." *Journal of Personality and Social Psychology* 55:580–587.

Driskell, James E., and Brian Mullen. 1990. "Status, Expectations, and Behavior: A Meta-Analytic Review and Test of the Theory." *Personality and Social Psychology Bulletin* 16:541–553.

Dugger, Karen. 1988. "Social Location and Gender-Role Attitudes: A Comparison of Black and White Women." *Gender and Society* 2:425–448.

Dunning, David, and David A. Sherman. 1997. "Stereotypes and Trait Inference." *Journal of Personality and Social Psychology* 73:459–471.

Eagly, Alice H. 1987. *Sex Differences in Social Behavior: A Social-Role Interpretation.* Hillsdale, NJ: Lawrence Erlbaum.

———. 1995. "The Science and Politics of Comparing Women and Men." *American Psychologist* 50:145–158.

Eagly, Alice H., Anne E. Beall, and Robert J. Sternberg (Eds.). 2004. *Psychology of Gender*, 2nd Ed. New York: Guilford.

Eagly, Alice H., and Linda L. Carli. 2003. "The Female Leadership Advantage: An Evaluation of the Evidence." *Leadership Quarterly* 14:807–834.

———. 2007. *Through the Labyrinth: The Truth about How Women Become Leaders.* Cambridge, MA: Harvard Business School Press.

Eagly, Alice H., and Amanda B. Diekman. 2003. "The Malleability of Sex Differences in Response to Changing Social Roles." Pp. 103–115 in *A Psychology of Human Strengths: Fundamental Questions and Future Directions for a Positive Psychology*, edited by L. G. Aspinwall and U. M. Staudinger. Washington, DC: American Psychological Association.

Eagly, Alice H., Mary C. Johannesen-Schmidt, and Marloes L. van Engen. 2003. "Transformational, Transactional, and Laissez-Faire Leadership Styles: A Meta-Analysis Comparing Women and Men." *Psychological Bulletin* 129:569–591.

Eagly, Alice H., and Stephen J. Karau. 1991. "Gender and the Emergence of Leaders: A Meta-Analysis." *Journal of Personality and Social Psychology* 60:685–710.

———. 2002. "Role Congruity Theory of Prejudice towards Female Leaders." *Psychological Review* 109:573–579.

Eagly, Alice H., Steven J. Karau, and Mona G. Makhijani. 1995. "Gender and the Effectiveness of Leaders: A Meta-Analysis." *Psychological Bulletin* 117:125–145.

Eagly, Alice H., and Anne M. Koenig. 2006. "Social Role Theory of Sex Differences and Similarities: Implications for Prosocial Behavior." Pp. 161–194 in *Sex Differences and Similarities in Communication*, 2nd Ed., edited by K. Dindia and D. J. Canary. Mahwah, NJ: Lawrence Erlbaum.

Eagly, Alice H., Mona G. Makhijani, and Bruce G. Klonsky. 1992. "Gender and the Evaluation of Leaders: A Meta-Analysis. *Psychological Bulletin* 111:543–588.

Eagly, Alice H., and Antonio Mladinic. 1989. "Gender Stereotypes and Attitudes toward Women and Men." *Personality and Social Psychology Bulletin* 15:543–558.

———. 1994. "Are People Prejudiced against Women? Some Answers from Research on Attitudes, Gender Stereotypes, and Judgments of Competence." Pp. 1–35 in *European Review of Social Psychology*, Vol. 5, edited by W. Stroebe and M. Hewstone. New York: Wiley.

Eagly, Alice H., and Valerie J. Steffen. 1984. "Gender Stereotypes Stem from the Distribution of Women and Men into Social Roles." *Journal of Personality and Social Psychology* 46:735–754.

———. 1986. "Gender and Aggressive Behavior: A Meta-Analytic Review of the Social Psychological Literature." *Psychological Bulletin* 100:309–330.

Eagly, Alice H., and Wendy Wood. 1999. "The Origins of Sex Differences in Human Behavior: Evolved Dispositions versus Social Roles." *American Psychologist* 54:408–423.

Eagly, Alice H., Wendy Wood, and Amanda B. Diekman. 2000. "Social Role Theory of Sex Differences and Similarities: A Current Appraisal." Pp. 123–173 in *The Developmental Psychology of Gender*, edited by T. Eckes and H. M. Trautner. Mahwah, NJ: Lawrence Erlbaum.

Eckles, Jacquelynne S., Bonnie Barber, and Debra Jozefowicz. 1999. "Linking Gender to Educational, Occupational, and Recreational Choice: Applying the Model of Achievement-Related Choices." Pp. 153–191 in *Sexism and Stereotypes in Modern Society: The Gender Science of Janet Taylor Spence*, edited by W. B. Swann, J. H. Langlois, and L. A. Gilbert. Washington, DC: American Psychological Association.

Edelman, Lauren B., and Stephen Petterson. 1999. "Symbols and Substance in Organizational Response to Civil Rights Law." *Research in Social Stratification and Mobility* 17:107–136.

Elliot, James R., and Ryan A. Smith. 2004. "Race, Gender, and Workplace Power." *American Sociological Review* 69:365–386.

Ellyson, Steve L., John F. Dovidio, and Clifford E. Brown. 1992. "The Look of Power: Gender Differences and Similarities." Pp. 50–80 in *Gender, Interaction, and Inequality*, edited by C. Ridgeway. New York: Springer-Verlag.

Emerson, Richard. 1962. "Power-Dependence Relations." *American Sociological Review* 27:31–41.

———. 1972. "Exchange Theory, Part II: Exchange Relations and Networks." Pp. 58–87 in *Sociological Theories in Progress*, Vol. 2, edited by J. Berger, M. Zelditch Jr., and B. Anderson. Boston: Houghton-Mifflin.

England, Paula. 1992. *Comparable Worth: Theories and Evidence*. New York: Aldine.

———. 2006. "Toward Gender Equality: Progress and Bottlenecks." Pp. 245–264 in *The Declining Significance of Gender?* edited by F. D. Blau, M. C. Brinton, and D. B. Grusky. New York: Russell Sage Foundation.

England, Paula, Paul Allison, Su Li, Noah Mark, Jennifer Thompson, Michelle Budig, and Han Sun. 2007. "Why Are Some Academic Fields Tipping toward

Female? The Sex Composition of U.S. Fields of Doctoral Degree Receipt, 1971–2002." *Sociology of Education* 80:23–42.

England, Paula, Michelle Budig, and Nancy Folbre. 2002. "Wages of Virtue: the Relative Pay of Care Work." *Social Problems* 49:455–473.

England, Paula, and Su Li. 2006. "Desegregation Stalled: The Changing Gender Composition of College Majors, 1971-2002." *Gender and Society* 20:657–677.

England, Paula, Lori Reid, and Barbara S. Kilbourne. 1996. "The Effect of the Sex Composition of Jobs on Starting Wages in an Organization: Findings from the NLSY." *Demography* 33:511–521.

England, Paula, Emily Fitzgibbons Shafer, and Alison C. K. Fogarty. 2008. "Hooking-up and Forming Romantic Relationships on Today's College Campuses." Pp. 531–547 in *The Gendered Society Reader*, 3rd ed., edited by M. S. Kimmel and A. Aronson. New York: Oxford University Press.

Epstein, Cynthia. 1988. *Deceptive Distinctions: Sex, Gender, and the Social Order*. New York and New Haven, CT: Yale University Press and Russell Sage Foundation.

Evertsson, Marie, and Magnus Nermo. 2004. "Dependence within Families and the Division of Labor: Comparing Sweden and the United States." *Journal of Marriage and Family* 66:1272–1286.

Fenstermaker, Sarah. 1996. "The Dynamics of Time Use: Context and Meaning." *Journal of Family and Economic Issues* 17:231–243.

Fernandez, Roberto, and Colette Friedrich. 2007. "Job Queues: Gender and Race at the Application Interface." Paper presented at the annual meeting of the American Sociological Association on August 11, 2007. New York, NY.

Fernandez, Roberto, and M. Lourdes Sosa. 2005. "Gendering the Job: Networks and Recruitment at a Call Center." *American Journal of Sociology* 111:859–904.

Ferree, Myra Marx, and Patricia Yancey Martin. (Eds.). 1995. *Feminist Organizations*. Philadelphia: Temple University Press.

Filardo, Emily K. 1996. "Gender Patterns in African American and White Adolescents' Social Interactions in Same-Race, Mixed-Sex Groups." *Journal of Personality and Social Psychology* 71:71–82.

Fiske, Susan T. 1998. "Stereotyping, Prejudice, and Discrimination." Pp. 357–411 in *The Handbook of Social Psychology*, 4th ed., edited by D. T. Gilbert, S. T. Fiske, and G. Lindzey. New York: McGraw-Hill.

Fiske, Susan T., Amy J. Cuddy, Peter Glick, and Jun Xu. 2002. "A Model of (Often Mixed) Stereotype Content: Competence and Warmth Respectively Follow from Perceived Status and Competition." *Journal of Personality and Social Psychology* 82:878–902.

Fiske, Susan T., Monica Lin, and Steven Neuberg. 1999. "The Continuum Model: Ten Years Later." Pp. 231–254 in *Dual Process Theories in Social Psychology*, edited by S. Chaiken and Y. Trope. New York: Guilford.

Fiske, Susan T., and Laura E. Stevens. 1993. "What's So Special about Sex? Gender Stereotyping and Discrimination." Pp. 173–196 in *Gender Issues in Contemporary Society*, edited by S. Oskamp and M. Costanzo. Newbury Park, CA: Sage.

Fiske, Susan T., and Shelly E. Taylor. 1991. *Social Cognition*, 2nd ed. New York: McGraw-Hill.

Foschi, Martha, Larissa Lai, and Kirsten Sigerson. 1994. "Gender and Double Standards in the Assessment of Job Applicants." *Social Psychology Quarterly* 57:326–339.

Geis, Florence L., Virginia Brown, Joyce Jennings, and Denise Corrado-Taylor. 1984. "Sex vs. Status in Sex-Associated Stereotypes." *Sex Roles* 11:771–785.

Gerber, Gwendolyn L. 1996. "Status in Same-Gender and Mixed-Gender Police Dyads: Effects on Personality Attributions." *Social Psychology Quarterly* 59:350–363.

Giddens, Anthony. 1984. *The Constitution of Society: Outline of the Theory of Structuration*. Cambridge, MA: Polity.

Glass, Jennifer. 2004. "Blessing or Curse? Work-Family Policies and Mother's Wage Growth over Time." *Work and Occupations* 31:367–394.

Glenn, Evelyn Nakano. 1999. "The Social Construction and Institutionalization of Gender and Race: An Integrative Framework." Pp. 3–43 in *Revisioning Gender*, edited by M. M. Ferree, J. Lorber, and B. B. Hess. Thousand Oaks, CA: Sage.

Glick, Peter, and Susan T. Fiske. 1999a. "Gender, Power Dynamics, and Social Interaction." Pp. 365–398 in *Revisioning Gender*, edited by M. M. Ferree, J. Lorber, and B. B. Hess. Thousand Oaks, CA: Sage.

———. 1999b. "Sexism and Other "Isms": Interdependence, Status, and the Ambivalent Content of Stereotypes." Pp. 193–221 in *Sexism and Stereotypes in Modern Society*, edited by W. B. Swan, J. H. Langlois, and L. A. Gilbert. Washington, DC: American Psychological Association.

Glick, Peter, Maria Lameiras, Susan T. Fiske, Thomas Eckes, Barbara Masser, Chiara Volpato, Anna Maria Manganelli, Jolynn C. X. Pek, Li-li Huang, Nuray Sakalli-Ugurlu, Yolanda Rodriguez Castro, Maria Luiza D'Avila Pereira, Tineke M. Willemsen, Annetje Brunner, Iris Six-Materna, and Robin Wells. 2004. "Bad but Bold: Ambivalent Attitudes toward Men Predict Gender Inequality in 16 Nations." *Journal of Personality and Social Psychology* 86:713–728.

Goffman, Erving. 1959. *The Presentation of Self in Everyday Life*. Garden City, NY: Doubleday.

———. 1967. *Interaction Ritual: Essays on Face-to-Face Behavior*, 1st ed. Garden City, NY: Anchor.

Goldin, Claudia. 1995. "Career and Family: College Women Look to the Past." National Bureau of Economic Research Working Paper No. W5188. Available at SSRN: http://ssrn.com/abstract=225251.

Gorman, Elizabeth H. 2005. "Gender Stereotypes, Same-Gender Preferences, and Organizational Variation in the Hiring of Women: Evidence from Law Firms." *American Sociological Review* 70:702–728.

———. 2006. "Work Uncertainty and the Promotion of Professional Women: The Case of Law Firm Partnership." *Social Forces* 85:865–890.

Gorman, Elizabeth H., and Julie A. Kmec. 2009. "Hierarchical Rank and Women's Organizational Mobility: Glass Ceilings in Corporate Law Firms." *American Journal of Sociology* 114:1428–1474.

Greenstein, Theodore N. 2000. "Economic Dependence, Gender, and the Division of Labor in the Home: A Replication and Extension." *Journal of Marriage and Family* 62:322–335.

Guerrero, Laura K., Susanne M. Jones, and Renee Reiter Boburka. 2006. "Sex Differences in Emotional Communication." Pp. 241–261 in *Sex Differences and Similarities in Communication*, 2nd ed., edited by D. J. Canary and K. Dindia. Mahwah, NJ: Lawrence Erlbaum.

Gupta, Sanjiv. 1999. "The Effects of Transitions in Marital Status on Men's Performance of Housework." *Journal of Marriage and Family* 61:700–711.

———. 2007. "Autonomy, Dependence, or Display? The Relationship between Married Women's Earnings and Housework." *Journal of Marriage and Family* 69:399–417.

Hall, Judith A. 1984. *Nonverbal Sex Differences: Communication Accuracy and Expressive Style*. Baltimore: Johns Hopkins University Press.

———. 2006. "Nonverbal Behavior, Status, and Gender: How Do We Understand Their Relations?" *Psychology of Women Quarterly* 30:384–391.

Hamilton, Laura, and Elizabeth A. Armstrong. 2009. "Gendered Sexuality in Young Adulthood: Double Binds and Flawed Options." *Gender & Society* 23:589–616.

Hardin, Curtis D., and Terri D. Conley. 2001. "A Relational Approach to Cognition: Shared Experience and Relationship Affirmation in Social Cognition." Pp. 3–18 in *Cognitive Social Psychology: The Princeton Symposium on the Legacy and Future of Social Cognition*, edited by G. B. Moskowitz. Mahwah, NJ: Lawrence Erlbaum.

Hardin, Curtis D., and E. Tory Higgins. 1996. "Shared Reality: How Social Verification Makes the Subjective Objective." Pp. 28–84 in *The Handbook of Motivation and Cognition: The Interpersonal Context*, Vol. 3, edited by R. M. Sorrentino and E. T. Higgins. New York: Guilford.

Hays, Sharon. 1996. *Cultural Contradictions of Motherhood*. New Haven, CT: Yale University Press.

Heilman, Madeline E. 1983. "Sex Bias in Work Settings: The Lack of Fit Model." *Research in Organizational Behavior* 5:269–298.

Heilman, Madeline E., Caryn J. Block, Richard F. Martell, and Michael C. Simon. 1989. "Has Anything Changed? Current Characterizations of Men, Women, and Managers." *Journal of Applied Psychology* 74:935–942.

Heilman, Madeline E., and Elizabeth J. Parks-Stamm. 2007. "Gender Stereotypes in the Workplace: Obstacles to Women's Career Progress." Pp. 47–77 in *Social Psychology of Gender, Advances in Group Processes*, Vol. 24, edited by S. J. Correll. San Diego, CA: Elsevier.

Hewstone, Miles. 1994. "Revision and Change of Stereotypic Beliefs: In Search of the Elusive Subtyping Model." Pp. 69–109 in *European Review of Social Psychology*, Vol. 5, edited by W. Stroebe and M. Hewstone. Chichester, UK: Wiley.

Hogg, Michael A. 2001. "A Social Identity Theory of Leadership." *Personality and Social Psychology Review* 5(3):184–200.

———. 2003. "Intergroup Relations." Pp. 479–502 in *Handbook of Social Psychology*, edited by J. D. Delamater. New York: Kluwer Academic/Plenum.

Hook, Jennifer. 2010. "Gender Inequality in the Welfare State: Sex Segregation in Housework, 1965–2003." *American Journal of Sociology* 115:1480–1523.

Hoyt, Crystal L., and Jim Blascovich. 2007. "Leadership Efficacy and Women Leaders' Responses to Stereotype Activation." *Group Processes & Intergroup Relations* 10: 595–616.

Huber, Joan. 2007. *On the Origins of Gender Inequality.* Boulder, CO: Paradigm.

Hyde, Janet S. 2005. "The Gender Similarities Hypothesis." *American Psychologist* 60:581–592.

Hyde, Janet S., and Elizabeth Ashby Plant. 1995. "Magnitude of Psychological Gender Differences: Another Side to the Story." *American Psychologist* 50:159–161.

Ibarra, Herminia. 1992. "Homophily and Differential Returns: Sex Differences in Network Structure and Access in an Advertising Firm." *Administrative Science Quarterly* 37:422–447.

Institute for Women's Policy Research. 2010. "Factsheet: The Gender Wage Gap: 2009." Retrieved June 29, 2010 (http://www.iwpr.org/pdf/C350.pdf).

Ito, Tiffany A., and Geoffrey R. Urland. 2003. "Race and Gender on the Brain: Electrocortical Measures of Attention to the Race and Gender of Multiply Categorizable Individuals." *Journal of Personality and Social Psychology* 85(4):616–626.

Jackman, Mary R. 1994. *The Velvet Glove: Paternalism and Conflict in Gender, Class, and Race Relations.* Berkeley: University of California Press.

Jackson, Lynne M., Victoria M. Esses, and Christopher T. Burris. 2001. "Contemporary Sexism and Discrimination: The Importance of Respect for Men and Women." *Personality and Social Psychology Bulletin* 27:48–61.

Jackson, Robert M. 1998. *Destined for Equality: The Inevitable Rise of Women's Status.* Cambridge, MA: Harvard University Press.

James, Deborah, and Janice Drakich. 1993. "Understanding Gender Differences in Amount of Talk: A Critical Review of Research." Pp. 281–312 in *Gender and Conversational Interaction*, edited by D. Tannen. New York: Oxford University Press.

Johannesen-Schmidt, Mary C., and Alice H. Eagly. 2002. "Another Look at Sex Differences in Preferred Mate Characteristics: The Effects of Endorsing the Traditional Female Gender Role." *Psychology of Women Quarterly* 26:322–328.

Johnson, Cathryn, Jody Clay-Warner, and Stephanie J. Funk. 1996. "Effects of Authority Structures and Gender on Interaction in Same-Sex Task Groups." *Social Psychology Quarterly* 59:221–236.

Jost, John T., and Mahzarin Banaji. 1994. "The Role of Stereotyping in System-Justification and the Production of False Consciousness." *British Journal of Social Psychology* 33:1–27.

Jost, John T., Diana Burgess, and Cristina O. Mosso. 2001. "Conflicts of Legitimation among Self, Group, and System: The Integrative Potential of System Justification Theory." Pp. 363–390 in *The Psychology of Legitimacy*, edited by J. T. Jost and B. Major. New York: Cambridge University Press.

Kalev, Alexandra. 2009. "Cracking the Glass Cages? Restructuring and Ascriptive Inequality at Work." *American Journal of Sociology* 114(6):1591–1643.

Kalev, Alexandra, Frank Dobbin, and Erin Kelly. 2006. "Best Practices Guesses? Assessing the Efficacy of Corporate Affirmative Action Policies." *American Sociological Review* 71:589–617.

Kane, Emily. 2000. "Racial and Ethnic Variations in Gender-Related Attitudes." *Annual Review of Sociology* 26:419–436.

Kanter, Rosabeth M. 1977. "Some Effects of Proportions on Group Life: Skewed Sex Ratios and Responses to Token Women." *American Journal of Sociology* 82:965–990.

Kessler, Suzanne J., and Wendy McKenna. 1978. *Gender: An Ethnomethodological Approach*. New York: Wiley.

Kilbourne, Barbara S., Paula England, George Farkas, Kurt Beron, and Dorothea Weir. 1994. "Returns to Skill, Compensating Differentials, and Gender Bias: Effects of Occupational Characteristics on the Wages of White Women and Men." *American Journal of Sociology* 100:689–719.

Koenig, Anne M., and Alice H. Eagly. 2005. "Stereotype Threat in Men on a Test of Social Sensitivity." *Sex Roles* 52:489–496.

———. 2006. "A Unified Theory of Stereotype Content: How Observations of Groups' Social Roles and Intergroup Relations Produce Stereotypes." Northwestern University, Evanston, IL. Unpublished paper.

Kroska, Amy. 2004. "Divisions of Domestic Work." *Journal of Family Issues* 25:900–932.

Kunda, Ziva, and Steven J. Spencer. 2003. "When Do Stereotypes Come to Mind and When Do They Color Judgment? A Goal-Based Theoretical Framework for Stereotype Activation and Application." *Psychological Bulletin* 129(4):522–554.

LaFrance, Marianne, Marvin A. Hecht, and Elizabeth Levy Paluck. 2003. "The Contingent Smile: A Meta-Analysis of Sex Differences in Smiling." *Psychological Bulletin* 129:305–334.

Lepowsky, Maria A. 1993. *Fruit of the Motherland: Gender in an Egalitarian Society*. New York: Columbia University Press.

Lightdale, Jennifer R., and Deborah A. Prentice. 1994. "Rethinking Sex Differences in Aggression: Aggressive Behavior in the Absence of Social Roles." *Personality and Social Psychology Bulletin* 20:34–44.

Lorber, Judith. 1994. *Paradoxes of Gender*. New Haven, CT: Yale University Press.

Lueptow, Lloyd B., Lori Garovich-Szabo, and Margaret B. Lueptow. 2001. "Social Change and the Persistence of Sex Typing: 1974–1997." *Social Forces* 80:1–36.

Lyness, Karen S., and Madeline E. Heilman. 2006. "When Fit Is Fundamental: Performance Evaluations and Promotions of Upper-Level Female and Male Managers." *Journal of Applied Social Psychology* 91:777–785.

Maccoby, Eleanor E. 1998. *The Two Sexes: Growing Up Apart, Coming Together*. Cambridge, MA: Belknap Press of Harvard University Press.

MacGeorge, Erina L., Bo Feng, Ginger L. Butler, and Sara K. Budarz. 2004. "Understanding Advice in Supportive Interactions: Beyond the Facework and Message Evaluation Paradigm." *Human Communication Association* 30(1):42–70.

Macrae, C. Neil, Kimberly A. Quinn, Malia F. Mason, and Susanne Quadflieg. 2005. "Understanding Others: The Face and Person Construal." *Journal of Personality and Social Psychology* 89(5):686–695.

Mark, Noah. 1999. "The Emergence of Status Inequality." Paper presented at the annual meeting of the American Sociological Association, Chicago, August 1999.

Mark, Noah, Lynn Smith-Lovin, and Cecilia Ridgeway. 2009. "Why Do Nominal Characteristics Acquire Status Value? A Minimal Explanation for Status Construction." *American Journal of Sociology* 115:832–862.

Martin, Joanne. Forthcoming. "Does Gender Inequality Ever Disappear? In *Gender, Work, and Organization Handbook*, edited by E. Jeanes, D. Knights, and P. Y. Martin. Oxford: Blackwell.

Martin, Joanne, Kathleen Knopoff, and Christine Beckman. 1998. "An Alternative to Bureaucratic Impersonality and Emotional Labor: Bonded Emotionality in the Body Shop." *Administrative Science Quarterly* 43:115–139.

Martin, Joanne, and Debra Meyerson. 1998. "Women and Power: Conformity, Resistance, and Disorganized Co-Action." Pp. 311–348 in *Power and Influence in Organizations*, edited by R. Kramer and M. Neale. Thousand Oaks, CA: Sage.

Martin, Patricia Yancey. 1996. "Gendering and Evaluating Dynamics: Men, Masculinities, and Managements." In *Men as Managers, Managers as Men*, edited by D. Collinson and J. Hearn. London: Sage.

———. 2003. "Said and Done versus Saying and Doing: Gendering Practices, Practicing Gender at Work." *Gender & Society* 17:342–366.

Maume, David J. 1999. "Occupational Segregation in the Career Mobility of White Men and Women." *Social Forces* 77:1433–1459.

McCall, Leslie. 2001. *Complex Inequality: Gender, Class, and Race in the New Economy.* London: Routledge.

McIlwee, Judith S., and J. Gregg Robinson. 1992. *Women in Engineering: Gender, Power, and Workplace Culture.* Albany: State University of New York Press.

McPherson, J. Miller, Lynn Smith-Lovin, and James M. Cook. 2001. "Birds of a Feather: Homophily in Social Networks." *Annual Review of Sociology* 27:415–444.

Mead, George H. 1934. *Mind, Self, and Society: From the Standpoint of a Social Behaviorist.* Chicago: University of Chicago Press.

Megargee, Edwin I. 1969. "Influence of Sex Roles on the Manifestation of Leadership." *Journal of Applied Psychology* 53:377–382.

Milkie, Melissa A. 1999. "Social Comparison, Reflected Appraisals, and Mass Media: The Impact of Pervasive Beauty Images on Black and White Girls' Self-Concepts." *Social Psychology Quarterly* 62:190–210.

Miller, Dale T., and William Turnbull. 1986. "Expectancies and Interpersonal Processes." *Annual Review of Psychology* 37:233–256.

Munch, Allison, J. Miller McPherson, and Lynn Smith-Lovin. 1997. "Gender, Children, and Social Contact: The Effects of Childrearing for Men and Women." *American Sociological Review* 62:509–520.

Nelson, Robert, and William Bridges. 1999. *Legalizing Gender Inequality: Courts, Markets, and Unequal Pay for Women in America*. New York: Cambridge University Press.

Nosek, Brian A., Mahzarin R. Banaji, and Anthony G. Greenwald. 2002. "Math = Male, Me = Female, Therefore Math ☐ Me." *Journal of Personality and Social Psychology* 83:44–59.

Ogburn, William Fielding. 1957. "Cultural Lag as Theory." *Sociology and Social Research* 41:167–174.

Orbuch, Terri J., and Sandra L. Eyster. 1997. "Division of Household Labor among Black Couples and White Couples." *Social Forces* 76:301–332.

Padavic, Irene, and Barbara Reskin. 2002. *Women and Men at Work*. Thousand Oaks, CA: Pine Forge.

Petersen, Trond, and Laurie A. Morgan. 1995. "Separate and Unequal: Occupation-Establishment Sex Segregation and the Gender Wage Gap." *American Journal of Sociology* 101:329–365.

Petersen, Trond, and Itzhak Saporta. 2004. "The Opportunity Structure for Discrimination." *American Journal of Sociology* 109(4):852–901.

Phillips, Damon J. 2005. "Organizational Genealogies and the Persistence of Gender Inequality: The Case of Silicon Valley Law Firms." *Administrative Science Quarterly* 50:440–472.

Pierce, Jennifer L. 1995. *Gender Trials: Emotional Lives in Contemporary Law Firms*. Berkeley: University of California Press.

Powell, Gary N., D. Anthony Butterfield, and Jane D. Parent. 2002. "Gender and Managerial Stereotypes: Have the Times Changed?" *Journal of Management* 28:177–193.

Prentice, Deborah A., and Erica Carranza. 2002. "What Women and Men Should Be, Shouldn't Be, Are Allowed to Be, and Don't Have to Be: The Contents of Prescriptive Gender Stereotypes." *Psychology of Women Quarterly* 26:269–281.

———. 2004. "Sustaining Cultural Beliefs in the Face of Their Violation: The Case of Gender Stereotypes." Pp. 259–280 in *The Psychological Foundations of Culture*, edited by M. Schaller and C. S. Crandall. Mahwah, NJ: Lawrence Erlbaum.

Pugh, Meredith D., and Ralph Wahrman. 1983. "Neutralizing Sexism in Mixed-Sex Groups: Do Women Have to Be Better Than Men?" *American Journal of Sociology* 88:746–762.

Rab, Sara. 2001. "Sex Discrimination in Restaurant Hiring." Unpublished MA thesis, University of Pennsylvania.

Rashotte, Lisa Slattery, and Murray Webster Jr. 2005. "Gender Status Beliefs." *Social Science Research* 34:618–633.

Reskin, Barbara. 1988. "Bringing the Men Back In: Sex Differentiation and the Devaluation of Women's Work." *Gender and Society* 2:58–81.

Reskin, Barbara, and Denise D. Bielby. 2005. "A Sociological Perspective on Gender and Career Outcomes." *Journal of Economic Perspectives* 19:71–86.

Reskin, Barbara, and Debra Branch McBrier. 2000. "Why Not Ascription? Organizations' Employment of Male and Female Managers." *American Sociological Review* 65:210–233.

Reskin, Barbara, Debra Branch McBrier, and Julie A. Kmec. 1999. "The Determinants and Consequences of Workplace Sex and Race Composition." *Annual Review of Sociology* 25:335–361.

Reskin, Barbara, and Patricia Roos. 1990. *Job Queues, Gender Queues: Explaining Women's Inroads into Male Occupations*. Philadelphia: Temple University Press.

Reskin, Barbara, and Catherine E. Ross. "Jobs, Authority, and Earnings Among Managers: The Continuing Significance of Sex." Pp. 127–151 in *Gender Inequality at Work*, edited by Jerry A. Jacobs. Thousand Oaks, CA: Sage.

Ridgeway, Cecilia L. 1982. "Status in Groups: The Importance of Motivation." *American Sociological Review* 47:76–88.

———. 1991. "The Social Construction of Status Value: Gender and Other Nominal Characteristics." *Social Forces* 70:367–386.

———. 1993. "Gender, Status, and the Social Psychology of Expectations." Pp. 175–197 in *Theory on Gender/Feminism on Theory*, edited by Paula England. New York: Aldine de Gruyter.

———. 1997. "Interaction and the Conservation of Gender Inequality: Considering Employment." *American Sociological Review* 62:218–235.

———. 2000. "Social Difference Codes and Social Connections." *Sociological Perspectives* 43:1–11.

———. 2001a. "Gender, Status, and Leadership." *Journal of Social Issues* 57:637–655.

———. 2001b. "Social Status and Group Structure." Pp. 352–375 in *Blackwell Handbook of Social Psychology: Group Processes*, edited by M. A. Hogg and S. Tindale. Malden, MA: Blackwell.

———. 2006a. "Expectation States Theory and Emotion." Pp. 347–367 in *Handbook of Sociology of Emotions*, edited by J. E. Stets and J. H. Turner. New York: Springer.

———. 2006b. "Gender as an Organizing Force in Social Relations: Implications for the Future of Inequality." Pp. 265–287 in *The Declining Significance of Gender?* edited by F. D. Blau, M. C. Brinton and D. B. Grusky. New York: Russell Sage Foundation.

———. 2006c. "Linking Social Structure and Interpersonal Behavior: A Theoretical Perspective on Cultural Schemas and Social Relations." *Social Psychology Quarterly* 69:5–17.

———. 2006d. "Status Construction Theory." Pp. 301–323 in *Contemporary Social Psychological Theories*, edited by P. J. Burke. Stanford, CA: Stanford University Press.

Ridgeway, Cecilia L., Kristen Backor, Yan E. Li, Justine E. Tinkler, and Kristan G. Erickson. 2009. "How Easily Does a Social Difference Become a Status Distinction? Gender Matters." *American Sociological Review* 74:44–62.

Ridgeway, Cecilia L., and James W. Balkwell. 1997. "Group Processes and the Diffusion of Status Beliefs. *Social Psychology Quarterly* 60:14–31.

Ridgeway, Cecilia L., and Joseph Berger. 1986. "Expectations, Legitimation, and Dominance Behavior in Groups." *American Sociological Review* 51:603–617.

Ridgeway, Cecilia L., Joseph Berger, and LeRoy Smith. 1985. "Nonverbal Cues and Status: An Expectation States Approach." *American Journal of Sociology* 90:955–978.

Ridgeway, Cecilia L., and Chris Bourg. 2004. "Gender as Status: An Expectation States Approach." Pp. 217–241 in *Psychology of Gender*, 2nd ed., edited by A. H. Eagly, A. Beall, and R. J. Sternberg. New York: Guilford.

Ridgeway, Cecilia L., and Shelley J. Correll. 2000. "Limiting Gender Inequality through Interaction: The End(s) of Gender." *Contemporary Sociology* 29:110–120.

———. 2004a. "Motherhood as a Status Characteristic." *Journal of Social Issues* 60:683–700.

———. 2004b. "Unpacking the Gender System: A Theoretical Perspective on Cultural Beliefs and Social Relations." *Gender and Society* 18:510–531.

———. 2006. "Consensus and the Creation of Status Beliefs." *Social Forces* 85(1):431–453.

Ridgeway, Cecilia L., and Kristan G. Erickson. 2000. "Creating and Spreading Status Beliefs." *American Journal of Sociology* 106:579–615.

Ridgeway, Cecilia L., Elizabeth Heger Boyle, Kathy Kuipers, and Dawn T. Robinson. 1998. "How Do Status Beliefs Develop? The Role of Resources and Interactional Experience." *American Sociological Review* 63:331–350.

Ridgeway, Cecilia L., Cathryn Johnson, and David Diekema. 1994. "External Status, Legitimacy, and Compliance in Male and Female Groups." *Social Forces* 72:1051–1077.

Ridgeway, Cecilia L., and Lynn Smith-Lovin. 1999. "The Gender System and Interaction." *Annual Review of Sociology* 25:191–216.

Risman, Barbara J. 1998. *Gender Vertigo: American Families in Transition*. New Haven, CT: Yale University Press.

———. 2004. "Gender as a Social Structure: Theory Wrestling with Social Change." *Gender and Society* 18(4):429–450.

Ritter, Barbara A., and Janice D. Yoder. 2004. "Gender Differences in Leader Emergence Persist Even for Dominant Women: An Updated Confirmation of Role Congruity Theory." *Psychology of Women Quarterly* 28:187–193.

Romero, Mary. 1992. *Maid in the U.S.A.* New York: Routledge.

Rudman, Laurie A., and Kimberly Fairchild. 2004. "Reactions to Counterstereotypic Behavior: The Role of Backlash in Cultural Stereotype Maintenance." *Journal of Personality and Social Psychology* 87:157–176.

Rudman, Laurie A., and Peter Glick. 2001. "Prescriptive Gender Stereotypes and Backlash toward Agentic Women." *Journal of Social Issues* 57:743–762.

Rudman, Laurie A., and Stephanie A. Goodwin. 2004. "Gender Differences in Automatic In-Group Bias: Why Do Women Like Women More Than Men Like Men?" *Journal of Personality and Social Psychology* 87:494–509.

Rudman, Laurie A., and Stephen E. Kilianski. 2000. "Implicit and Explicit Attitudes toward Female Authority." *Personality and Social Psychology Bulletin* 26:1315–1328.

Rudman, Laurie A., Julie E. Phelan, Sanne Nauts, and Corinne A. Moss-Racusin. 2009. "Status Incongruity and Backlash toward Female Leaders: The Role of Proscriptive Stereotypes." Rutgers University, unpublished paper.

Sanchez, Laura, and Elizabeth Thompson. 1997. "Becoming Mothers and Fathers: Parenthood, Gender, and the Division of Labor." *Gender and Society* 11:747–772.

Schneider, Donald J. 2004. *The Psychology of Stereotyping*. New York: Guilford.

Sechrist, Gretchen B., and Charles Stangor. 2001. "Perceived Consensus Influences Intergroup Behavior and Stereotype Accessibility." *Journal of Personality and Social Psychology* 80:645–654.

Sewell, William H. 1992. "A Theory of Structure: Duality, Agency, and Transformation." *American Journal of Sociology* 98:1–29.

Shackleford, Susan, Wendy Wood, and Stephen Worchel. 1996. "Behavioral Styles and the Influence of Women in Mixed Sex Groups." *Social Psychology Quarterly* 59:284–293.

Shelly, Robert K., and Paul T. Munroe. 1999. "Do Women Engage in Less Task Behavior Than Men?" *Sociological Perspectives* 42:49–67.

Shelton, Beth Anne. 2000. "Understanding the Distribution of Housework between Husbands and Wives." Pp. 343–355 in *The Ties That Bind: Perspectives on Marriage and Cohabitation*, edited by L. J. Waite. New York: Aldine de Gruyter.

Shelton, Beth Anne, and Daphne John. 1996. "The Division of Household Labor." *Annual Review of Sociology* 22:299–322.

Shih, Margaret, Todd L. Pittinsky, and Nalini Ambady. 1999. "Stereotype Susceptibility: Identity Salience and Shifts in Quantitative Performance." *Psychological Science* 10:80–83.

Smith, Ryan A. 2002. "Race, Gender, and Authority in the Workplace: Theory and Research." *Annual Review of Sociology* 28:509–542.

Smith-Doerr, Laurel. 2004. *Women's Work: Gender Equality vs. Hierarchy in the Life Sciences*. Boulder, CO: Lynne Rienner.

Smuts, Barbara. 1995. "The Evolutionary Origins of Patriarchy." *Human Nature* 6:1–32.

South, Scott J., and Glenna Spitze. 1994. "Housework in Marital and Nonmarital Households." *American Sociological Review* 59:327–347.

Spence, Janet T., and Camille E. Buckner. 2000. "Instrumental and Expressive Traits, Trait Stereotypes, and Sexist Attitudes: What Do They Signify?" *Psychology of Women Quarterly* 24:44–62.

Spencer, Steven J., Claude M. Steele, and Diane M. Quinn. 1999. "Under Suspicion of Inability: Stereotype Threat and Women's Math Performance." *Journal of Experimental Social Psychology* 35:4–28.

Stangor, Charles, Laure Lynch, Changming Duan, and Beth Glass. 1992. "Categorization of Individuals on the Basis of Multiple Social Features." *Journal of Personality and Social Psychology* 62:207–218.

Steele, Claude M., and Joshua Aronson. 1995. "Stereotype Threat and the Intellectual Test Performance of African-Americans." *Journal of Personality and Social Psychology* 69:797–811.

Steinberg, Ronnie J. 1995. "Gendered Instructions: Cultural Lag and Gender Bias in the Hay System of Job Evaluation." Pp. 57–92 in *Gender Inequality at Work*, edited by J. A. Jacobs. Thousand Oaks, CA: Sage.

Stone, Pamela. 2007. *Opting Out? Why Women Really Quit Careers and Head Home*. Berkeley: University of California Press.

Strodtbeck, Fred, Rita James, and Charles Hawkins. 1957. "Social Status in Jury Deliberations." *American Sociological Review* 22:713–719.

Stryker, Sheldon, and Kevin D. Vryan. 2003. "The Symbolic Interactionist Frame." Pp. 3–28 in *The Handbook of Social Psychology*, edited by J. Delamater. New York: Kluwer Academic/Plenum.

Sullivan, Oriel. 2006. *Changing Gender Relations, Changing Families: Tracing the Pace of Change over Time*. New York: Rowman and Littlefield.

Swim, Janet K., Eugene Borgida, Geoffrey Maruyama, and David G. Myers. 1989. "Joan McKay versus John McKay: Do Gender Stereotypes Bias Evaluations?" *Psychological Bulletin* 105:409–429.

Swim, Janet K., and Lawrence J. Sanna. 1996. "He's Skilled, She's Lucky: A Meta-Analysis of Observers' Attributions for Women's and Men's Successes and Failures." *Personality and Social Psychology Bulletin* 22:507–519.

Tajfel, Henri, and John C. Turner. 1986. "The Social Identity Theory of Intergroup Behavior." Pp. 7–24 in *Psychology of Intergroup Relations*, edited by S. Worchel and W. Austin. Chicago: Nelson-Hall.

Tannen, Deborah. 1993. *Gender and Conversational Interaction*. London: Oxford University Press.

Tichenor, Veronica. 2005. *Earning More and Getting Less: Why Successful Wives Can't Buy Equality*. New Brunswick, NJ: Rutgers University Press.

Tilly, Charles. 1998. *Durable Inequality*. Berkeley: University of California Press.

Tomaskovic-Devey, Donald. 1993. "The Gender and Race Composition of Jobs and the Male/Female and White/Black Pay Gaps." *Social Forces* 72:45–47.

Tomaskovic-Devey, Donald, Catherine Zimmer, Kevin Stainback, Corre Robinson, Tiffany Taylor, and Tricia McTague. 2006. "Documenting Desegregation: Segregation in American Workplaces by Race, Ethnicity, and Sex, 1966–2003." *American Sociological Review* 71:565–588.

Turner, John C., Michael Hogg, Penelope J. Oakes, Stephen D. Reicher, and Margaret Wetherell. 1987. *Rediscovering the Social Group: A Self-Categorization Theory*. Oxford: Blackwell.

Twenge, Jean M. 2001. "Changes in Women's Assertiveness in Response to Status and Roles: A Cross-Temporal Meta-Analysis." *Journal of Personality and Social Psychology* 81:133–145.

Twiggs, Joan E., Julia McQuillian, and Myra Marx Ferree. 1999. "Meaning and Measurement: Reconceptualizing Measures of the Division of Household Labor." *Journal of Marriage and Family* 61:712–724.

U.S. Bureau of Labor Statistics. 2009. "Changes in Men's and Women's Labor Force Participation Rates." Retrieved June 17, 2009 (http://www.bls.gov/opub/ted/2007/jan/wk2/art03.htm).

———. 2010. "American Time Use Survey." Retrieved April 4, 2010 (http://www.bls.gov/tus/).

U.S. Census Bureau. 2009. "Families and Living Arrangements." Retrieved April 2, 2010 (http://www.census.gov/population/www/socdemo/hh-fam.html).

Valian, Virginia. 1999. *Why So Slow? The Advancement of Women*. Cambridge, MA: MIT Press.

von Hippel, William, Denise Sekaquaptewa, and Patrick T. Vargas. 1995. "On the Role of Encoding Processes in Stereotype Maintenance." *Advances in Experimental Social Psychology* 27:177–254.

Wagner, David G,. and Joseph Berger. 1997. "Gender and Interpersonal Task Behaviors: Status Expectation Accounts." *Sociological Perspectives* 40:1–32.

Wagner, David G., and Joseph Berger. 2002. "The Evolution of Expectation States Theories." Pp. 41–78 in *Contemporary Sociological Theories*, edited by M. Zelditch Jr. and J. Berger. New York: Rowman & Littlefield.

Wagner, David G., Rebecca S. Ford, and Thomas W. Ford. 1986. "Can Gender Inequalities Be Reduced?" *American Sociological Review* 51:47–61.

Weber, Max. 1946. "Class, Status, Party." Pp. 180–195 in *From Max Weber: Essays in Sociology*, translated by H. H. Gerth and C. Wright Mills. New York: Oxford University Press.

Webster, Murray Jr., and Martha Foschi. 1988. "Overview of Status Generalization." Pp. 1–20 in *Status Generalization: New Theory and Research*, edited by M. Webster and M. Foschi. Stanford, CA: Stanford University Press.

West, Candace, and Sarah Fenstermaker. 1993. "Power, Inequality, and the Accomplishment of Gender: An Ethnomethodological View." Pp. 151–174 in *Theory on Gender/Feminism on Theory*, edited by P. England. New York: Aldine de Gruyter.

West, Candace, and Don H. Zimmerman. 1987. "Doing Gender." *Gender and Society* 1:125–151.

Whittington, Kjersten Bunker. 2007. "Employment Sectors as Opportunity Structures: Male and Female: The Effects of Location on Male and Female Scientific Dissemination." Ph.D. dissertation, Stanford University.

Whittington, Kjersten Bunker, and Laurel Smith-Doerr. 2008. "Women Inventors in Context: Disparities in Patenting across Academia and Industry." *Gender and Society* 22:194–218.

Wight, Vanessa, Suzanne Bianchi, and Bijou Hunt. 2009. "Explaining Racial/Ethnic Variation in Partnered Women's and Men's Housework: Does One Size Fit All?" Department of Sociology, University of California, Los Angeles, CA. Unpublished paper.Williams, Christine. 1992. "The Glass Escalator: Hidden Advantages for Men in the 'Female' Professions." *Social Problems* 39:253–267.

Williams, Joan E. 2000. *Unbending Gender: Why Family and Work Conflict and What to Do about It*. New York: Oxford University Press.

Williams, John E., and Deborah L. Best. 1990. *Measuring Sex Stereotypes: A Multinational Study*. Newbury Park, CA: Sage.

Wisecup, Allison K., Miller McPherson, and Lynn Smith-Lovin. 2005. "Recognition of Gender Identity and Task Performance." Pp. 177–202 in *Social Identification in Groups*, Vol. 22, edited by S. R. Thye and E. J. Lawler. San Diego, CA: Elsevier.

Wood, Wendy, and Alice H. Eagly. 2002. "A Cross-Cultural Analysis of the Behavior of Women and Men: Implications for the Origins of Sex Differences." *Psychological Bulletin* 128:699–727.

———. 2010. "Gender." Pp. 629–667 in *Handbook of Social Psychology*, 5th ed., Vol. 1, edited by S. Fiske, D. T. Gilbert, and G. Lindzey. New York: Wiley.

Wood, Wendy, and Stephen J. Karten. 1986. "Sex Differences in Interaction Style as a Product of Perceived Sex Differences in Competence." *Journal of Personality and Social Psychology* 50:341–347.

Wood, Wendy, and Nancy Rhodes. 1992. "Sex Differences in Interaction Style in Task Groups." Pp. 97–121 in *Gender, Interaction, and Inequality*, edited by C. L. Ridgeway. New York: Springer-Verlag.

Yoder, Janice D. 1991. "Rethinking Tokenism: Looking Beyond Numbers." *Gender and Society* 5:178–192.

Zárate, Michael A., and Eliot R. Smith. 1990. "Person Categorization and Stereotyping." *Social Cognition* 8:161–185.

Zelditch, Morris Jr., and Anthony S. Floyd. 1998. "Consensus, Dissensus, and Justification." Pp. 339–368 in *Status, Power, and Legitimacy: Strategies and Theories*, edited by J. Berger and M. Zelditch. New Brunswick, NJ: Transaction.

Zemore, Sarah E., Susan T. Fiske, and Hyun-Jeong Kim. 2000. "Gender Stereotypes and the Dynamics of Social Interaction." Pp. 207–241 in *The Developmental Social Psychology of Gender*, edited by T. Eckes and H. M. Trautner. Mahwah, NJ: Lawrence Erlbaum.

Index

The letter f following a page number denotes a figure.

Bianchi, Suzanne, 140–41
biases
  communicative, 162;
    confirmation, 161–62, 163;
    employer, 106; in-group, 110–13,
    124, 178; informal, 178;
    workplace, 114, 122–23
biological imperative, 39
biological sciences, 174
biology, 18–23, 174
biotech firms, 174–77, 178, 181, 187, 196
biotechnology, 174, 187
birth control pills, 182
Blair, Sampson, 141, 143
Blair-Loy, Mary, 117, 129, 150
blueprints, organizational, 136, 173,
    179, 180–81, 188
breastfeeding, 22
Brewer, Marilynn, 37, 40–41
Bridges, William, 121
Brines, Julie, 144
Buckner, Camille, 166–67, 168
Budig, Michelle, 112
buffering processes, 161, 186
bureaucracy model, 179
bureaucratic rules, 179
Burke, Ronald J., 79

campuses, college, 182, 183, 184
careers. *See* employment
caregiving. *See* child care
caretakers, primary, 117, 119, 134
care work. *See* child care
Carli, Linda L., 87
Carranza, Erica, 169–70
Carrington, Christopher, 139–40
casual dates, 182, 183
categorical inequalities, 4, 66
categories
  age, 54; primary, 37–43, 69; race, 54;
    relations, 9; sex, 9, 38–43, 54, 67;
    sex/gender, 33, 40; shared category
    systems, 54; systems based on
    difference, 36–38

categorization, mutual, 36
    See also sex categorization
Cejka, Mary Ann, 101
Charles, Maria, 98
child care
  African Americans and, 134; gender
    division of, 140–41; men and, 138,
    145, 153–54, 194, 200; mothers
    and, 140; parental status and, 149–
    51; women and, 6, 63, 128, 130–31,
    137–38, 145, 149–51, 153–54, 199;
    worker's wages, 130
children
  household division of labor and, 150;
    raising, 67, 131, 151; sex-
    categorizing by, 42; *See also* child
    care
civil rights, 13
Clark, Anna, 162
codes, social difference, 37, 45, 49
cognition
  individual, 161, 186
  social, 161
cognitive competence, 168–69, 186
college campuses, 182, 183, 184
college majors, 107–8
college students, 181–84, 187, 188
commitment model, 179
common knowledge, 35–36, 56, 162–63
communality
  expectations for, 85–88; gender
    differences in, 171; gender
    stereotypes and, 73, 89, 117;
    qualities of, 63–64, 65, 73; traits
    of, 59, 186; women and, 86–88, 89,
    90, 117, 170
communal skills, 105
competence
  beliefs about, 194; cognitive, 60,
    168–69, 186; in gender
    stereotypes, 90; men's, 61, 193;
    status and, 60; stereotypes of
    differences in, 193
compliance procedures, 122

occupations. *See* employment
old boy networks, 178
opting-out, of paid labor force, 151
Orbuch, Terri, 146, 147
organizational blueprints, 136, 173, 179, 180–81, 188
organizational genealogies, 180
organizations
    economic and political, 13, 159; egalitarian practices, 198; female dominated, 113; job evaluation and pay systems, 121; make up of, 10–11; positional inequalities in, 11, 12, 14, 27–28, 30; positions in, 9, 95; social, 10–11; work, 30, 95, 113, 114
orgasm, 184

paid work. *See* employment
parental status
    child care and, 149–51
    housework and, 149–51, 154
parenthood, 149, 154
    See also fathers; mothers and motherhood
patents, 176, 178
pay. *See* wages
performance
    capacity, 60, 61, 193; evaluations, 104; expectations, 74–76, 78, 79, 84–85, 90
persistence, dynamics of, 14–16
personal agency, 198
personal ties, 104
Phillips, Damon, 180
physical sciences, 177, 187
political efforts, 13
political movements, feminist, 53
political organizations, 13, 159
politics, gender, 72
politics, racial, 72
positional inequalities, 10–14, 27–28, 30
positions
    executive, 5; in organizations, 9, 95; supervisory, 176

power
    control of, 4; differences based on race, 72; inequalities and, 10–11, 12, 14, 156–57; interpersonal, 181; physical, 14–15
power dependence theory, 10
preferred workers, 95, 101–3, 117–18, 120, 124, 129
premarital sex, 182
Prentice, Deborah, 26, 169–70
prescriptive beliefs, 169–71
primary caretakers, 117, 119, 134
primary categories, 37–43, 69
primary frame, for organizing social relationships, 33, 52–53, 88, 90, 96, 99, 122, 157, 190–91
primary identities, 69, 72, 191
productive roles, 64, 65, 89
productivity, 105–6
promotions. *See* hiring and promotions
providers, 129, 130
psychology, 17, 21
public sphere, 159

race, 54, 72, 146–47
Rashotte, Lisa, 60–61
relations and relationships
    categories of, 9; gender relations, 16, 88, 134, 173; interpersonal relations, 28; intimate relations, 161, 188; between men and women, 45; sexual relations, 183–84, 188; status relations, 60, 66; student-teacher relations, 70; work relations, 93–94, 123, 125–26
reproduction, 14, 15, 22, 39, 46
reputations, 184
resources
    control of, 4; dependence and power and, 14; inequalities and, 10–11, 12, 156–57; material, 4, 5, 17; social organizations and, 10–11
Ridgeway, Cecilia L., 48